11/12

D1117023

The Black Arts Enterprise and the
Production of African American Poetry

The Black Arts Enterprise and the Production of African American Poetry

Howard Rambsy II

The University of Michigan Press • Ann Arbor

Copyright © by the University of Michigan 2011
All rights reserved
Published in the United States of America by
The University of Michigan Press
Manufactured in the United States of America
♾ Printed on acid-free paper

2014   2013   2012   2011   4   3   2   1

A CIP catalog record for this book is available from the British Library.

Library of Congress Cataloging-in-Publication Data

Rambsy, Howard.
    The black arts enterprise and the production of African American
poetry / Howard Rambsy, II.
        p.   cm.
    Includes bibliographical references and index.
    ISBN 978-0-472-11733-8 (cloth : acid-free paper)
        1. American poetry—African American authors—History and
criticism.   2. Poetry—Publishing—United States—History—20th
century.   3. African Americans—Intellectual life—20th century.
4. African Americans in literature.   I. Title.
PS310.N4R35 2011
811'.509896073—dc22

2010043190

Dedicated to Donald Garcia, Maryemma Graham,
Cynthia Spence, Mae G. Williams, and Jerry W. Ward Jr.

A Preface

"We Will Change the World Before Your Eyes"

At some point during the late 1960s, black poetry reached a tipping point. No fewer than sixty anthologies featuring African American verse appeared between 1965 and 1976 alone. This flourishing of black poetry was Harlem Renaissance 2.0 and then some. A large number of African American poets enjoyed unprecedented popular and critical success—their images regularly appeared in magazines, their words were frequently published in periodicals, and their voices resonated alongside the sounds of jazz musicians and gospel choirs on albums. Their poetry and pronouncements were sometimes forceful, sometimes outrageous, and often infused with a militant, black nationalist ethos. "We are building publishing houses, and newspapers, and armies, and factories," wrote Amiri Baraka. "We will change the world before your eyes." An explanation of the forces that created an environment for the display of these kinds of provocative statements constitutes the major focus of this study.

The Black Arts Enterprise and the Production of African American Poetry illuminates the often underexamined publishing factors that facilitated one of the most decisive moments in American literary history. In particular, this book explains how a diverse range of writers, editors, publishers, illustrators, and musicians collaborated to enact a dynamic cultural movement. The central argument of this project is that the coordinated and innovative efforts of black artists and their supporters greatly increased the visibility and implications of African American poetry. An examination of the production—not merely the composition—of black verse from the late 1960s to the mid-1970s reveals what made the Black Arts Movement such an enduring cultural enterprise.

Acknowledgments

Years ago, I informed the people in my circles that I was writing a book. They somehow misheard me and thought I said I was building a house. So for some time now, they have been offering all kinds of assistance and materials for a project much larger than a study of poetry and publishing history.

First, my mom and dad, my siblings, Kenton and Phillis, and my extended family gave invaluable support when I was laying my earliest groundwork. Later, at Pennsylvania State University, Bernard Bell, Keith Gilyard, William Harris, and James Stewart—all wonderful builders—provided me with formal direction on developing a solid foundation. Later still, Aldon Nielsen, Lovalerie King, Earleen Patterson, James Smethurst, Vorris Nunley, Stefan Bradley, and my big sister Alondra Nelson gave me stimulating and diverse models for envisioning the types of structures that I wanted to create.

I have benefited from a broad range of building support, including grants from the Woodrow Wilson Foundation and Southern Illinois University Edwardsville (SIUE) and assistance from Julie Hansen in tracking down rare materials. Emily and Scott VanDette, my friends and colleagues at SIUE and in the College Language Association, and my fellow travelers with the SIUE Black Studies Program, were tremendously supportive at all stages of the process. LeAnn Fields and the good people at the University of Michigan Press have generously provided a platform for what I produced.

At a crucial moment in the project, I met Psyche Southwell, and her generosity and intellectualism inspired me to think and then build in new and exciting ways. Finally, I could never say enough about all I have gained observing and tracing the workings of that wonderful East St. Louis, world-traveling architect Eugene B. Redmond.

Contents

Introduction

"A Group of Groovy Black People"

In the June 1965 issue of *Liberator,* Larry Neal described the arrival of the Black Arts School in Harlem, which opened on April 30 with "an explosive evening of good poetry." According to Neal, however, the most memorable event of the black arts weekend was the parade held that Saturday morning in Harlem. "Imagine jazz musicians, African dancing, and a group of groovy black people swinging down Lenox Avenue," wrote Neal. "It was Garvey all over again. It was informal and spontaneous and should illustrate something of the potential for creative encounter existing in our community." Just in case readers needed help envisioning the scene, a photograph accompanied the story showing two men leading a group down the middle of the street, carrying a large flag that read, "The Black Arts Repertory Theatre/School." The caption for the photo identified "LeRoi Jones and Hampton Clanton leading the Black Arts parade down 125th Street, New York City."[1] They were on a mission, on the move. As a result, when Neal assessed the activities of these groovy black people a few years later, he defined their efforts as a movement, a Black Arts Movement.

The operation of the Black Arts School in Harlem was relatively brief; however, the spirit of activism and explosiveness expressed by those black artists "swinging down Lenox Avenue" typified the vitality and outlook of African American writers and organizers across the country during the time period. Those writers who ventured to take literary art to the people in such dramatic fashion suggested that they wanted to expand and transform conventional notions about what it meant to be artists. Not content with being only composers of verse and prose, they sought to become active on multiple fronts in the processes of artistic production. In fact, given Larry Neal's abilities crafting insightful essays about the nature of black art, Amiri Baraka's talents constructing compelling artistic productions, and Hoyt Fuller's and Dudley Randall's significant work designing sites of publication, there is little wonder as to why observers often refer to these figures, among others, as "architects" of the Black Arts Movement. Their collective artistic activities and organizing efforts were integral to the construction of an extensive series of interconnected cultural productions.

During the 1960s, a large number of poets achieved unprecedented levels of exposure in the literary marketplace and academy. This is not to say that the Harlem Renaissance was anything less than a crucial moment in American and African American literary history. The New Negro Movement of the 1920s certainly paved the way for the New Black Poetry of the 1960s. Yet the tremendous body of writings produced by and about African American poets between 1965 and 1976 was unparalleled. Even if we accept the assessment of critic Henry Louis Gates Jr. that the Black Arts Movement "was the most short-lived of all" African American literary movements, we would be hard-pressed to identify a moment in literary history with such a remarkable and memorable attentiveness to black poets and poetry.[2]

But of course, the characterization "most short-lived" is untenable, especially since the legacies of the Black Arts Movement are continually unfolding. Consider, for instance, that the first edition of Gates and Nellie McKay's *Norton Anthology of African American Literature* (1997) presents "The Black Arts Movement: 1960–1970," while the second edition, released in 2004, presents "The Black Arts Era, 1960–1975." The shifting views of the Black Arts Movement (or is it the Black Arts Era?) testify to the substantial yet elusive power of a diverse range of artists and cultural activists to affect the shape of literary history. An investigation into the series of smaller movements—of poets, of poems, of books, of magazines—that comprised the Black Arts Movement reveals what made it such a fascinating and apparently difficult to define artistic enterprise. In particular, an examination of the transmission of poems and the socialization of poets illuminates the operations of the larger cultural movement.

The publishing history of Amiri Baraka's now well-known poem "Black Art" indicates the importance of transmission and socialization in the production of poetry during the era. At the time that "Black Art" was composed, Baraka was known as LeRoi Jones, and his poem initially appeared in 1965 on jazz drummer Sonny Murray's album *Sonny's Time Now;* the album was released under the imprint of Baraka's publishing company, Jihad Productions. In January 1966, "Black Art" was published in *Liberator* magazine; consequently, the cover of that issue featured a photograph of Baraka. "Black Art" was subsequently printed in Baraka's volumes of poetry and in such anthologies as *Black Fire* (1968), *Black Poetry* (1969), *The Black Poets* (1971), *Modern and Contemporary Afro-American Poetry* (1972), and *Understanding the New Black Poetry* (1973), becoming one of the most widely circulating poems of the era. In recent years, the poem has appeared in *The Amiri Baraka Reader*, *Call and Response: The Riverside Anthology of the African American Literary Tradition*, and *The Norton Anthology of African American Literature*. The appearance of "Black Art" in multiple sites over the years has helped solidify the poem and Baraka's centrality to the canon of African American literature.

The militant tone and profane use of language in "Black Art" and its message that "poems are bullshit" unless they advance political interests are hardly the only factors that give Baraka's poem significance. Instead, the different forms and sites in which the poem circulated, the relationship of the poem's title to the cultural activities known as the Black Arts Movement, and the status of the poem's author also contributed to why "Black Art" appeared so frequently and became such a regularly cited poem. Baraka composed the poem, but a range of editors, scholars, and general readers ensured its broad circulation. In order to account for the increased rotation of Baraka's "Black Art" and several other writings that circulated widely during the time period, including Nikki Giovanni's "Nikki-Rosa," Larry Neal's "The Black Arts Movement," Margaret Walker's "For My People," and Robert Hayden's "Runagate Runagate," we must pursue close readings of publishing venues and consider how factors such as poets' participation in literary activities and their social standing affect the reception of their works. Analyzing the circulation of literary texts and the ways that poets access various, interrelated modes of publication to engage distinct readerships enhances our understanding of what made the production of African American poetry during the 1960s and 1970s such a special moment in American literary history.

Transmitting Poetry, Socializing Poets

The most notable contribution of this project to the study of African American literature is the focus on factors of transmission and socialization in the presentation of black verse. Definitions of transmission and socialization actually overlap, but for the purposes of this study, *transmission* refers to the material production and circulation of writers' compositions. *Socialization* connotes how writers interact with fellow writers, audiences, and various discourses. Processes of transmission and socialization ultimately shape the visibility and value of poets and their works. These processes are also fundamental yet underexamined factors that often influence what gets classified as "African American literature," "black poetry," and "the Black Arts Movement." The publication of spirituals in Dudley Randall's *The Black Poets* (1971) and the appearance of folk songs, spirituals, and blues lyrics in Stephen Henderson's *Understanding the New Black Poetry* (1973) may have anticipated the now established practice among editors of presenting song lyrics in poetry anthologies. Transmuting aural forms of expression to words on a page expands views of what constitutes black literary art and at the same time underscores the connections between auditory art forms and print-based compositions. Highlighting the connections between musical and literary forms was especially important for black poets, many of whom preferred to align themselves and their work with African American sonic traditions as opposed to what they perceived as the more restricting conventions of white or Eurocentric literary traditions. Of course, aural and print-based forms are integral to a wide range of literary traditions, but the social dynamics of the 1960s often led black artists and observers to encourage the auditory and performative features of African American verse.

The perception that there were culturally distinct roles and select methods of writing that progressive, socially committed black writers must address in their work was a pervasive force within African American artistic communities. "Black art must expose the enemy, praise the people and support the revolution," declared Maulana Karenga, one of many observers to weigh in on what black art and artists *must* do (Ron Karenga, "Black Cultural Nationalism," 6). Ultimately, such prescriptive declarations were limiting and failed to adequately acknowledge the innumerable functions of black artistic production. Nonetheless, even prominent writers who resisted the idea that their creative works should correspond to a particular agenda had a hard time avoiding the prevalent influence of the politically charged movements that determined the shape of African American literary culture of the era. Drawing on the spirit and rhetoric of Black Power and nationalist ideology, leading African American writers fashioned themselves as fiery artist-activists who were willing to advance a wide array of political interests.

Poets discovered that fashioning themselves as artists and activists could be liberating. For one, those poets who viewed themselves as artists felt freer to cross genres and compose plays, prose, and audio recordings as well as verse. As self-proclaimed artists and not simply writers, poets were more inclined to celebrate and emulate a wider range of subject positions such as performers, musicians, and streetwise orators as opposed to only literary models. This poet-as-artist model also prompted writers to actively seek collaborations with musicians, visual artists, dancers, and other writers working in a variety of genres in order to produce mixed-media black art. The conception of poets as activists equipped writers with a presumably higher, purpose-driven calling than those poets who seemingly wrote poetry for its own sake. Unlike those so-called nonpolitical poets who wrote flowery verse, militant black poets advocated the use of "words as weapons," a proposition that Richard Wright, a respected figure among the writers, had advanced decades prior to the 1960s. Formulating words as weapons gave poets the opportunity to envision themselves "like little black spears," to apply Henry Dumas's phrasing, hurling militant critiques at barriers of injustice. Finally, the poet as artist-activist would, at least in theory, increase the likelihood of changes in literature and society that black arts participants were calling for.

The shifts from writers to black artists and from artists to artist-activists represented crucial social transformations adopted and adapted by African American poets. Beyond these distinct social transformations, however, what gave the poets' works a definite place in literary history related to the nature of their transmission. What served as the indispensable links between the poets and a variety of readerships were a select group of influential literary magazines and a wide assortment of anthologies. Nonetheless, few studies have analyzed the roles and implications of these particular modes of transmission, despite their historical and continuing importance for the display and distribution of poetry. The prevalence of black poetry and the Black Arts Movement in general, this study contends, was predicated on the activities of African American literary magazines and collections featuring black writing.

Magazine editors and anthologists, along with support from publishers, offered increased publishing opportunities for emergent poets and for earlier generations of poets such as Phillis Wheatley, Langston Hughes, Countee Cullen, and Paul Laurence Dunbar. *Liberator, Negro Digest/Black World, Freedomways,* the *Journal of Black Poetry,* and *Black Dialogue,* to name a few of the magazines, created the occasions for the publication of hundreds of poets, as well as reviews of volumes of poetry and essays on poetics. Arnold Adoff's *I Am the Darker Brother* (1968), June Jordan's *soulscript* (1970), Gwendolyn Brooks's *Jump Bad* (1971), and Woodie King's *Black Spirits* (1972), along with the dozens and dozens of other anthologies produced during the time period, brought together several diverse poets in a common setting, and publishers, such as Broadside Press and Third World Press, further expanded the prospects of poets circulating their works among African American readerships. Based on shared editorial and publishing practices, these magazines, anthologies, and publishers represented interconnected sites of publication, and the strong ties between the various publishing venues assisted in generating the perception that the varied literary activities among black writers constituted a collective enterprise.

Textual scholars and editorial theorists such as Jerome McGann, George Bornstein, D. C. Greetham, Peter Shillingsburg, and Robin Schulze have developed a useful vocabulary and body of ideas for explaining the significance of editorial practices in literary production.[3] Particularly pertinent is McGann's notion that we must interpret a text's "bibliographic codes," such as its price, dedication, page format, and typeface, in order to gain a fuller understanding of how the text conveys meaning among readers and in the marketplace. Generally speaking, textual scholarship offers important frameworks for investigating the transmission and material production of African American writings, especially since so much editing, reprinting, and anthologizing has occurred over the last several years.[4] For the most part, however, leading textual scholars have focused their analyses on white writers. But there are exceptions. James D. Sullivan's *On the Walls and in the Streets: American Poetry Broadsides from the 1960s* utilizes aspects of McGann's methodology in order to show "how graphic design and text interact to produce literary meanings" in relation to the broadsides produced by Broadside Press.[5]

In addition, in his essay "Killing John Cabot and Publishing Black: Gwendolyn Brooks's *Riot,*" Sullivan applies concepts relating to editorial theory to explain the importance of what occurred when "Brooks materially removed her work from a white context and placed it into a black context," as she began publishing her works with Broadside Press.[6] Following the lines of thinking established by textual scholars, Sullivan observes how issues such as price, book design, and the back-cover author photo factor in the overall implications of Brooks's *Riot.* According to

Sullivan, "The challenge here for the criticism of African American literature is to recognize that literature always appears under the name not only of an author, but also of a racially marked publishing institution whose mission always inflects the work" (568). Consequently, black poetry of the 1960s and 1970s appeared under the names of racially marked publishing entities, and more important, the poetry appeared under the banner of a larger racially marked cultural movement.

The recent scholarship on writers and writings of the black arts era covers considerable ground. Margaret Reid, Kimberly Benston, Cheryl Clarke, Aldon Nielsen, Lorenzo Thomas, and Tony Bolden, to name a few, have produced studies that analyze stylistic and thematic features of poetry during the time period.[7] My study complements these studies, as I explain how the design and circulation of texts, as well as the production of a cultural movement, influenced how readers viewed poetry and poets at a particular historical moment. My objective of treating the literary histories of the black arts era makes my work especially congruent with Melba Boyd's *Wrestling with the Muse: Dudley Randall and the Broadside Press* (2003) and James Smethurst's *The Black Arts Movement: Literary Nationalism in the 1960s and 1970s* (2005), two studies that chart the literary activities of principal figures. I do, however, take the material production of black poetry and its distinct socialization as my main areas of concern. My project explains how Broadside Press, to take one example, fashioned literary products to appeal to the nationalist sensibilities of its audiences and at the same time to display a sense of black solidarity among its authors.

Smethurst's book represents the most thorough treatment of 1960s artistic productions and organizing efforts among writers and creative intellectuals. His book pays special attention to the "regional variations" of the Black Arts Movement "while delineating how the movement gained some sense of national coherence institutionally, aesthetically, and ideologically, even if it never became exactly homogenous."[8] My understanding of the local developments of the movement draws on Smethurst's work, but at the same time, I take a somewhat panoramic view, or macro approach, to examining the time period. Rather than focus in detail on developments taking place within particular geographic locations, as Smethurst does, I concentrate on sites of publication and publishing practices that brought the work of several poets from across the country and from historical time periods together in common settings. My focus allows me to pinpoint how writers, editors, and publishers utilized particular modes of transmission to popularize poetry and to elevate the status of black poets in literary history and the marketplace.

My interest in the popularization of poetry means that my study, more so than many modern literary histories, recognizes the ascent of Nikki Giovanni as a notable achievement worthy of scholarly consideration. Relatively few poets, especially African American women poets, ever received substantial national acclaim. Yet Giovanni achieved famed status (she was often referred to as "the princess of black poetry") and became one of the movement's most iconic figures. Her poetry remains in print, and her work continues to appeal to large, diverse audiences. Indeed, Giovanni stands as yet another counterpoint to the charge that the Black Arts Movement was short-lived.

Despite Giovanni's prominence, however, she is routinely excluded from critical examinations. Her distancing from the movement's most visible political groups and grassroots organizations, her striking independence, her decision to publish with a mainstream press, and the view that her poetry does not meet certain criteria of literary sophistication might explain why critics have relegated Giovanni to the margins of academic discourse. In the context of this study, though, Giovanni's ascent and wide appeal reveal the significance of transmission and socialization in the popularization of an African American poet. The widespread presentation of her poems in numerous anthologies, the publication of her volumes of poetry by Broadside Press and the large corporate publishing entity William Morrow and Company, the release of her poems on audio CDs, and her extensive national public reading appearances accounted for Giovanni's extraordinary popularity as a poet. Her popularity among audiences and general readers gave her a special place in African American cultural history, regardless of the fact that her poetry has generated little critical acclaim. As suggested by Giovanni's career, scholarly indifference does not necessarily impede a poet from attaining widespread appeal.

At the same time, public expressions of disdain for a writer do not automatically translate into literary exclusion, a point made most apparent in the career of Robert Hayden, a seemingly unpopular poet whose publishing record flourished during the black arts era. During a black writers' conference at Fisk University in 1966, Hayden was quoted in *Negro Digest* as telling his audience, "Let's quit saying we're black writers writing to black folks—it has been given importance it should not have."[9] Hayden's sentiments opposed the proponents of black racial affirmation and cultural pride, thus making Hayden a target of militant black writers' countercritiques. In a 1968 issue of *Negro Digest,* for example, the editors observed that "Mr. Hayden does not hesitate to speak harshly of those militant writers who do not share his—and the Literary Establishment's—idea of what constitutes art in literature."[10] The editors' comments, which were congruent with those expressed by many, presented Hayden as a harsh critic of black arts writers and an ally of the presumably white "Literary Establishment."

Although Hayden was viewed with derision by several militant writers, anthologists did not always show contempt toward the elder poet, at least not when it came to selecting his works for inclusion in their collections. In fact, Hayden became one of the most widely anthologized poets of the period; his works appeared in as many anthologies as those of leading militant poets. Even though he had published poems prior to the 1960s, his writings began to enjoy their widest circulation during the Black Arts Movement. Similar to the varied dissemination of Amiri Baraka's "Black Art," the publishing history of Hayden's "Runagate Runagate" illustrates the consequential role that transmission plays in the production of poetry.

"Runagate Runagate," which presents episodes from the first-person perspectives of a group of runaway slaves being led by Harriet Tubman, was initially published in Langston Hughes and Arna Bontemps's *The Poetry of the Negro* (1949). During a visit to Fisk University in 1963, anthologist Rosey Pool read "Runagate Runagate" to an audience where Hayden was also in attendance. For years, Hayden had put "Runagate Runagate" aside, viewing it "as another of my many failures." However, when Pool read the poem at Fisk, Hayden changed his mind and concluded that his poem "was not so bad as I'd thought." Accordingly, he made revisions to the poem and sent the new version to Pool. In the June 1966 issue of *Negro Digest,* Pool published a laudatory assessment of Hayden's poetry; her essay was followed by two different versions of "Runagate Runagate."[11] This same issue of the magazine, by the way, contained the Fisk writers' conference report that portrayed Hayden as an adversary of militant black writers. Thus, whereas *Negro Digest* raised the visibility of Hayden's disapproval of activist writers, it may have also increased the visibility of the second version of "Runagate Runagate," which editors began to frequently reprint in their anthologies.

The increased circulation of Hayden's poems during the late 1960s and early 1970s—despite his disagreements with militant poets—illustrates the abilities of anthologists to accommodate multiple, seemingly conflicting interests among poets. Similarly, although Phillis Wheatley was thought to be totally dismissed for her supposed conservative ideology, the publishing record suggests otherwise, as her poems appeared in several collections during the period. Along with Hayden and Wheatley, a number of other older poets, including Paul Laurence Dunbar, Langston Hughes, and Margaret Walker, benefited from the new and expanded channels for presenting African American poetry.

Establishing a Black Arts Discourse

Amiri Baraka's "Black Art" and Larry Neal's essay "The Black Arts Movement" are among the most frequently referenced texts associated with the movement. The very titles of Baraka's poem and Neal's essay have come to represent foundational phrases and concepts in the vocabulary created and utilized to describe the cultural activities enacted by African American artists during the 1960s and 1970s. The development and use of distinct terms, names, phrases, symbols, and images in common sites of publications associated with artistic productions of the era constitute what I refer to as "black arts discourse." This discourse gave a sense of cohesion to a rather large and diverse network of literary artists, cultural workers, and readerships interested in topics relating to African Americans and artistic productions. That writers utilized a common discourse does not mean that they held the same values and agreed on a common set of goals. They did, however, draw on loosely interrelated modes of communication, and their creative works regularly appeared in common publishing venues.

The development of a black arts discourse was an empowering process for writers and their audiences. In her essay "Black Power Is Black Language," the sociolinguist Geneva Smitherman explains that "the power of the word lies in its enabling us to translate vague feelings and fleeting expressions into forms that give unity, coherence and expression to the Inexpressible. The process of composing becomes a mechanism for discovery wherein we may generate illuminating revelations about a particular idea or event."[12] Smitherman views the abilities of black people to create and adapt their own approaches to communication as significant acts of self-determination. Consequently, the frequent appearance of words and phrases like "Black," "Black Art," "the Black Arts Movement," "Black Artists," "Black Aesthetic," and "the

New Black Poetry" functioned to "generate illuminating revelations" about the activities taking place among African American artists.

The publication of striking images and photographs further conveyed the spirit of a militant nationalist ethos in the context of literary art. A photograph of LeRoi Jones speaking angrily into a microphone on the cover of the January 1966 issue of *Liberator* magazine visually communicated the idea of the poet as activist, a popular conception in black arts discourse. The cover of the Spring 1969 issue of the *Journal of Black Poetry* includes drawings of Malcolm X, along with excerpts from some of his speeches regarding self-determination, such as, "You get freedom by letting your enemy know that you'll do anything to get your freedom." Most notably, *Negro Digest/Black World* regularly presented photographs of black writers and images of African artifacts as a way of appealing to the visual and cultural sensibilities of black readerships.

Generally speaking, black arts discourse was characterized by expressions of militant nationalist sensibilities, direct appeals to African American audiences, critiques of antiblack racism, and affirmations of cultural heritage. With anthologies bearing such titles as *Black Fire, New Black Voices, soulscript, I Am the Darker Brother, We Speak as Liberators,* and magazines *Black World* and the *Journal of Black Poetry,* editors and publishers highlighted the racial and cultural imperatives of their contributors. Poets of the era frequently composed poems that advanced their commitment to militant sensibilities. In his poem "Let's Get Violent!" published in *Negro Digest* in 1969, Ted Joans utilizes violent and nationalist rhetoric to encourage his presumably black audience to liberate their minds from the hegemony of whiteness. He urges readers to "ATTACK THE WHITEWASH / ICING CAKED / ON OUR BLACK MINDS / LETS GET VIOLENT THAT WE LEAVE that white way / of thinking / IN THE TOILET BENEATH OUR BLACK BEHINDS."[13] Similarly, Giovanni displays the aggressive approach to liberation discussed among African Americans in her poem "The True Import of Present Dialogue: Black vs. Negro." In the poem, she raises the questions, "Can a nigger kill / Can a nigger kill a honkie / Can a nigger kill the Man / Can you kill nigger / Huh?"[14] She closes her poem by asserting that the possibility of African Americans becoming "Black men" rests on whether "we learn to kill WHITE for BLACK / Learn to kill niggers" (319). Magazine editors, anthologists, and publishers, of course, determined that poems promoting militancy would be recurrent features of the discourse.

The poets often expressed the viewpoint that important battles for black liberation and social justice would occur along cultural fronts. From this perspective, poems could be used as viable means for inspiring African Americans to become more politically conscious and active. In Calvin Hernton's "Jitterbugging in the Streets," Hernton writes that there will be no typical Fourth of July celebration this year. In its place, "the rage of a hopeless people" will be their dancing or "jitterbugging in the streets." They will jitterbug in the streets across the country "To ten thousand rounds of ammunition / To waterhoses, electric prods, phallic sticks / hound dogs, black boots stepping in soft places / of the body."[15] Hernton predicts that African Americans will respond to the "TERROR" of impoverished living conditions with a powerful cultural form, a black dance. More precisely, they will counter the terror with fierce, erratic, and expressive movements.

Hernton's "Jitterbugging in the Streets" was published in *Black Fire* (1968), along with several other poems that emphasize the idea that black people could and should utilize cultural practices to liberate themselves from forms of oppression. While many political activists certainly would not have offered music and dance as methods for achieving freedom, there were large numbers of artists and creative intellectuals who believed that distinct African American cultural practices were essential to how a group of people would attain degrees of freedom. In June 1964 in Harlem, for instance, Malcolm X read the "Statement of Basic Aims and Objective of Organization of Afro-American Unity." Section 6 of the document focuses on culture and states that African Americans "must recapture our heritage and our identity if we are ever to liberate ourselves from the bonds of white supremacy. We must launch a cultural revolution to unbrainwash an entire people." The document goes on to state, "Culture is an indispensable weapon in the freedom struggle."[16] Accordingly, it becomes clear, as in the case of Hernton's poem, how a black dance might serve as a viable weapon in struggles for freedom or why poets viewed music as a powerful force for combating injustice.

Amiri Baraka had expressed the idea that black music contains hidden radical messages in his 1964 play *The Dutchman*. Toward the end of the play, the main character Clay explains that a musician such as Bessie Smith was really telling white people to "kiss my black unruly ass" and that Charlie Parker would not have needed to play another "note of music if he just walked up to East Sixty-seventh Street and killed the first ten white people he saw."[17] In his poem "Don't Say Goodbye to the

Pork-Pie Hat," Larry Neal observes that "all over America black musicians" are picking up their instruments and "preparing to blow away the white dream. you can / hear them screeching love in rolling sheets of sound." In her "liberation / poem," Sonia Sanchez explains that the blues are "sounds of / oppression / against the white man's / shit." But, upon hearing the "soft / soul / ful / sighs" of Billie Holiday, the poet is no longer blue; instead, "i'm blk / & ready."[18] As these poets suggested, black musicians served as models for enacting progressive change.

In the process of combining militant agendas with affirmations of black cultural practices, several militant writers abandoned what they saw as the Eurocentric idea of the genteel poet, disconnected from the masses. As Nikki Giovanni observes in her poem "For Saundra," she would prefer to "clean my gun / and check my kerosene supply," rather than write poems about nature.[19] The poets actively sought to construct new possibilities for their roles and responsibilities as literary artists. Askia Toure's "Notes from a Guerilla Diary (for Marvin X and Che Guevara)," for example, asserts that the social and political conditions of black and Third World peoples demand that African American poets avoid becoming conventional isolated writers and pursue more militant goals. "I wanted to be an artist," writes Toure, but that was "before revolution turned me / towards / Islam and Malcolm's eyes glowing with compassion over / dope- / infested ghettoes of our fears." He goes on to note that "dreams are beautiful," yet "Reality's blonde / wig smothers the Afros of our souls." As a result of the harsh conditions confronted by black people, Toure decides to forgo his initial wish to become an artist in any traditional sense. Instead, he will go "back to cutting throats and cleaning guns; even / *that* / can be a form of art!"[20] Similar to Giovanni's "For Saundra" and Baraka's "Black Art," Toure's poem promotes the idea that poets must do more than simply write poems if they are to realize their fullest potential as black artists.

What gave the militant, nationalist spirit of the poems such wide visibility was the strong support that they received from magazine editors, anthologists, publishers, and a select group of literary and cultural critics. As I discuss more thoroughly in chapter 1, the editorial and publishing activities of *Negro Digest/Black World*, edited by Hoyt Fuller, were indispensable to the increased prominence of black poetry. Under Fuller's leadership, the periodical became a defining force for the circulation of poetry, as the magazine published hundreds of poems, essays, and reviews of poetry volumes. The magazine consistently publicized poets' activities and printed images of writers interacting with fellow poets and diverse audiences. Overall, *Negro Digest/Black World* amplified dominant themes in black arts discourse and consolidated the interests of a wide range of poets by getting them on the same pages, so to speak.

Anthologies served as another invaluable mode of transmission for the dissemination of black poetry and the expression of a common agenda among diverse groupings of writers. The publication and arrangement of anthologies, not simply the content of the poems, shaped how readers would view poetry of the black arts era. As explained in chapter 2, the editorial practices of anthologists, including their publication of a common group of writers and poems, contributed to establishing the defining perceptions of black arts poetry. In addition to publishing countless emergent poets, anthologists kept previous generations of writers in print as well, demonstrating that collections of black writing could serve as platforms for showcasing "new" and "old" black poetry.

Anthologies and magazines were important platforms for the display of black poetry, but they were certainly not the only distinct methods used to transmit verse. Chapter 3 highlights how the formats of books and audio texts expanded the possibilities for presenting and experiencing poetry. Poets and illustrators collaborated to juxtapose images and words in the compositions of texts that appealed to the linguistic and visual sensibilities of readers. For some time now, scholars have discussed the importance of performance in the presentation of poetry, but what about the significance of audio recordings of literary products that could expand and diversify the composition of black arts literature? Amiri Baraka, Jayne Cortez, Nikki Giovanni, and a number of other poets produced audio recordings, thus further aligning their poetry with black music and making the sound of verse and the presence of recordings central to the nature of black arts publishing history.

If venues such as anthologies and magazines served as important networks for bringing large numbers of writers together, then certainly poets' decisions to write about overlapping subjects also advanced the impression that they shared a common agenda. The composition of tributes to black historical figures and writings displaying principles of jazz were among the most pervasive kinds of poems written by poets of the era. Not surprisingly, then, there was a proliferation of poetry focused on Malcolm X and John Coltrane. Featuring Malcolm and Coltrane in their poems enabled poets and editors to popularize their movement more effectively, as those two figures were admired by audiences well beyond the realm of poetry. Malcolm and Coltrane also represented important models for the poets, who frequently projected public personas as political figures and musicians. The discussion of poems focusing on Malcolm and Coltrane in chapter 4 reveals that the poets' concentration on common themes and techniques heightened the interconnectivity of their varied literary activities.

Poets of the black arts era did not wait for literary historians to "rediscover" their works or for critics to assess the value of their writings. Instead, many poets fashioned themselves as artist-critics and actively participated in the critical valuation of black literary art, a subject described more fully in chapter 5. As essayists, book reviewers, literary historians, and theorists, poets influenced the shape of black arts discourse and the conversations about poetry and artistic production. Larry Neal was a particularly important figure in this regard. He was a fairly well-known poet, but his well-placed and illuminating essays amount to his most important contribution to black arts discourse. In addition to Neal, artist-critics such as Carolyn Rodgers and Eugene B. Redmond also produced influential prose on African American poetry and artistic culture and thus further solidified the presence of poets in the forefront of critical discussions.

Topics concerning "black aesthetics" initiated provocative, if not controversial, conversations regarding the valuation and composition of black literary art. Notably, creative artists took leading roles in these wide-ranging conversations about the interpretation, valuation, and production of African American literary art. Addison Gayle's widely cited collection of essays *The Black Aesthetic* (1971) contains works by such figures as Amiri Baraka, Dudley Randall, Keorapetse William Kgositsile, Sarah Webster Fabio, Larry Neal, and Langston Hughes, making it difficult to imagine discussions of black aesthetics without the contributions of poets. The active participation of poets at so many levels in the production and appreciation of African American literature represents an important moment in literary history, especially given the decreasing significance of black poetry in scholarly discourses from the mid-1970s onward.

The final chapter of this book identifies and explains important social forces and modes of transmission that have shaped perceptions of black arts discourse. An analysis of the first and second editions of *The Norton Anthology of African American Literature* reveals how these and other anthologies present the movement's contributors to modern readers. A consideration of the decline of the Black Arts Movement indicates that this so-called decline is not as fixed as some commentators have proposed. The production of militant, nationalist poetry certainly has no definite closure, as younger generations of artists frequently fashion themselves as extensions, if not continuations, of the Black Arts Movement's more progressive tenets.

An examination of the methods by which publishing venues and editorial practices advanced an artistic movement is long overdue. *The Black Arts Enterprise and the Production of African American Poetry* seeks to make vital, though regularly overlooked, publishing factors central to the operations of Black Arts Movement more apparent. In particular, this study seeks to deepen our understanding of literary art by explaining significant ways that processes of transmission and socialization shaped the rise of black arts poetry. We will gain a broader knowledge concerning the production of poetry when greater attention is paid to roles played by anthologies, literary magazines, and audio recordings, for instance. Our knowledge of the production of poetry will also expand as we examine more closely the ways that writers positioned themselves in relation to one another, their audiences, and literary and cultural traditions.

1 • Getting Poets on the Same Page

The Roles of Periodicals

The efforts of prolific poets did not dictate the extraordinary proliferation of black poetry during the 1960s and 1970s. That is to say, the presentation of hundreds of poems in centralized sites of publication was hardly achieved because of poets' prolificacy and desire to reach large numbers of readers. Writing regularly and having a strong desire to get published does not always translate into publication results. In fact, the belief that writing hard and writing well will necessarily lead to publication is as flawed as the dream that states that hard work will automatically lead to wealth. Writers, as we know, need more than a strong work ethic to develop distinguished publication records. Literary artists of the black arts era, consequently, relied heavily on a network of supportive publishing institutions and editors to ensure the broad circulation of their works.

"Nowhere is the new Black Renaissance more evident than in the number of talented poets who are emerging upon the scene," announced an introductory note to the 1968 annual special section on poetry in *Negro Digest*. Most of the poets "are confronting their experiences and giving vent to their imaginations without apology," explained the editors, "thanks—in large measure—to the growing number of literary outlets for their works."[1] The editors of the magazine were reminding its readers that the emergence of new black poets was being facilitated by black publishing venues. According to literary critic Carolyn Gerald, "The direction and developing quality of black literature can be but imperfectly seen if these journals are ignored." She goes on to write that African American literary magazines and journals "are an important index of the measure and meaning of the sixties."[2]

The selection and presentation of poems, the promotion of poets, and the assessment of volumes of poetry constitute central activities performed by periodicals in the material production of verse. In addition, literary magazines and journals serve as those indispensable outlets that mediate poets' initial exposure to large readerships. Nonetheless, relatively little scholarship has examined the essential roles of periodicals in the publication of African American poetry. Taken together, writings produced by James Hall, Abby Arthur Johnson and Ronald Maberry Johnson, Eugene B. Redmond, and Julius Thompson do offer a useful set of historical surveys of literary magazines in general.[3] More detailed analyses will be necessary, though, in order to account for the role of periodicals in the representation of poets and the broad circulation of poetry during the era.

Literary magazines such as *Liberator,* the *Journal of Black Poetry, Negro Digest/Black World, Black Dialogue, Soulbook,* and *Freedomways* were collectively and largely responsible for providing widespread exposure to both the writings and the activities of black poets during the 1960s and 1970s. The tendency of these publications to publish a common group of writers who wrote on overlapping, culturally distinct topics actually advanced the pervasive sense of "nationality," as Redmond observes, that characterized black arts discourse.[4] The literary magazines and journals published poems, articles on poetics, reviews of poetry, and news regarding African American literary activities and thus operated as invaluable venues for the presentation and appreciation of black poetry and poets. In many instances, these periodicals served as the preliminary site of publication for poems that would later appear in anthologies and volumes of poetry. Moreover, periodicals regularly participated in augmenting the messages of poems, as editors of publications made key decisions concerning presentation.

For instance, Mari Evans's poem "The Black Woman" appears on the cover of the September 1969 annual poetry issue of *Negro Digest,* joined by a photograph of the author, thus showcasing the poet and her poem for readers in ways that Evans could not have done alone. The appearance of the poet and her poem on the front cover of the magazine in 1969 also provided Evans with major publicity for her then upcoming volume of poetry *The Black Woman* (1970). *Negro Digest*'s method of presentation also prompted reader-viewers to link the words of the proud and strong black woman in the poem with the accompanying image. Similarly, *Black Dialogue*'s presentation of Sonia Sanchez's "a ballad for stirling street" juxtaposes poem and image and thus complements the poet's words with a concrete vision. "Someone shud write" a book about "stirling street," proposes Sanchez, to showcase the street's "beauty of blk / culture" and to celebrate "brothers / TCBing on stirling street."[5] Sanchez's poem is accompanied by a photo of two black men, one playing a guitar and another one dancing. The image prompts readers to conclude that the street in the background is the "stirling street" that Sanchez refers to in her poem and that the men pictured are taking care of business. As the presentations of Sanchez's and Evans's poems suggest, magazine editorial decisions such as the fusion of poems and photographs in the presentation of literary art can influence how audiences perceive poets' works.

Of the several periodicals that contained verse, *Negro Digest/Black World* was arguably the most influential venue for the publication and discussion of African American poetry and poets. The magazine's wide circulation, its inclusion of so many leading poets, and its prominent role initiating and showcasing particular concerns related to black writers made it a defining outlet in the transmission of black literary art and an important social force for getting poets on the same page. This magazine was actually one among a number of publications, including *Liberator,* the *Journal of Black Poetry, Soulbook, Freedomways,* and *Black Dialogue.* These and other publications were certainly important to the presentation of black verse as well. However, *Negro Digest/Black World* requires special attention for understanding the production of black poetry during the 1960s and 1970s.

Setting the Stage for Black Arts Literature

According to Larry Neal, *Negro Digest/Black World* "had the most consistent effect on contemporary black letters." Neal goes on to observe that the magazine's "strong influence on the new literary movement derives from the fact that it is the most stable and widely read of the magazines concerned with the full range of issues confronting the black artistic community."[6] The editorial staff of the magazine included Hoyt Fuller, David Llorens, Carole Parks, Herbert Temple, Ariel Strong, and Robert Fentress. Fuller, Llorens, and Parks, in particular, assisted in increasing the visibility of black poets and poetry by providing coverage of literary conferences and events during the era. The collective efforts of these writers and editors served as a foundation for the reports and editorials focusing on black artistic production presented in the magazine. The editorial staff, or more specifically the design and layout artists, created dynamic displays of poetry and images appealing to a black nationalist ethos.

Among other African American literary magazines of the era, *Negro Digest/Black World* "had more tangible marks of outward success: a longer history and a larger circulation and readership," observe Abby Johnson and Ronald Johnson.[7] John H. Johnson's financial backing gave the publication unparalleled resources, especially for a magazine that regularly featured writings and news on African American literary art. For example, the periodical had a circulation of thirty thousand, by far the largest circulation among magazines that regularly published black poetry. The relationships between *Negro Digest/Black World* and other African American literary magazines of the era were often interactive. The smaller publications influenced and were influenced by the Johnson-financed magazine.

Although Abby Johnson and Ronald Johnson's assessment that *Negro Digest/Black World* had more outward markers of success than other magazines has some validity, it is worth noting that *Liberator,* the *Journal of Black Poetry, Freedomways,* and *Black Dialogue* served different purposes and should perhaps be evaluated in slightly different categories. *Liberator,* for instance, concerned itself with concentrated regional interests. In particular, the editors oriented their material to the arts and political scenes of New York and especially Harlem. In the process, the magazine appealed to its local readership and offered publishing opportunities more frequently to those in the area. The *Journal of Black Poetry* also tended to have a regional focus, this one on the West Coast, though the periodical did have a news and announcements section that provided national news on literary events. As the title of the publication suggests, though, the *Journal of Black Poetry* concentrated primarily on African American verse. The magazine effectively published a range of materials by established and emergent poets; the publication's attention to verse meant that it would present a large number of writers in each issue. To the extent that the material from so many of the African American periodicals of the era influenced a common group of poets and readerships, viewing their overall achievements as interrelated is necessary.

Published monthly, *Negro Digest/Black World* could be found on newsstands and in bookstores across the country in major black-populated areas. First published in 1942, *Negro Digest* thrived in securing a large African American middle-class readership, as its owner Johnson capitalized on "an almost insatiable thirst by African Americans to hear about themselves."[8] Indeed, Johnson, who later founded *Ebony, Jet,* and

Tan, proved to have keen insight and much success in black capitalist enterprises. As James Hall notes, "Johnson perceived potentially lucrative opportunities in packaging a product sensitively aimed at the social, cultural, and psychological particularities of the black consumer." Johnson's major accomplishment was therefore "his significant insight into the psychology of American capitalism."[9]

Modeled on *Reader's Digest, Negro Digest* initially reprinted news articles focusing on African Americans from a variety of sources.[10] The publication became profitable early on but was surpassed by Johnson's "picture-focused periodical" *Ebony,* which began in 1945. With the rising interest in *Ebony,* Johnson discontinued publication of *Negro Digest* in 1951 because of a decrease in profits. The magazine reappeared in 1961, however, with Hoyt Fuller as its new managing editor. "Fuller transformed *Negro Digest* from a publication that merely reprinted articles to one that showcased all forms of original scholarly and creative expression," writes literary historian Clovis Semmes (xi). As managing editor of a widely distributed magazine that gave substantial coverage to African American literary culture, Fuller, according to Semmes, "became a major architect of the Black Arts and Black Consciousness movement of the mid-1960s and 1970s" (xii).

Under Fuller's leadership, *Negro Digest/Black World* was a premier magazine that published a tremendous amount of poems and articles related to poetry. Kalamu ya Salaam observes that Fuller "published a variety of viewpoints but also insisted on editorial excellence and thus made *Negro Digest/Black World* a first-rate literary publication."[11] To be sure, between 1965 and 1976, *Negro Digest/Black World* published over three hundred poets and more than 750 poems.[12] Fuller's column "Perspectives (Notes on Books, Writers, Artists, and the Arts)" informed readers about publishing opportunities, upcoming conferences, and the latest book releases. In his column, Fuller presented the names of writers in bold lettering, which highlighted artists and creative intellectuals of the era. He also provided mailing addresses of black-owned presses, making them more available to potential book buyers. As the facilitator of such an expansive site regarding African American literature and the contemporary arts scene, Fuller established the publication as an invaluable resource and venue for black literary art.

Fuller also utilized his column to celebrate and critique trends in the literary marketplace and to warn African American writers and readers in general about what he viewed as the antiblack racist practices of the mainstream publishing industry. In the December 1970 issue of the publication, Fuller placed an inquiry in a small box at the bottom of the first page of his column: "Question: Why would a writer who makes a big production of being 'just a writer, not a Negro writer,' accept a contract from a publisher to collect material for—and serve as editor of—an anthology of Afro-American literature?"[13] The question and critique most likely referred to Robert Hayden, who had edited *Kaleidoscope: Poems by American Negro Poets* and who had also been criticized for taking a seemingly conservative position regarding his racial identity as a writer. Fuller's question functioned to raise suspicions about writers who avoided being referred to as "black" yet still pursued opportunities to profit from labeling their works under categories related to African American literature. Fuller's critique echoed 1960s debates, as well as prior disagreements regarding how African American writers should define themselves and their relationship to white and black audiences. Langston Hughes addressed the degree to which black writers embraced their cultural and racial identities in his essay "The Negro Artist and the Racial Mountain," initially published in 1926. The appearance of Fuller's critique in such a popular venue gave potential editors and writers a sense of the consequences that might befall them if they misaligned themselves with black militancy.

Negro Digest/Black World increased the visibility of black writers in a number of ways. For one, the magazine published poems, short stories, and essays by leading black writers, including Amiri Baraka, Larry Neal, Nikki Giovanni, Dudley Randall, Haki Madhubuti (Don Lee), and Sonia Sanchez. The periodical also published reports on literary conferences, publicized events organized by writers, and announced the publication of recent books and recipients of literary awards. Further, the periodical published articles focusing on African American literature and hundreds of reviews. Finally, the magazine regularly published photographs of black writers and thus familiarized readers with visual images of literary artists. The "Perspectives" section of the July 1968 issue of the magazine, for example, announced that "the first Conrad Kent Rivers Memorial Fund Award was presented to Carolyn Rodgers" and included a photograph of the poet alongside the announcement.[14] The constant presentation of poet photographs greatly increased poets' popularity, making it possible for audiences to establish visual connections with the black literary figures.

Like most magazines, *Negro Digest/Black World* utilized images to accentuate the writings in the publication and to appeal to both the linguistic and the visual sensibilities of readers. The editors often relied on

that Giovanni published in *Negro Digest,* in 1966 and in 1969, that criticized the chauvinism of male cultural nationalists. In "First Steps toward a True Revolution," Giovanni asked, "Is it necessary that I cease being a Black woman so that he [a black man] can be free?"[29] Here, in the pages of *Negro Digest,* Giovanni articulated concerns about the relegation of black women to less important roles in the movement in the interest of advancing black men. In her essay "Black Poets, Poseurs and Power," Giovanni questioned the "latent militarism of the artistic community." According to Giovanni, at a conference in Philadelphia, all the artists had military attachments. "The conference had guards; the artists had guards; the guards had guards," wrote Giovanni comically. Giovanni concluded that this "artist-guard syndrome" resulted from black male artists wanting to impress "the white community with [their] militancy and the guards [wanting to] impress the Black community with their power. It's a sick syndrome with, again, the Black community bring the loser."[30]

Overall, Giovanni's comments in "Black Poets, Poseurs and Power," as well as in her 1966 article "First Steps toward a True Revolution," are notable in that they demonstrate the willingness of a leading black arts poet to critique sexism in the movement. Moreover, the appearance of her article in *Negro Digest* demonstrated the publication's willingness to provide a platform for the kinds of ideas expressed by Giovanni. *Negro Digest* apparently offered Giovanni an opportunity to critique the sexism of black men in the midst of the movement. As a result, the publication provided space for both the promotion and the critique of leading black artists and African American cultural figures in general. Clearly, *Negro Digest/Black World* made expanding the views of African American cultural figures and literature one of its central missions.

Contemporary critics often charge that black arts writers lacked appreciation for the African American writers who preceded them. However, these critics seem to have overlooked the editorial practices of *Negro Digest/Black World.* The articles and special issues published in the magazine on writers such as Richard Wright, Ralph Ellison, Sterling Brown, and Harlem Renaissance writers reveal that recovery projects constituted a major aspect of Fuller's editorial vision. Also, notably, in terms of representing black women literary predecessors, Alice Walker has often been credited with "launching a [Zora Neale] Hurston revival" with the publication of her article on Hurston in *Ms.* Magazine in March 1975.[31] In praising Walker, however, the critics fail to point out that *Black World* played a role in that "revival" with its August 1974 issue, which carried a photo of Hurston on the cover with a caption reading "Black Women Image Makers." The late literary critic Barbara Christian took interest in the edition of *Black World* featuring Hurston because of "the tone of the individual pieces," which were by and about African American women, "and the effect of their juxtaposition." According to Christian, "What the configuration of the August 1974 *Black World* suggested to me, as I am sure it did to others, was the growing visibility of Afro-American women and the significant impact they were having on contemporary black culture."[32] The editorial leadership of Hoyt Fuller and his staff at *Negro Digest/Black World* contributed to this increased exposure of black women writers. Whereas the publication performed many services in the presentation of African American literary art and artists of the 1960s and 1970s, the periodical was especially important for displaying and promoting black poetry.

Transmitting the New Black Poetry

As mentioned, *Negro Digest/Black World* published a few hundred poets, reviews of volumes of poetry, and essays on poetics. Where else but in *Negro Digest/Black World* could issues regarding black poetry receive a regular readership of thirty thousand? Few popular venues in the history of African American literature dedicated so much space to black poets and their writings. The editorial staff utilized several modes of transmission in order to shape views of African American poetry. In particular, the timing and arrangement of poems presented in the periodical, the recurring types of poetry published, the number and popularity of the magazine's contributors, and the wide-ranging coverage of issues pertaining to poetry in general represented central editorial practices utilized by *Negro Digest/Black World*. These editorial practices, in short, mediated the publication, circulation, and reception of black poetry.

As the crucial links between poets and readerships, magazine editors played major roles in how poems would be presented and possibly interpreted. The dates or the timing of publication in *Negro Digest/Black World* constituted a subtle yet significant factor in a poem's delivery. LeRoi Jones's "A Poem for Black Hearts," which memorializes Malcolm X, appeared in the September 1965 of *Negro Digest,* seven months after the leader was slain, thus placing Jones, his poem, and the site of publication in the forefront in terms of the flood of elegies to Malcolm that would follow.[33] In February 1966, *Negro Digest* commemorated the one-year anniversary of Malcolm's assassination by publishing David Llorens's memorial poem dedicated to the Muslim leader, entitled "One Year Ago."[34] A month after Martin Luther King Jr. was assassinated, the May 1968 issue of *Negro Digest* published poems by Mari Evans and Zack Gilbert focusing on King's life and death.[35] The July 1968 issue of *Negro Digest* published Joseph Bush's "Trane's Tracks," while the September–October issue of 1968 contained LeRoi Jones's "The Evolver." Both poems pay tribute to John Coltrane. Interestingly, the publication of Bush's tribute poem in July marked the one-year anniversary of Coltrane's death, and Jones's poem about Trane appeared in the special September issue, the month of the saxophonist's birthday.

Conventional analyses of the aforementioned poems might provide an understanding of the writers' individual, isolated messages. Yet analyses of only the poems and not the timing of publication overlook the efforts made by editors to situate poems and poets within distinct social and historical narratives. Making publishing decisions based on noteworthy dates in African American history enabled the editors to display some of the poems they published in accordance with a black "cultural calendar."[36] Strategically publishing poems to coincide with the chronology of significant events constituted an editorial practice that kept noteworthy African American events and persons on the mindscapes of audiences.

In many instances, the timing and arrangement of poems in the periodical contributed to the messages and values the editors conveyed to their audiences. In the September 1970 issue of the magazine, *Black World* published poems by Charles Moreland and Charyn Sutton that publicized the deaths of members of the Black Panther Party.[37] Notably, Moreland's and Sutton's poems appear next to each other in the publication, thus amplifying the documentation of violence committed against African Americans, as well as the willingness of the editorial staff to catalog such injustices. The editors could present their own disdain for the plight of black activists by endorsing these kinds of poems. In the January 1976 issue of *Black World,* the magazine covered the tenth-anniversary celebration of Broadside Press.[38] Before and after the article on the celebration, poems by Sterling Plumpp and Gwendolyn Brooks paid tribute to Broadside Press founder Dudley Randall and thus indicated *Black World*'s appreciation for the publisher/poet.[39] Fuller and his staff frequently published tribute poems like those by Plumpp and Brooks to convey their overall valuation of notable figures, and in the process they helped raise the visibility of poetry.

The note for Haki Madhubuti's poem "One-Sided Shoot-Out," published in the January 1970 issue of *Negro Digest,* reads, "(for fred hampton & mark clark, murdered 12/4/69 by chicago police at 4:30 AM while they slept)."[40] Notably, the poem appeared a month after the two men were killed. In the poem, Madhubuti explains that despite all the "rhetoric and seriousness," the murder of Hampton and Clark provided evidence that black people were not taken seriously by most Americans. Madhubuti explains that the two men would be memorialized in the usual ways that African American victims of violence were memorialized, yet the violence against black people would continue. In retrospect, the appearance of the poem so shortly after the incident reflects a swift collaboration between *Negro Digest* and Madhubuti in contributing to the wide range of publicity of the murders of Hampton and Clark. Unfortunately, these murders were not officially recognized as crimes by the government until decades later.

Similar to Madhubuti's "One-Sided Shoot-Out," the note for June Jordan's "Poem," published in the March 1973 issue of *Black World,* reads, "On the Murder of Two Human Being Black Men, Denver A. Smith and Leonard Douglas Brown, at Southern University, Baton Rouge, Louisiana, November 1972."[41] With a bitter and sarcastic tone, Jordan addresses the killing of the two student protesters, noting that their lives and the lives of black people in general are viewed as "light-stuff" in comparison to the private property and "heavy real estate" that belong to those in power. Against private property and heavy real estate, "the lightstuff be quite blown away" (64). Jordan goes on to write, "if you have 300 unarmed students / running away from tear gas fired / by / 150 gorillas decked with shotguns / and / two of the students fall down shot / by shotguns / shot and killed," then the mystery becomes "who shot the two Black men who died?" (64). It is a mystery that "Nobody official anywhere could solve"; however, "the Governor / and the mayor / they said / at anyrate the homicide was justified" (64). Jordan closes her poem informing her audience, "what you have to realize / is / Amerika will kill you / Amerika will kill you / Amerika will kill you / *too*" (65). Publishing poems such as Madhubuti's "One-Sided Shoot-Out" and Jordan's "Poem" allowed *Negro Digest/Black World* to actively participate in addressing the injustices committed against African Americans. The poems indicate the writers' sense of rage at these acts of violence, and the publication of these poems in such a popular venue shows the extent to which *Black World* could collaborate with poets to address injustice.

Publishing memorial poems that focus on slain activists enabled poets and the editors of *Negro Digest/Black World* to chronicle current tragedies in a widely read venue and highlight a distinct and poetic sense of black anger. Occasionally, the poems also familiarized readers with the plight of African-descended people in countries outside the United States. In his poem "Lumumba Section," published in the July 1968 issue of *Negro Digest,* the exiled South African writer Keorapetse William Kgositsile laments the 1961 torture and assassination of Patrice Lumumba, the first prime minister of the independent Republic of the Congo. "Searching past what we see and hear," wrote Kgositsile in the poem, which addressed a deceased Lumumba, ". . . We see the gaping wounds where / Those murderers butchered your flesh / As they butchered the flesh of our land."[42] The appearance of Kgositsile's poem on Lumumba reveals *Negro Digest*'s commitment to addressing the struggles and injustices on the African continent. Further, the publication of Kgositsile's poem anticipates *Negro Digest*'s developing focus on "black world" issues beyond the United States. Overall, *Negro Digest/Black World* honed and amplified the collective rage expressed by several black poets through the publication of numerous poems relating to violence against black people.

In addition to memorial poems, the periodical frequently published tribute or praise poems, which honored the lives and achievements of African American political figures, musicians, and writers. These displays of poems advanced the objectives of celebrating black people, history, and culture and of displacing the dominance of Eurocentrism. As Haki Madhubuti wrote, "We must destroy Faulkner, dick, jane and other perpetuators of evil. It's time for Du Bois, Nat Turner and Kwame Nkrumah."[43] In terms of tribute poems, the elegies to Malcolm X seemed to predominate. Among the posthumously published poems by Conrad Kent Rivers that appeared in the September 1975 issue of *Black World* was his "Malcolm, A Thousandth Poem." The poet views Malcolm as a major inspiration: "When brothers build a city / Down in valleys / And through mountains, / Across plains slashed by winds / Forever African; / Your flame fires them on."[44] *Negro Digest/Black World* contributed to keeping Malcolm and his black radical vision on the minds of readers. Typically appealing to the visual sensibilities of its audience, the cover of the November 1968 issue of the publication carries a drawing of Malcolm X with the caption "Brother Malcolm and the Black Revolution."

The editors regularly published poems by poets paying tribute to fellow writers. In "Don L. Lee Is a Poem," published in the September 1969 issue of *Negro Digest,* Marvin X describes the walk, talk, and being of Madhubuti as a poem. Marvin X observes that "Don don't smoke pot / He always loaded / on his poems."[45] Alicia L. Johnson's "To (2) Poets," published in the same issue, commemorates the deaths of Christopher Okigbo and Conrad K. Rivers. Johnson explains that the poets passed like the wind but would return in new forms: "they are not / dead / they have only passed / through / HEAVENSGATE."[46] The magazine also published tributes by poets celebrating the movement's leading figure, Amiri Baraka. In the August 1968 issue, Lennox Raphael opens his poem "Roi" by pointing out that "LeRoi Jones roams the blues of night with sweet and gentle / courage of awakening, as black, as man, as brother, as Roi."[47] Poet-to-poet tribute poems further underscored the periodical's sense of camaraderie among black writers.

Celebrations of black music and musicians constituted the most frequently recurring types of tributes published in *Negro Digest/Black World.* Etheridge Knight celebrates one of the famous sidemen of John Coltrane in his poem "Elvin Jones: Jazz Drummer." Jones "has fire and steel in his hands," observes Knight. "ELVIN JONES / thumps the big circle in bare feet, / opens wide the big arms and, / like the sea, / swallows us."[48] In her poem "Tribute to Duke," Sarah Webster Fabio celebrates the composer Duke Ellington: "Right on, Duke / Do your thing, / your own thing. / And, Man, / the word's out / when you / get down / Bad / it's good, / Real good."[49] In a reverent poem for John Coltrane published in *Negro Digest,* Amiri Baraka writes, "The power of John Coltrane / The power of God / The worship of Soul-Ra / The worship of God / The feeling of the infinite / The shadows and suns upon our bodies and minds / The power of John Coltrane / The worship of God."[50] The editors' publication of tribute poems extended the widespread practice among creative intellectuals of continually emphasizing the connections between poetry and music. When readers encountered a grouping of poems in *Negro Digest/Black World,* they were likely to come across references to black music.

Praise poems and elegies were hardly the only kinds of poetry published in *Negro Digest/Black World.* However, their strong presence throughout the pages of the publication is quite evident, as is the appearance of these kinds of writings throughout black arts discourse. The types of poems published by the most visible magazine of the era had far-reaching effects. The regular publication of praise poems and elegies in *Negro Digest/Black World* influenced the subject matter that poets chose to write about and helped determine what they eventually chose to submit for possible publication. Based on the large number of elegies and praise poems that appeared in the publication, it seems apparent that the editorial staff of the publication valued these modes of writing. The poems that the magazine decided to publish confirm that *Negro Digest/Black World* was certainly not a neutral venue, seeking to present any and all kinds of writings. Instead, the magazine had an agenda that involved celebrating black historical figures and cataloging injustices committed against African Americans. Further, *Negro Digest/Black World* framed the contours of black poetry by promoting particular kinds of poems.

Whereas the types of poems *Negro Digest/Black World* published are important, the periodical also shaped the production of poetry based on the number of poems it presented and the degree to which the periodical featured black poetry in general. The September issues represented one of the publication's most impressive contributions to the transmission of black poetry. These special issues included between twenty-five and forty poets and articles on major literary figures or trends occurring in literary culture with regard to poetry. The magazine presented poems by writers from all over the country and occasionally from countries in Africa. *Negro Digest/Black World*'s presentation, in a single issue, of African American poets who represented various ages, regions of the country, poetic styles, and political persuasions indicated the diversity among black poets. At the same time, the magazine provided a common publishing venue and hence a sense of unity among a variety of different poets and poems. Not all the poets who published in *Negro Digest/Black World* are commonly referred to as black arts poets. For instance, although writers such as Audre Lorde and Michael Harper were published in black publications, they are not usually associated with the same kind of militant stances taken by writers such as Askia Toure, Haki Madhubuti, and Sonia Sanchez. Nonetheless, publishing various kinds of black writers in a common site gave the impression, at least, that there were some commonalities among the poets. If nothing else, these writers met the selection criteria of the editorial staff of *Negro Digest/Black World*.

Presenting a sense of unity among writers was integral to the notion of a black artistic movement. The appearance of several poets at one time in the September issues of the magazine suggested that the writers were on the same page, committed to similar causes. While most issues of *Negro Digest/Black World* dispersed poems randomly and separately throughout the periodical, the special September issues on poetry always grouped many of the poets together in a section labeled "Portfolio of Poetry." The poems were displayed using a common format—same typeface and font size, and the author's name at the end of each poem—making it possible for readers to move easily through the various poems and poets in the magazine. The regular appearance of established and popular poets in *Negro Digest/Black World* contributed to the periodical's reputation as a major venue for African American literary art. Leading poets of the era—Sonia Sanchez, Haki Madhubuti, Dudley Randall, Amiri Baraka, Carolyn Rodgers, Nikki Giovanni, and Gwendolyn Brooks—all published in the magazine, and writings by the poets appeared in the special September issues. The positioning of their names on the cover and in the pages of the publication demonstrated the periodical's association with some of the most popular and prominent poets of the time period.

The cover designs for the special issues increased the exposure of poets and emphasized the significance of the New Black Poetry. The cover of the September–October 1968 issue of *Negro Digest* displays an assortment of African American publications, including several volumes of poetry, the *Journal of Black Poetry,* and *Umbra.* Superimposed over the images of the books and magazines, the publication announces, "THE ANNUAL POETRY ISSUE / Black Poets and Their Publications." The cover goes on to note that the issue contains poems by Gwendolyn Brooks, Dudley Randall, Sonia Sanchez, LeRoi Jones, and Mari Evans, as well as articles by Don L. Lee, Sarah Webster Fabio, and Keorapetse William Kgositsile. The cover of the September 1972 issue of *Black World* displays a drawing by Jon Onye Lockard of Gwendolyn Brooks sporting an afro. The cover informs readers that the issue includes an excerpt from Brooks's autobiography and the annual "PORTFOLIO OF POETRY." The cover of the September 1974 issue displays a Yoruba sculpture of a "horse and rider." Along the left side of the cover, the publication announces its annual poetry issue and lists the names of featured poets, including Johari Amini, Alvin Aubert, Gwendolyn Brooks, Julia Fields, Michael Harper, David Henderson, Doc Long, Audre Lorde, Dudley Randall, and Ron Welburn. Placing the names and images of well-known poets on the cover of the magazine simultaneously confirmed and extended the writers' popularity among readers.

In addition to presenting dozens of poets in the "Portfolio of Poetry" section, the September issues included a "Poetry Features" section. This section contained a series of poems by three or more poets, providing them with more space to share their work than the single poems representing other writers in the issue. The annual poetry issue also contained articles on black poetry. Some of the articles focused on historically significant poets such as Jean Toomer, Langston Hughes, and Sterling Brown. The essays in the September issues also addressed contemporary trends in poetry, including discussions of black aesthetics and articles such as "Black Poetry—Where It's At" and "Images of Black Women in Afro-American Poetry."

The 1972 September issue contains an excerpt from the autobiography of Gwendolyn Brooks, an article by Ted Joans entitled "The Langston Hughes I Knew," and an article by Barbara Christian entitled "Whatever Happened to Bob Kaufman." The "Portfolio of Poetry" section presents thirty-two poets, including Zack Gilbert, Dudley Randall, August Wilson, Sonia Sanchez, and David Henderson. The issue's featured poets are Julia Fields, Ibrahima Diallo, and Herbert Clark Johnson. The September 1974 issue contains an article on Jean Toomer by Bernard Bell, an essay on the black aesthetic by Addison Gayle, and an essay-review of Sterling Plumpp's *Steps to Break the Circle* by Keorapetse William Kgositsile. The "Portfolio of Poetry" section includes twenty-two poets, and the featured poets for the issue are Mari Evans, Alvin Aubert, and Johari Amini. As the tables of contents of these two issues suggest, the special poetry issues showcased a range of issues pertaining to black poetry.

Several poets published reviews and essays in *Negro Digest/Black World*. Carolyn Rodgers, Amiri Baraka, Haki Madhubuti, and Larry Neal, to name a few, contributed articles focusing on poetics and poetry. As a result, these and several other poets who published in the magazine contributed to the larger critical conversations concerning African American literary art of the era. Nikki Giovanni, Keorapetse William Kgositile, Sterling Plumpp, Dudley Randall, Julia Fields, Johari Amini, and Carolyn Rodgers were among the most frequent reviewers of poetry in the publication.[51] That the periodical's reviewers were leading poets illustrates that they were actively involved in the assessment and valuation of contemporary black literature. Most important, the regular appearance of poetry reviews gave poets and discussions of verse increased exposure.

Negro Digest/Black World played an especially important role in providing coverage of Chicago-area poets. In particular, the magazine frequently published writers associated with the Organization of Black American Culture (OBAC). As a cofounder of OBAC and chairperson of the writers' workshop for OBAC, Hoyt Fuller was in a position to showcase members of the group in his publication. Indeed, he published members of the workshop regularly in the magazine. Moreover, he provided the group with free publicity. For instance, in an article explaining the origins of OBAC, *Negro Digest* stated that in order to reach the people, members of the writers' workshop "went to taverns where adults congregated and to community centers where young people assembled. Poetry, they found, is welcome entertainment if it speaks to the people."[52] The anonymous article projected the popular sentiment among writers of the era that African American poets frequently functioned in the role of community activists. As managing editor of a major black arts publication, Fuller ensured publicity and publishing opportunities for members of OBAC.

In the August 1968 issue of *Negro Digest,* the magazine provided a profile article entitled "Chicago's OBAC: Portrait of Young Writers in a Workshop." The article opens by noting that for the OBAC writers' workshop "literature is a truly lively art. For more than a year, the pursuit of literary reflection of The Black Experience has animated the writers and their weekly sessions." With individual photos of over ten writers in the workshop accompanying the essay, the article announces recent and upcoming publications by the group's members, including Jewell Latimore, Don L. Lee, Carolyn Rodgers, and Kharlos Wimberli. Finally, the article emphasizes the group's connection to established African American writers by noting that Gwendolyn Brooks, who "contributed $200 toward the publication of the group's anthology," also worked closely with the writer's workshop.[53] In addition, the workshop members organized a benefit for LeRoi Jones to help pay his court costs in a case in which he was charged with possession of a firearm. Calling attention to their relationship to well-known writers such as Brooks and Jones, and reporting on their activities in the community in *Negro Digest/Black World,* established the image of OBAC writers as committed and politically active artists. Ultimately, the magazine increased the visibility of OBAC members by providing them with regular coverage and publishing opportunities.

The seeming favoritism that *Negro Digest/Black World* showed toward Chicago poets led poets from other areas of the country to critique the publication's preferences. Moreover, despite all of its achievements, the periodical had several limitations. As Eugene Redmond suggested, although the magazine published the widest number of poems and poets, it was less likely than the *Journal of Black Poetry* to publish experimental verse.[54] In this view, the publication was not necessarily the most cutting-edge publisher of the New Black Poetry. Looking over past issues of the *Journal of Black Poetry* shows that this publication took a more grassroots and experimental approach to the publication of verse. Joe Goncalves, founding editor of the publication, regularly allowed guest editors to take the lead. Goncalves's publication had a far more limited budget in comparison to *Negro Digest/Black World*. Thus, the *Journal of Black Poetry* relied on seemingly cruder yet more artistically engaging blends of words and images. Rather than printing photographs alongside poems, the *Journal of Black Poetry* was more likely to present drawings and more abstract images to complement poems. As a result, the *Journal of Black Poetry* displayed a more vernacular aesthetic than *Negro Digest/Black World*.

Some observers maintained that the periodical was quite limited in its assessment of the conditions facing African Americans. According to writers Ishmael Reed and Amiri Baraka, its writers offered fairly conventional and thus insufficient critiques of antiblack racism. As Reed explains, "*Black World* thought it was a simple matter of white faces being white racists. It should be so easy."[55] Reed also suggests that the favoritism shown some writers and schools of thought led the publication to dismiss, if not mistreat, several other writers, including Ralph Ellison, John Williams, and Al Young. Baraka charged that the publication was "schizophrenic," an accusation that "meant that even in the same issue they'd have widely differing stances and attitudes, some positive, some absolutely backwards, some irrelevant, lifeless academic set pieces to get somebody an A+ in Boredom, and now and again a couple fragments, poems, etc."[56] Moreover, Baraka viewed *Negro Digest/Black World* as "simply the petit bourgeoisie at work, defending as usual, objectively, a bourgeoisie, which is classically their gig." The assessments by Reed and Baraka carried some validity: *Negro Digest/Black World*'s ability to publish such a wide range of writers and views was one of its strengths, but perhaps, the magazine's well-financed capabilities were also a weakness. With such a broad focus and commercial backing, the magazine could certainly not meet all expectations. Further, among the range of writers the magazine did publish, there would inevitably be conflicting ideologies presented. Because Fuller and his staff chose sides and had preferences, they gained supporters as well as detractors.

Along with its strengths and weaknesses, *Negro Digest/Black World* was central to the transmission of new black poetry. The decline of the Black Arts Movement and the demise of *Black World,* in fact, seem interconnected. John Johnson, publisher of the magazine, discontinued the publication after the April 1976 issue.[57] Consequently, several scholars identify 1976 as a defining year in terms of when the movement subsided. "The death of *Black World*," explain Abby Arthur Johnson and Ronald Maberry Johnson, "was a convincing sign that the Black Arts movement was no longer the dominant voice in African American literature."[58] Hoyt Fuller went on to create another literary journal, *First World*. He drew on the large network of writers and creative intellectuals whom he worked with over the course of his tenure at *Negro Digest/Black World* to found *First World*. Houston Baker Jr., Toni Cade Bambara, Ossie Davis, Sarah Webster Fabio, Addison Gayle, Haki Madhubuti, Kalamu ya Salaam, Geneva Smitherman, Darwin Turner, and Shirley Anne Williams were among the editorial advisors and contributors for *First World*.[59] Lacking the financial support that Fuller had at *Black World*, however, Fuller's new publication was far less influential. Thus, the discontinuation of *Black World* in 1976 meant the end of one of the most visible and defining platforms for the publication of African American poetry.

Publicizing Amiri Baraka

Poets who become widely known among the countless number of published writers during any particular era must have an edge. Factors beyond the value of their individual poems and volumes of poetry determine the degree to which these writers might achieve popular and critical acclaim. Consequently, the coverage and publicity provided by magazines serve to increase poets' popularity among readers and potential book buyers. Few black arts poets were as widely publicized in magazines as Amiri Baraka. There is arguably a direct correlation between his status as the movement's leading figure and the frequency with which he was featured in various periodicals during the 1960s and early 1970s. A brief consideration of the coverage of Amiri Baraka offers an idea of how magazine exposure presented one poet to a wider readership and conveyed ideas about larger currents in African American literature and culture by highlighting a single writer.

In an article published in *African American Review*, James Smethurst reminds us that Baraka was "but one voice among many" of those who contributed to the Black Arts Movement. Although Smethurst's article appears in a special issue dedicated to Baraka, Smethurst seeks to "avoid the sort of great-man theory in which Baraka's work becomes a metonymy for all Black Arts literature, drama, criticism, and so on."[60] The positioning of Baraka as the movement's representative figure, as Smethurst's comments suggest, suppresses narratives about the diversity among a large number of black writers. Presenting Baraka as a representative black artist also diminishes the numerous contributions of other writers and at the same time overlooks the fact that Baraka's tremendous reception was quite exceptional. His pre- and post-1960s achievements, as well as his extensive and ongoing critical acclaim, make the trajectory of his career uncommon among poets. So whereas Baraka was hardly the leader per se of the Black Arts Movement, he was certainly the era's most revered and *leading* figure. His status as the movement's leading figure might help explain how the methods magazines used to publicize Baraka extended his popularity and simultaneously increased the movement's black radical visibility.

Larry Neal's appraisals of Baraka in magazines were particularly notable since Neal was identifying Baraka as the movement's principal figure just as the movement was unfolding. In a February 1965 *Liberator* review of Baraka's plays *The Slave* and *The Toilet,* Neal praises Baraka's works as "attempts to break down the barriers separating the artist from the audience to whom a work must ultimately address itself." Neal goes on to note that Baraka's "plays are the verbal companions to the expressions that have reached their greatest intensity in the music of Coltrane, Ornette Coleman, and more lately Archie Shepp." Neal thus opens his review with assessments that would become recurring themes in black arts discourse, namely, praising writers who directly address black audiences and whose work demonstrates the qualities of music, especially free jazz. Neal closes his review by stating that Baraka's "plays are among the most socially-conscious literary works in the history of Afro-American and American drama. Both are steps toward building a body of literature to which black people can point with pride, and which can be assimilated into the life-and-death drama which is the coming black revolution in America."[61] Here, Neal proclaims the significance of Baraka's plays in literary history, and he also predicts that Baraka's art will prove beneficial to black folks preparing for an imminent revolution in America. Overall, Neal's article promotes Baraka as both an artist who engages African American audiences and an agent for inspiring black political action.

Neal's positioning of Baraka within the unfolding narratives of Black Power and nationalist discourse would become more apparent in two articles featuring Baraka published in the January and February 1966 issues of *Liberator*. In the first article, Neal opens by pointing out that "LeRoi Jones is Black, is thirty-one years old, is a man dedicated to the liberation of his people by any means necessary." Again, Neal links Baraka to national political activity; most notably, the "by any means necessary" comment links Baraka to Malcolm X. Neal follows his opening statement by observing that Baraka was actually one of many artists from his generation committed to black liberation. What distinguished Baraka from his contemporaries, however, was "his public image," as "for about a year now, and especially since Malcolm's death, Jones has been projected by the news media as a venom-filled monster oozing with hate of the white man." Neal identifies the *Village Voice,* the *Herald Tribune,* the *World-Telegram,* "and a myriad of television stations" as the news media organizations taking part in the distortion of Baraka's "public image."[62] Notwithstanding the negative attention he was receiving, Baraka's visibility in media outlets was certainly making him more widely known.

Neal's article indicates that as early as 1965, Baraka possessed what relatively few poets ever obtain: a national public image. If the news media seemed to focus on distorting Baraka's image by asserting his "hate of the white man," then certainly magazine articles by writers like Neal were preoccupied with *undistorting* his image by giving attention to Baraka's commitment to "his people." An introductory editorial note to the second part of Neal's series "Development of LeRoi Jones" mentions that these articles on Baraka were necessary "in order to clarify certain misinformation concerning LeRoi Jones. Much of this misinformation has come from the white power establishment which stands opposed to any Black man asserting his manhood and integrity." Pitting him against white adversaries, the editors of *Liberator* could, in a nationalist context, make Baraka seem more endearing to a black readership. The article also includes a photograph of Baraka surrounded by a group of white men; the photo contains a caption that reads, "LeRoi Jones and his critics."[63]

A close inspection of the photo shows that Baraka and the men are in a somewhat relaxed setting, a reception perhaps. They do not necessarily look like adversaries. However, the caption accompanying the photo is clearly designed to convey the idea that whites are hostile to Baraka's work, which complements Neal's claim in the article that Baraka was "a welcomed member of the white literary world" when his works were perceived as only *literary* (18). According to Neal, however,

Baraka was less favored by the white literary establishment now that the poet was directing "his tremendous talents, towards meaningful activities in the Black community" (19). Neal's assessment of Baraka, as well as his contemplations of the radical possibilities of black art in his *Liberator* articles, anticipates his most widely circulated essay, "The Black Arts Movement," in which he identifies Baraka as the movement's "prime mover and chief designer."[64] Appearing first in the *Drama Review* in 1968, Neal's "The Black Arts Movement" circulated widely during the 1960s and 1970s. Echoing his comments on Baraka provided in *Liberator,* Neal's extended and positive treatment of Baraka in the essay helps explain why readers were likely to view Baraka as the movement's leading figure. "The Black Arts theatre, the theatre of LeRoi Jones," writes Neal, "is a radical alternative to the sterility of the American theatre" (33). Linking Baraka's individual productions to the overall identity and function of black arts theater identifies him as integral to the emergence of the movement.

Neal's praise for Baraka was infectious. Throughout the era, poets and various commentators extolled Baraka's talents as an artist and his *by any means necessary* commitments to *his people*. In addition to publishing Baraka's artistic productions, magazines also frequently published his image. As a result, they gave Baraka—and not simply his writings—increased visibility. Although photographs of writers that appeared in magazines rarely appeared in bibliographies, the pervasive publication of Baraka images certainly had to contribute to how he was envisioned by readers. It would be difficult to say exactly how images of writers influence interpretations of their work. The presentation of Baraka's images in magazines, however, did suggest to readers/viewers that whoever this artist was, he was important.

Liberator magazine was especially involved in presenting images of Baraka that linked him with black arts activities. An image of Baraka adjoins an article that describes a program produced by "a new theatre group called The Black Arts" in the April 1965 issue of *Liberator*.[65] Two months later, a photo showing "LeRoi Jones and Hampton Clanton leading the Black Arts parade down 125th Street, New York City," accompanies Larry Neal's article "The Cultural Front," which reports on the opening of the Black Arts Repertory/Theatre School in Harlem.[66] In the July 1965 issue, a photograph of Baraka and John Oliver Killens appears along with Baraka's essay "The Revolutionary Theatre."[67] And most visibly, a photograph of Baraka speaking assertively into a microphone appears on the cover of the January 1966 issue of *Liberator*. Notably, just as the black arts enterprise was getting under way in 1965 and 1966, *Liberator* was publishing Baraka's poems, featuring articles on the implications of his work and trajectory of his career, and also regularly presenting striking photographs of the artist. For *Liberator*'s readers, at least, Baraka was easily the most identifiable face of black arts.

With more national exposure than *Liberator*, *Negro Digest/Black World* participated in the presentation of Baraka's images. In a September 1964 report on a writers' conference, *Negro Digest* published various photographs of conference participants. The only photo featuring an individual artist, however, was the image of Baraka, who is shown seated in front of a large window-shaped brick structure. The image—Baraka's juxtaposition with his background—gives the sense that he is sitting on a kind of throne. The caption for the photo reads, "Framed by soaring backdrop, LeRoi Jones ponders questions during one of series of informal seminars. The Dead Lecturer is his latest book."[68] The April 1966 issue of *Negro Digest* presents an image of Baraka with a group of people on the steps of a building with the Black Arts Repertory Theatre flag; the image adjoins Baraka's essay "In Search of the Revolutionary Theatre."[69] A photo of Baraka that accompanies his article "Toward the Creation of Political Institutions for All African Peoples," published in the October 1972 issue of *Black World*, promotes Baraka as a political figure more than a conventional writer. In the photograph, Baraka stands at a podium that has several microphones; he is apparently taking questions, as if he is at a press conference.[70] The top portion of the cover of the November 1972 issue of the magazine shows a profile view of Baraka with an intense look on his face as he sports an afro and full goatee. To the left of his image, the magazine notes, "Position Paper: 'Toward Ideological Clarity' by Imamu Amiri Baraka."

Of course, African American magazines regularly published photographs of black writers and political figures. *Negro Digest/Black World*, in particular, frequently published images of emergent black poets. What distinguished the photographic presentations of Baraka, however, were the methods and frequency with which his images appeared throughout African American publications. More so than the typically static photographs of poets on the back covers of their books, magazines could show artists in a variety of poses and situations. The visual coverage of Baraka often gave special attention to his activist participation and blurred his status as a poet and a political figure. The early presentations by *Liberator* and *Negro Digest* of Baraka as a militant writer

closely associated with black arts activities and committed to the liberation of African Americans contributed to the idea that Baraka was the
movement's leading figure. Perhaps the most widely circulating article
on Baraka among a black readership—which blended striking images
and praises—appeared in *Ebony* magazine.

In August 1969, *Ebony* published an issue entitled "The Black Revolution," which included articles on jazz and contemporary black poetry
by A. B. Spellman and Larry Neal, respectively, as well as a feature article on Baraka by David Llorens—who was on the staff of *Negro Di-
gest/Black World.*[71] With *Ebony*'s wide circulation and notable influence
among African Americans, the magazine's profile on Baraka was certain
to further increase his national visibility. Llorens's profile, "Ameer
(LeRoi Jones) Baraka," echoes the sentiments of Larry Neal in his essay
"The Black Arts Movement" by identifying Baraka as the most prominent figure of the movement. "That LeRoi Jones would be heir to the
literary baton that had passed from Richard Wright to Ralph Ellison to
James Baldwin became apparent a few years after he set foot on the
track. Fools alone doubted his speed and ability," writes Llorens.[72] Here,
Baraka is favorably identified as the successor to three of the most
widely known and established African American writers.

Baraka "is regarded by those closest to black art," writes Llorens,
"as the nation's leading black writer, which of course suggests that no
other, however talented, has proven—in this time and place—more
valuable to *black people*" (75). Again echoing sentiments expressed by
Larry Neal, Llorens associates Baraka's artistry with his *value* to black
people. Llorens goes on to describe Baraka's literary career and his role
as an organizer. Emphasizing the idea that Baraka represents "the prototype of the poet as newest cultural hero in the black community,"
Llorens focuses more broadly on Baraka's political views as opposed to
the specifics of his poetry (83).

The images that accompany Llorens's story project a striking visual
narrative as well. Beneath the title in bold letters—**AMEER (LEROI
JONES) BARAKA**—and below the two opening paragraphs of the article, the first page of the story presents a photo of Baraka that con-
sumes nearly three-fourths of the page. In the photograph, Baraka is
looking to his left and smiling at someone in the direction in which he is
facing. He has an afro and full beard, wears beads with a medallion, and
is dressed in an orange African-style shirt. His attire and appearance
project an afrocentric fashion sensibility, which was popular among
some African Americans and some nationalists in particular. That the

image of Baraka is in such a prominent position suggests that the image of the writer is as important as the words about him. The design of the page, which emphasizes the photograph of the poet, amplifies or actually anticipates Llorens's opening opinion in the article that Baraka must be *seen* as more than a writer. Other additional photographs in the article show Baraka performing a marriage ceremony, and he is identified in one of the captions as an Orthodox Muslim and "a minister of the Kawaida faith" (76).

Another photograph in the series of images accompanying the story shows black women dressed in African attire—some sport afros, others wear head-wraps. The caption for the photographs informs readers that the women attend classes at an "African Free School where they study works of LeRoi Jones, Maulana Karenga, and other black thinkers of both the New World and the Old" (78). Overall, the photographs of Baraka dressed in African attire, as well as the images of black women, children, and men involved with organizations led by the writer-minister, validate Baraka's role as a committed cultural worker who apparently has a following. Moreover, the attire of Baraka and his supporters, as well as their engagement in cultural activities, presents a visual narrative that emphasizes Baraka's relationship to black people and an African aesthetic. The images indicate Baraka's connectedness to a black nationalist ethos quite vividly.

Presenting black poets as politically engaged, socially committed activists became the recurring practice of a number of magazines. In addition to the article on Baraka, *Ebony* ran feature profiles on Haki Madhubuti and Nikki Giovanni; the profile articles assisted in confirming and extending the importance of these leading poets as popular cultural figures. In the photographs that accompany the article on Haki Madhubuti (then known as Don Lee), the poet sports an afro, an African-print shirt, and dark sunglasses as he stands at a podium. The image of Madhubuti is accompanied by a photograph of an auditorium crowded with white people. Later in the article, Madhubuti is pictured reading his work to a group of African Americans. Collectively, the photographs project the idea of Madhubuti's wide appeal.

Llorens opens the article by reporting Gwendolyn Brooks's complimentary appraisal of Madhubuti as a poet and militant. According to the article, when an observer informed Brooks that Madhubuti "frightens me," Brooks responded, "He should."[73] That opening exchange between "an ingratiating black matron" and Brooks presents Madhubuti as a poet who makes some viewers and listeners uneasy. The idea that his persona and poetry might frighten some observers would give Madhubuti more credibility as a militant figure. Continuing the depiction of a defiant poet, Llorens characterizes Madhubuti and his work as "transcending customs. Niceties. Platitudes. Seeking no approval. No applause. No contest. Just making people hear their own silence. A disquieting experience" (72). Later, Llorens points out that Madhubuti's work reflects "a revolutionary black consciousness" (75). Throughout the article, Llorens intersperses excerpts from Madhubuti's poems to support observations about the political position of the poet. Linking Madhubuti's overall objectives with those of other black artists of the day, Llorens notes that "the young writers with whom [Madhubuti] shares fraternity have in no uncertain terms declared white critics unqualified to evaluate and judge their works. They have rejected, as parochial, the Western theory of an aesthetic." Instead, black poets' "consciousness is directed toward a *black aesthetic.*" That aesthetic involves Madhubuti and others "communicating with black people" (77).

Presenting Madhubuti as a militant poet, showing his popularity among large audiences, and revealing his specific concerns with a black aesthetic and the conditions of African Americans, Lloren actually promotes the idea of Madhubuti as a major force in black poetry. Like his profile of Baraka, Llorens's feature article on Madhubuti in *Ebony* reports on and ultimately expands the poet's popularity for a black readership. Whereas Baraka and Madhubuti were widely known in literary and cultural circles by 1969, the *Ebony* articles projected complimentary descriptions and striking visual images of the poets on a larger black stage. In the February 1972 issue of *Ebony,* the magazine ran a similar feature profile on Nikki Giovanni.

Similar to the articles on Madhubuti and Baraka, the profile on Giovanni foregrounds her connections to black nationalist sensibilities visually and linguistically. Like Madhubuti and Baraka, Giovanni is African American, sports an afro, and is pictured interacting with various groups of black people. The profile also shows a private side to Giovanni. A full-page photograph of Giovanni sitting on the floor of an apartment reading a book to a toddler, identified in the caption as her son, Tommy, adjoins the first page of the article. The caption for the photo explains that Giovanni authored a children's book, *Spin a Soft Black Song,* "because I wanted Tommy to have something to read and relate to." Another photograph shows Giovanni and actor Ossie Davis being interviewed on the set of a New York television show, *Straight Talk.* The caption notes that Giovanni "has been increasingly busy since release of her successful record album, *Truth Is On Its Way.*" At the bottom of the page, a note in bold letters points out that "poetry excerpts [that will appear in the article] are from *Black Feeling, Black Talk/Black Judgement* by Nikki Giovanni (William Morrow & Co., Inc., New York, 1970)."[74] In the process of documenting her accomplishments, the profile effectively provides publicity for Giovanni's current projects.

Slightly deviating from the articles on Madhubuti and Baraka, the profile on Giovanni presents her differences from leading male black artists. For one, in the title, Giovanni is quoted as saying, "I Am Black, Female, Polite." The foregrounding of "female" and "polite" do not fit neatly within the masculine and militant paradigms associated with black radical nationalism. Furthermore, whereas Baraka, Madhubuti, and black activist-poets in general were presented as selfless cultural workers for black people, Giovanni is presented as something of an individualist. "I write out of my own experiences—which also happen to be the experiences of my people," Giovanni is quoted as saying. "But if I had to choose between my people's experiences and mine, I'd choose mine because that's what I know best. That way I don't have to trap the people into some kind of *dreams* that I have about what they should be into" (49). Here, Giovanni's comments provide a critique of seemingly overbearing, confrontational black militant *spokesmen* who were proscriptive regarding what black people should do. "Unlike some I-am-a-Black-Militant speakers," explains Bailey, Giovanni "does not seek to make young blacks feel that they are traitors for even being in college" (50). Bailey's comments present Giovanni as distancing herself from several of her more militant counterparts.

Unlike the typical presentation of a militant black poet, the Giovanni article foregrounds the poet's protofeminist consciousness. Other leading black women poets, such as Sonia Sanchez, Carolyn Rodgers, and Audre Lorde, provided critiques of masculine paradigms in their work. However, the high visibility and commercial success of Giovanni made her critiques of black male nationalist ideology especially notable. The last page of the profile on Giovanni shows another photo of the poet with her son. The caption notes that Giovanni "was not married when her son was born" and quotes Giovanni as saying, "I had a baby at 25 because I *wanted* to have a baby and could *afford* to have a baby. I didn't get married because I didn't *want* to get married and I could *afford* not to get married" (56). Giovanni suggests that her desires and financial success provided her with a degree of autonomy from men and traditional ideas of family. The feminist consciousness displayed by Giovanni would represent a kind of threat to the more traditional concepts of black nationalist ideology.[75]

Another major factor that placed Giovanni at a distance from several other leading black writers, if not at odds with them, and that at the same time gave her more popularity as a leading poet related to her album *Truth Is On Its Way.* On the album, Giovanni reads her poetry and is accompanied by a gospel choir. The album was a huge commercial success, selling thousands of copies. Whereas militant poets tended to distance themselves from Christian ideology, not only does Giovanni's *Truth Is On Its Way* include gospel music, but the music, in fact, holds as prominent a place on the album as Giovanni's poetry. According to Giovanni, utilizing gospel music ensured that she could appeal to an older generation who usually felt alienated by young and militant black poets. Producing works that might appeal to an older generation, as well as publishing children's books, accounted for Giovanni's wide-ranging popularity among African Americans. Giovanni's commercial success certainly drew critiques. As one anonymous observer associated with "the black power literary establishment" is quoted as saying, Giovanni's "talent doesn't match her reputation. She needs to retire for a while and develop her talent rather than continue the quest to be a personality" (52). Whatever the case, what remains notable about the profile on Giovanni in this context is that Giovanni is described as a figure who both embodies and pushes the limits of what it means to be a black arts poet. Like the previously discussed articles on Baraka and Madhubuti, the coverage provided by *Ebony* assisted in expanding Giovanni's popularity for a large African American readership.

Ebony feature articles on Baraka, Madhubuti, and Giovanni provided the poets with significant exposure. The striking visual narratives and complimentary words utilized to describe the poets in *Ebony* projected them in a positive light for an African American readership much wider than the readership for typical black arts publications. The feature profiles in *Ebony* were unique opportunities for these three poets in particular and the larger movement among black poets in general. The favorable coverage provided readers, including other writers, with an idea of what it meant to be leading black poets.

Liberator, Black Dialogue, the *Journal of Black Poetry,* and especially *Negro Digest/Black World* regularly provided photographic and journalistic coverage of poets engaged in activities and political organizing. While scholars commonly document the critical attention placed on writers, the recurring and highly visual coverage of Baraka in particular suggests that his popular appeal, not simply his critical acclaim, deserves notice as well. In many respects, given the early coverage of Baraka, he became a visible blueprint, a model even, for what a black artist should look like and do. More important for the purposes of this study, the coverage of Baraka confirms the defining role that magazines played in popularizing a select group of artists. *Negro Digest/Black World*'s wide circulation, its commitment to a black readership, and its ability to present a wide range of issues pertaining to African American verse enabled the publication to establish itself as one of the most influential vehicles for the production of black poetry. The magazine served as a crucial common venue for the publication of hundreds of poets, and by continually publishing essays and reviews focusing on poetry, as well as presenting photographic and journalistic coverage of writers, *Negro Digest/Black World* increased the visibility of poets, their writing, and their allegiances to black militant causes. Under Hoyt Fuller's direction, the periodical significantly shaped black arts discourse, and *Negro Digest/Black World* ultimately contributed to the enterprise of getting poets and their readers on the same page.

2 • Platforms for Black Verse

The Roles of Anthologies

The back cover of Dudley Randall's 1969 anthology *Black Poetry: A Supplement to Anthologies which Exclude Black Poets* notes that "because students at the University of Michigan complained that anthologies used in introductory poetry courses contained no Black poets, Broadside Press was asked to compile a sample collection."[1] Randall's forty-eight-page collection contains poems by Langston Hughes, Jean Toomer, Gwendolyn Brooks, Etheridge Knight, and LeRoi Jones, among others. Interestingly, only two years later, when Randall published his anthology *The Black Poets,* he somewhat shifted his focus. Rather than concentrating on efforts to supplement anthologies that exclude black poets, Randall was in the position of justifying the need for yet another collection of African American verse. Partly because of the Black Arts Movement, explained Randall, "there are so many anthologies of black poetry that each editor must justify the publication of a new one."[2] Dudley's *The Black Poets* was one among at least sixty other anthologies published between 1965 and 1976 that served the crucial role of extending the visibility of African American poetry. The publication of so many anthologies featuring black verse contributed significantly to the idea that the poets were engaged in a coordinated and collective enterprise.

Although literary journals publish hundreds of poets, anthologies tend to be especially helpful in extending the shelf life, literally and figuratively, of poets and poems. Indeed, anthologies are among the most important platforms for the presentation and preservation of poetry. As literary critic Cary Nelson observes, "the only sure way to keep a poem alive is to anthologize it."[3] During the time period, editors and publishers ensured that poems initially published in literary journals and volumes of poetry would have new and extended lives in anthologies. In addition, editors utilized anthologies as platforms from which to express their political commitments and literary-cultural values. The use of a common discourse, as well as the inclusion of an interconnected group of writers, highlighted the links among the numerous anthologies published during the time period.

The anthologies of the black arts era frequently characterized poets as political activists; promoted ideas of liberation; and celebrated the dynamics of African American expressive culture, most notably by drawing attention to connections between black music and poetry. Between the late 1960s and the early 1970s, editors of African American anthologies published a fairly select group of poets and drew frequently from such sources as *Negro Digest/Black World,* the *Journal of Black Poetry, Black Dialogue,* and *Freedomways.* Even though anthologies played a defining role in the transmission of poetry, few studies have examined how and to what ends these collections functioned. Paying attention to the operations of anthologies reveals their importance in the production of literature. More specifically, "editorial organizing" represented integral practices in the construction of black arts anthologies—those multiauthored texts that assisted in shaping the contours of the movement.

Editorial organizing, especially as envisioned in this chapter, comprises the decision-making processes that inform the production of anthologies, such as titling; selecting entries; arranging the selections; and framing the overall entries in the introduction, afterword, and contributor notes. Whereas editorial organizing is typically attributed to the editor or coeditors of a single anthology, these efforts actually always represent the results of collaborations with authors, copyright holders, and publishing institutions. A focus on editorial organizing sheds light on how the design and function of anthologies affected the circulation of a broad range of African American poetry. How do the arrangements of poems in anthologies influence how readers might interpret those selections and their authors individually and collectively? In what ways do editors construct their anthologies in order to appeal to particular readerships? How did the design and proliferation of anthologies relate to the progression of the Black Arts Movement? This line of inquiry indicates the types of questions and issues raised in an approach based on editorial organizing.

The organizing efforts of anthologists shape the presentation of poets and poems in a number of ways that determine the circumstances by which readers encounter the writers and their selections. For one, the arrangement of poems in an anthology based on specific themes could reveal common interests among a group of diverse poets. An anthology arranged chronologically, for example, situates poems and poets in history more readily for readers. Also, editors often decide how a single poet might be represented based on the selections chosen for inclusion by that writer. An editor wanting to display the fiery and confrontational features of militant black poetry would be more inclined to publish Nikki Giovanni's "The True Import of Present Dialogue: Black vs. Negro," which includes the recurring line "Nigger Can you kill," as opposed to the more personal and reflective poems in her volume of poetry *My House*. When trying to account for the extensive production of poetry during the black arts era, factors associated with editorial organizing cannot be overlooked.

Historically, anthologies have been crucial to the transmission of black literary art. In a survey of African American anthologies, literary critic Keneth Kinnamon observes that "several anthologies appeared in the 1920s, few in the 1930s and 1940s, almost none in the 1950s." Not surprisingly, then, anthologies of the 1920s, most notably *The New Negro*, were associated with the Harlem Renaissance, while the paucity of anthologies in the three subsequent decades might explain why so many African American poets of those eras had to be "rediscovered" during more modern times. Kinnamon goes on to note that "beginning in the 1960s, the production of anthologies accelerated."[4] Indeed, the increased publication of African American anthologies during the era served the interests of cultural workers seeking to advance a movement among literary artists, and anthologies continue to shape how readers envision the tradition of African American literature. *The Norton Anthology of African American Literature*, one of the more well-known contemporary anthologies, contains many of the most critically acclaimed black writers in literary history and shapes how students around the world view the tradition of African American literature. Anthologies often function to present a wide range of writers in a common site. As a result, these collections bring more attention to racial and cultural connections among the contributors' literary art. Projecting a united front and underscoring the links among various writers were evidently defining features of black arts discourse.

A Collective Enterprise

Anthologists who regularly presented African American poetry designed their collections to coincide with developing political and cultural movements of the time period. For one, the titles, arrangement of selections, introductions, and other features associated with the design of anthologies contributed to how effectively these collections solidified the formation of a distinct discourse and a canon of black poetry. In addition, anthologists regularly showcased poems that promoted black consciousness and made direct appeals to African American audiences. In the process, anthologists facilitated the connections between poets and readerships interested in African American concerns and went well beyond simply compiling a selection of writings. Along with publishers, anthologists often made editorial decisions that influenced the ways readers might view the poets, their poems, and the collective enterprise among poets.

The titles of anthologies enabled editors and publishers to situate their books within a common African American discourse. Consider the following brief listing of anthologies: *Black Fire* (1968), edited by LeRoi Jones and Larry Neal; *Dark Symphony* (1968), edited by James Emmanuel and Theodore L. Gross; *For Malcolm* (1969), edited by Dudley Randall and Margaret Burroughs; *Black Voices* (1968) and *New Black Voices* (1972), edited by Abraham Chapman; *Black Arts* (1969), edited by Ahmed Alhamisi and Harum Kofi Wangara; *soulscript* (1970), edited by June Jordan; *On Being Black* (1970), edited by Charles T. Davis and Daniel Walden; *We Speak as Liberators* (1970), edited by Orde Coombs; *The New Black Poetry* (1970), edited by Clarence Major; *Natural Process* (1970), edited by Ted Wilentz and Tom Weatherly; and *Black Spirits* (1972), edited by Woodie King. As these titles suggest, anthologists often relied on racially marked language to frame their books. These book titles alerted readers that they were preparing to enter a distinct cultural space or African American discourse community.

Editors frequently drew on nationalist discourse by using the word *black,* African American terminology, and concepts associated with liberation in the titles and subtitles of their anthologies. Doing so enabled them to appeal more directly to the sensibilities of black readerships. The culturally distinct titles of the anthologies appealed to audiences interested in African American issues and also functioned as important framing devices for situating the contents of the collections. Editors also utilized concepts of newness to frame their books—an indication that the materials in their collections were at the vanguard of poetic production. The titles of anthologies edited by Chapman, Henderson, Major, and Wilentz and Weatherly underscored the "new" label placed on black poetry of the 1960s and implied to audiences that they were reading fresh, cutting-edge material.

The inclusion of poets in anthologies helped to confirm their membership within a common African American discourse, regardless of any differences they may have held. The introductions to these anthologies certainly suggest that the contributors were pursuing a common enterprise. "Black poets here," writes Clarence Major in the introduction to *The New Black Poetry,* "are practically and magically involved in collective efforts to trigger real social change, correction throughout the zones of this republic."[5] In the introductory comments to *Black Arts,* Ahmed Alhamisi explains that the essays and poems included represent "the chants the prayers songs drumbeats of warriors and lovers."[6] In the foreword to *Black Fire,* Baraka introduces the contributors by explaining that "these are the founding Fathers and Mothers, of our nation. We rise, as we rise (agin)." He goes on to conclude, "We are presenting. Your various selves. We are presenting, from God, a tone, your own. Go on. Now."[7] As Major's, Alhamisi's, and Baraka's introductions imply, despite geographical, political, and ideological differences, the anthologists linked several different poets to overlapping agendas relating broadly to black people and social activism.

The sense of solidarity produced by anthologies overshadowed what may have been vital dissimilarities among contributors. James Smethurst's meticulous study of the development of the Black Arts Movement pays careful attention to the distinct regions and varied approaches of poets and black arts activists. His book illuminates the divergent interests, generational differences, and dissimilar approaches to writing poetry that existed among a large group of writers. These writers were, nonetheless, frequently categorized under the label "black arts." The different writing styles and geographic locations of a Gwendolyn Brooks and a Larry Neal, for instance, or a Lance Jeffers and a Carolyn Rodgers, did not prevent anthologists from including their works in the same collections. The routine publication of diverse writers in common venues perhaps downplayed views of their differences while highlighting their commonalities.

What about writers such as Al Young, Robert Hayden, and Lucille Clifton, who are not typically identified as black arts poets? Their appearance in so many African American anthologies associated with the cultural movement reveals that they were indeed contributors to black arts discourse. As mentioned previously, the disdain that some younger writers expressed toward Robert Hayden was well publicized, but editors did not seem as dismissive of his works. The appearance of Hayden's poems in collections published during the late 1960s and 1970s made several of his poems widely available. Editors most often selected Hayden's "Ballad of Remembrance," "Frederick Douglass," "Homage to the Empress of the Blues," "Middle Passage," and "Runagate Runagate" for inclusion. Notably, "Runagate Runagate" and "Frederick Douglass" appeared in approximately twenty anthologies between 1968 and 1974. The anthologists effectively inscribed Hayden and his poem into the canon of black writing.

A close look at the design and arrangement of *For Malcolm, Black Fire,* and *Understanding the New Black Poetry* reveals more clearly how editorial decisions utilized in the production of these popular collections extended the vision of a cultural movement with poets at the forefront. *For Malcolm,* edited by Dudley Randall and Margaret Burroughs, was one of the most well-known anthologies published by an African American press. The anthology suggests that Malcolm X was a major source of creative and political inspiration for black poets. The book's subject matter, organization, and supporting materials shape the overall function of the individual poems. The anthology opens with a photo of Malcolm X dated February 1965, the month and year that the minister was assassinated, and the book is dedicated to "Mrs. Betty Shabazz," Malcolm's widow. In addition to featuring selections by poets, the anthology presents readers with several other writings that help frame how they might engage the poems. The table of contents arranges the poems into four sections: "The Life," "The Death," "The Rage," "The Aftermath." The book contains two indexes, one of authors and one of poems.

Near the beginning of the book, *For Malcolm* also contains a six-page biography of the leader, a preface by Ossie Davis explaining why he eulogized Malcolm X, and an introduction by the editors that explains the back story of the book's publication. After "hearing Margaret Walker read her poem on Malcolm X at the Fisk University Writers' Conference in April 1966," Dudley Randall and Margaret Burroughs explain, they decided to publish a book of poems dedicated to the late leader.[8] Randall and Burroughs go on to note the large and diverse group of poets who submitted works, including prominent poets such as Gwendolyn Brooks, Robert Hayden, and LeRoi Jones; "prolific and much-published poets" such as Clarence Major, John Sinclair, and Ted Joans; and "talented young poets" such as Sonia Sanchez, Mari Evans, and Larry Neal (xx). Randall and Burroughs's explanation of how the anthology came into being suggests a grassroots effort among poets. According to Randall and Burroughs, *For Malcolm* emerged out of an impulse on the part of writers to organize around a political subject and direct their concerted efforts at memorializing a figure who "didn't bite his tongue, but spelled out the evil done by the white man and told him to go to hell" (xxi). The editors highlight the range of poets and poetic styles included in their book and showcase the existence of a diverse body of writings among African American poets. Actually, the book also contains a few white writers as well.

The editors of *For Malcolm* influenced how readers might view the contributors beyond their poems by including extensive biographical notes, which contain information on the lives of the poets, their publication records, their works in progress, and a list of their awards and other achievements. Just in case these biographical details are not enough, the book also includes photographs of the contributors. Near the end of the collection, the editors provide a bibliography of works by and about Malcolm X and a reprint of Ossie Davis's popular eulogy. The assortment of short essays, photos, and biographical information in *For Malcolm* situates the poets and their poems within a common African American literary and sociopolitical enterprise. That enterprise was part of the larger black arts discourse that praised Malcolm X, celebrated black people, and promoted political and cultural liberation.

The appearance of several poets in the common site of an anthology influenced the implications of individual poems. Part of what makes single Malcolm X poems by writers Larry Neal, Sonia Sanchez, Etheridge Knight, and Margaret Walker carry particular significance is that they were published together in one venue. Certainly, each individual poem can be analyzed for its own literary merits. However, individual poems published in anthologies sometimes rely on the larger collection to communicate meaning. Consider Mari Evans's poem "The Insurgent." The speaker of the poem mentions seeking freedom and liberty. However, nowhere in the poem is that speaker directly identified as Malcolm X. If the poem was published individually or in another site, how would readers know that the poem was paying homage to Malcolm? The appearance of Evans's "The Insurgent" in *For Malcolm* becomes crucial for readers to know that the poem refers to Malcolm. In short, Evans's poem relies on its site of publication, a collection on Malcolm, to fill in the spaces that the poem may leave blank.

For Malcolm, explains James Smethurst, "is truly a national anthology with a range of poets from the East and West coasts and, to a lesser extent, the South." And more so than the more popular *Black Fire,* observes Smethurst, Randall and Burroughs's anthology "attempts to bridge the generations and eras of political activism while maintaining a militant, nationalist stance." Further, Smethurst finds *For Malcolm* "anomalous," based on "the presence of several white radical poets among the contributors."[9] The publication of white poets in an African American anthology was in fact fairly unique. However, the editing of African American anthologies by white men was more common. Daniel Walden, Keneth Kinnamon, Abraham Chapman, and Arnold Adoff all edited or coedited anthologies featuring African American writings. Their contributions, not to mention the fact that most anthologies were financed by nonblack presses, reveal that the production of African American collections was hardly a black-exclusive endeavor.

Still, the Broadside Press imprint on *For Malcolm* signaled audiences that the book was produced in a black context and in the interests of an African American readership. In retrospect, publishing so many prominent and emerging African American writers in a single collection helped establish Broadside Press's reputation as a respected and influential black publishing institution. *For Malcolm* was one of the earliest book projects of Broadside Press and thus linked the press to one of the movement's most revered figures.[10] Therefore, just as the founders of the Black Arts Repertory Theater/School in Harlem associated the origins of their enterprise with the untimely death of Malcolm, Broadside Press similarly marked its beginnings in publishing by focusing on the slain leader as well. Overall, the arrangement and confluence of poetry, prose, and photographs in *For Malcolm,* as well as the reputations of the anthology's contributors and publisher, affected the collection's importance in African American literary culture.

Although *For Malcolm* was one of the earliest anthologies to include several writers who would later become associated with the New Black Poetry, Larry Neal and Amiri Baraka's anthology *Black Fire* may have been the era's single most influential anthology in terms of visibly promoting the agenda of militant black poetry and its proponents. Published in 1968, *Black Fire* is a multigenre anthology that includes essays, poetry, fiction, and drama. The writings in *Black Fire* cover a range of topics and issues including nationalism, black music, the effects of antiblack racism, and self-determination. More important for this discussion, however, the visual presentation, the varied contributions, and the statements by the editors of *Black Fire* contributed to the anthology's status as one of the most popular collections of the black arts era.

On the center of the cover of the anthology, an orange and fiery background displays the black lettering of the title. Below the title, the anthology's subtitle, "An Anthology of Afro-American Writing," and the names of its editors, LeRoi Jones and Larry Neal, appear in cursive writing. The blend of black and orange used on the cover accentuates the idea of black explosiveness, expressed in the main title of the collection. The book was published the same year as the assassination of Martin Luther King Jr. and during an era when African Americans participated in riots in cities across the United States, so the ideas of fire and rage were certainly on the minds of large numbers of black people. So even before readers opened the book, the title of Jones and Neal's collection oriented them to a strong sense of rage among African American writers. Significantly, the title of the anthology foregrounds the writers' relationship to political activism.

In addition to the title, several other features relating to the organization and presentation of the book operate to situate the anthology and frame its contributors within the larger currents of a black and emergent movement. Though more subtle than the title, the designation "writing" in the subtitle of the book is noteworthy, as the reference to the selections in the anthology as "Afro-American Writing" distances the contributors and their works from more formal traditions of "literature." On the credits page, the anthology acknowledges a number of publications for granting reprinting rights. Notably, the most frequent sources for reprints were *Negro Digest, Liberator,* and other African American periodicals. As a result, the acknowledgment pages at the beginning of the book provide evidence that many of the writings in *Black Fire* were linked to a network of black publishing sites.

Baraka's foreword and Neal's afterword function as important documents in defining for readers the mission of the contributing poets. Written in a "strange new grammar and syntax,"[11] Baraka's foreword suggests that the contributors to the anthology are involved in an endeavor larger than only producing literature. "We are being good. We are the beings of goodness, again," Baraka writes. "We will be righteous and our creations good and strong and righteous, and teaching" (xvii). Referring to the contributors as "poet/philosophers" and black artists as "warriors," Baraka seeks to orient readers to a view of writers that goes beyond conventional definitions. According to Baraka, the writers in *Black Fire* are doing work of a higher calling: "We are presenting, from God, a tone, your own, Go on. Now" (xviii). Baraka explains that the writers are involved in a common agenda and that they are acting on behalf of black people.

Larry Neal's often-cited afterword, entitled "And Shine Swam On," charts the objectives of new black artists. "We don't have all the answers," writes Neal, "but have attempted, through the artistic and political work presented here to confront our problems from what must be called a radical perspective."[12] Neal goes on to make connections and draw contrasts between the cultural movement among artists of the 1960s and past African American cultural movements. He elaborates on how African American poets seeking to utilize radical perspectives in their writings and appeal to black audiences must incorporate the spirit of Malcolm X and musicians such as John Coltrane and James Brown in their writings.

Neal closes his essay by informing readers that "the artist and the political activist are one. They are both shapers of the future reality" (656). Baraka's foreword and Neal's afterword establish motives and explanations for the poetry and other writings included in their anthology. The editors' statements prompt readers on how they might interpret and recognize the connections between the various contributors and poems of *Black Fire*. Framed within the spaces of a fiery cover, acknowledgments to black sources, a foreword by Baraka, an afterword by Larry Neal, essays on one side and fiction and drama on the other, the fifty-plus poets and over 140 poems included in *Black Fire* gain meaning in part because of the site where they appear. Baraka and Neal contextualize the contributions of the anthology within an emerging black radical movement in literature and refer to black writers as activists, "warriors, priests, lovers and destroyers," thus representing the multidimensional nature of black arts writers (Neal, "And Shine Swam On," 656).

The contributors' notes to *Black Fire* allow the writers to identify their publication record and also express their commitment to African Americans and various activist organizing projects. The contributors represent themselves in their author biographies as activists and writers. As a result, many of these notes emphasize that they are not poets in the conventional sense. After identifying where Askia Toure's poems have appeared, for instance, the biographical note informs readers, "He is one of the prime movers of the new spirit in Black Art. He is an extremely active poet, reading his works wherever Black people gather."[13] Similarly, biographical notes on Bob Bennet and Edward Spriggs reveal their involvement with black communities. In his statement, Norman Jordan explains that he has "stopped trying to have my poetry published" in mainstream venues. "As long as I am having my work produced here for black people, my black people, I am happy" (665). Like

Black Fire, several other anthologies such as *Black Spirits, We Speak as Liberators, The Forerunners,* and *Natural Process* include biographical sketches that highlight the experiences of contributors as poets and as organizers and activists within African American communities. For many of the contributors, it appears, revealing their activist involvement with black folks was as important as revealing their publication records.

Another intriguing example of how Baraka and Neal helped shape views of the New Black Poetry in their anthology appears as a "note to the first paperback edition of *Black Fire.*" Here, Baraka and Neal observe that "it is obvious that work by: Don Lee, Ron Milner, Alicia Johnson, Carl Boissiere, Katibu (Larry Miller), Halisi, Quincy Troupe, Carolyn Rodgers, Jayne Cortez, and Jewell Latimore shd be in this collection."[14] Unfortunately, though, "various accidents" prevented works by these artists from appearing in the first edition of *Black Fire.* The editors state that "these devils," presumably their white publisher, claimed that reprint costs were too expensive to include the aforementioned artists in the paperback edition. Thus, the editors expressed their hope that they could include the absent writers in the second edition. In a direct address to their audience, they conclude, "The frustration of working thru these bullshit white people shd be obvious" (xvi). Baraka and Neal's critique of their white publisher functions as a humorous and biting rhetorical display. Their note also confirms that the writers were attempting to communicate directly to a black audience or an audience sympathetic to African Americans. The willingness of the editors to openly criticize their publisher and speak of its management as "devils" authenticates Baraka and Neal's stance as militant black writers and enables them to further mark their anthology as a black-controlled space. That black space was also a white space.

Although seemingly quiet and unassuming in the process, the publishing house in question, William Morrow, actively contributed to the production of *Black Fire.* The officials at William Morrow, not Baraka and Neal, for instance, had the final word on whether the critical "note to the first paperback edition of *Black Fire*" would appear in the anthology. Maybe the publisher was not threatened by the comments of the editors. Or perhaps they figured that including Baraka and Neal's complaint could actually help sell more books. Whatever the case, although the editors were speaking to African Americans, they were able to reach such a wide black and nonblack audience in large part because they spoke through a publishing outfit financed by a mainstream white publisher. Actually, quiet as it's kept, William Morrow played a crucial role in publishing key African American and black arts texts during the 1960s and 1970s. Amiri Baraka's *Blues People, Black Music,* and his plays *The Dutchman* and *The Slave;* Harold Cruse's *The Crisis of the Negro Intellectual;* volumes of poetry by Nikki Giovanni; Stephen Henderson's *Understanding the New Black Poetry;* and plays by Ed Bullins—all were published by William Morrow. The publisher was an indispensable facilitator of black poetry and writings by African American artists in general. Grove Press, Random House, and Doubleday all played significant roles in publishing African American and black arts literature during the era as well.[15] Whereas black arts writers often promoted African American institution building and encouraged writers to publish with black-owned presses, the national exposure that African American poetry received was definitely a result of support provided by mainstream publishers.

While *For Malcolm* and *Black Fire* oriented readers to the interest poets had in addressing black nationalist politics, *Understanding the New Black Poetry: Black Speech and Black Music as Poetic References,* edited by Stephen Henderson. revealed an even broader sense of the place of the New Black Poetry in the history of African American expressive culture. Henderson's introduction, as well as the range and number of poets and writings that he included in his anthology, made the collection an impressive display of black verse. Henderson's lengthy introduction details the operations of the poetry in a formal, academic style, and rather than limit his discussion to only those poems composed during the 1960s and early 1970s, Henderson makes connections between black verse of the 1960s and earlier traditions of African American poetry. He also discusses verbal forms such as blues lyrics, folk poetry, and street poetry in order to suggest the "*continuity* and the *wholeness* of the Black Poetic tradition in the United States."[16]

To redress the systematic misunderstandings of African American poetry by literary critics, on the one hand, and to draw attention to the connections between the written and the oral, on the other hand, Henderson offers a "critical framework, an organizing principle, other than chronology" (3). Although scholars have debated the merits of Henderson's theories, few studies have discussed how the organizational features of his anthology influenced views of black poetry. Yet his editorial organizing, which links a wide range of poets, contributes to the visibility of his theories. The inclusion of such a diverse body of poets spanning generations displays the interconnections between writers, as well as expressive forms, and the arrangement of the selections in Henderson's anthology stands as a case in point to his theories.

Henderson's book opens with a seventy-page introduction, and the contents are organized into three sections. Section 1, "Pre-Harlem Renaissance and Soul-Field," contains Georgia Sea Island songs; folk rhymes; "The Judgment Day," by James Weldon Johnson; and poems by Paul Laurence Dunbar. Section 2, "The Harlem Renaissance and Afterward, Soul-Field," includes blues lyrics; poems by well-known figures of the New Negro era such as Hughes and Countee Cullen; and works by writers who came to prominence during the 1930s and 1940s, including Margaret Walker Alexander, Gwendolyn Brooks, Melvin Tolson, and Robert Hayden. The final and largest segment, "The New Black Consciousness, the Same Difference," consists of street poetry by H. Rap Brown and Reginald Butler and poems by Baraka, Madhubuti, Sanchez, Larry Neal, Carolyn Rodgers, and several other poets associated with black arts discourse.

Henderson's book presents the similarities between black poetry of the 1960s and 1970s and previous generations of writers, vernacular forms, and music by displaying a dynamic assortment of established and emergent poets. Placing Madhubuti, Giovanni, Carolyn Rodgers, and several other younger poets of the era in concert with Gwendolyn Brooks, Langston Hughes, and Paul Laurence Dunbar allowed Henderson to emphasize the *continuity* of the black poetic tradition. For Henderson, that tradition was composed not only of conventional literary works of art. His inclusion of song lyrics and street raps suggests that in order to understand the New Black Poetry, readers and scholars must consider a long history of black multigenre expressive forms—expressive forms informed by literature and music. Henderson's decision to include song lyrics in his anthology, as well as Dudley Randall's inclusion of spirituals in his anthology *The Black Poets,* anticipated the wide and regular practice among contemporary anthologists of presenting spirituals and song lyrics in literature collections.

The organization of Henderson's anthology also functions to present a view that the New Black Poets are more unified than they are fragmented. On the one hand, the poets featured in the third section comprise a diverse group of writers, but Henderson purposely downplays the differences among the poets in order to present the idea that "despite its variety the poetry of the sixties is informed and unified by the new consciousness of Blackness" (183). Henderson does not offer an extensive explanation of exactly what constitutes the new consciousness of blackness. Actually, he could exercise more flexibility regarding what poets and poems he could include in the section by avoiding a strict definition of exactly what that new consciousness entails. Rather than offer a precise and inevitably limited definition, Henderson reveals his view of the new consciousness by presenting a range of selections to readers. In fact, his eclectic selections disrupt conventional notions about what constitutes poetry.

A number of the "poems" in *Understanding the New Black Poetry* are not always identified as poems. The inclusion of Georgia Sea Island songs, folk rhymes, blues lyrics, and street poetry in the anthology enables Henderson to reveal that black musical forms could be presented and read as poetry. In his introduction, he also explains how music operates as a poetic reference in poetry, and he identifies at least ten ways that black music informs African American poetry, noting that the methods poets utilize to draw on music include generalized references to songs, song titles, quotations from songs, adaptations of song forms, tonal memories as poetic structure, musical notations in texts, emotional responses incorporated into poems, the figure of the musician as subject/poem/history/myth, language from jazz life, and poems as musical score or chart (47). To support his claims, Henderson offers examples from the poems included in his anthology for each of the categories (46–61).

Henderson further promotes the musicality of black poetry through his choice of selections. Several of the poems in *Understanding the New Black Poetry* focus on music and musicians. Percy Johnson's "'Round 'Bout Midnight, Opus 17," Le Roy Stone's "Flamenco Sketches," Lance Jeffers's "How High the Moon," Sarah Webster Fabio's "Tribute to Duke," Sonia Sanchez's "a/coltrane/poem," Nikki Giovanni's "Revolutionary Music," Larry Neal's "Don't Say Goodbye to the Pork-Pie Hat," Etheridge Knight's "To Dinah Washington," Haki Madhubuti's "Don't Cry, Scream," and Sharon Bourke's "Sopranosound, Memory of John" are among the many poems in the book that focus on black music and musicians. Henderson goes well beyond simply compiling a collection of poems and instead offers a framework for comprehending New Black Poetry, publishing a large number of poems that correspond to African American music. He also encourages his readers to pay attention to the musicality and orality of black verse, as well as the connections between contemporary poetry and a long-standing black poetic tradition.

The designs of *For Malcolm, Black Fire,* and *Understanding the New Black Poetry* oriented audiences to the prominence of a nationalist ethos of African American poetry. The titles, arrangement of selections, and introduction of these collections, and the popularity of the contributors, shaped views of African American verse and emphasized the connections among contemporary poets, black radical politics, and a variety of expressive traditions, including African American speech and music. *For Malcolm, Black Fire,* and *Understanding the New Black Poetry* were certainly not the only anthologies that played a role in shaping the New Black Poetry. Actually, it was the collective work of several editors and the circulation of so many anthologies that ensured the vibrant production of black poetry and the increased visibility of poets during the 1960s. Indeed, the collections made African American poetry, not to mention folklore, spirituals, and various other black expressive forms, available to large numbers of readers.

The Shape of Black Arts Anthologies

Editors provided readers with views of the era's major poets and dominant types of African American poetry, often featuring leading poets in comprehensive anthologies. Houston Baker's *Black Literature in America* (1971), Dudley Randall's *The Black Poets* (1971), Richard Barksdale and Keneth Kinnamon's *Black Writers of America: A Comprehensive Anthology* (1972), and Arnold Adoff's *The Poetry of Black America: Anthology of the 20th Century* (1973) contain selections by Nikki Giovanni, Etheridge Knight, Haki Madhubuti, and Sonia Sanchez, among others. Editors situated relatively young poets within the continuum of African American literature by including their works in collections along with older generations of writers. Poems by Phillis Wheatley and Jupiter Hammon appear early in Barksdale and Kinnamon's *Black Writers of America,* and toward the end of the collection, the anthology presents poems by Haki Madhubuti, Sonia Sanchez, and Nikki Giovanni. Anthologizing emergent poets in collections designed for classroom use helped solidify places for the writers in the canon of African American literature.

Academic anthologies and anthologists often function to assign or reinscribe literary value. Unlike *Black Fire,* which labels its contents as "writings," Baker's collection, as well as Barksdale and Kinnamon's, presents its contributions as "literature." In addition to offering a venue for a wide display of works by a group of writers, editors often provide introductions and background information in order to define poets' place in literary history and perhaps encourage readers to seek out more expansive presentations of the poets' work. In "The Present Generation:

Since 1945" section of their anthology, Barksdale and Kinnamon explain that "four relatively young Black poets who have been introduced, with remarkably provocative results, by Dudley Randall's Broadside Press are Don L. Lee [Haki Madhubuti], Sonia Sanchez, Nikki Giovanni, and Etheridge Knight. Rarely has a group of Black poets had such a constructively emotional impact on the collective racial ego of Black America, particularly the youth of Black America."[17] The anthology only includes one poem apiece by Giovanni and Sanchez and two poems each by Knight and Madhubuti. Perhaps the explanation that these four poets appeal to audiences, especially "the youth of Black America," was intended to prompt readers to consider the writers' significance beyond the small number of poems with which they are represented in the anthology. Interestingly, *Black Writers of America* hardly displays the range of the four writers' literary talents. Readers are made aware of the poets' significance based on how the editors describe them, more so than by the presentation of their actual poems.

Editors regularly included writings by Nikki Giovanni, Etheridge Knight, Haki Madhubuti, Larry Neal, Carolyn Rodgers, and Sonia Sanchez, as well as the work of elder writers Gwendolyn Brooks and Dudley Randall. And of course, Amiri Baraka (LeRoi Jones) was one of the most recognizable and recurring names to appear in African American anthologies of the era, notwithstanding some regional collections. On the one hand, editors assisted these writers by making their names and poetry available to readers. At the same time, anthologists relied on the name recognition of Amiri Baraka, Sonia Sanchez, Haki Madhubuti, and other popular poets to appeal to the interests of their readership. The cover of Woodie King's *Black Spirits: A Festival of New Black Poets in America* suggests how an anthology might utilize popular black poets to draw reader interest. On the front of *Black Spirits,* in addition to providing the title and editor's name, the cover of the book announces, "ARTISTIC CONSULTANT IMAMU AMIRI BARAKA / WITH A FOREWORD / BY NIKKI GIOVANNI / AND INTRODUCTION / BY DON L. LEE." In 1972, when *Black Spirits* was published, Giovanni, Baraka, and Madhubuti (Lee) were among the most popular writers associated with the Black Arts Movement. Placing these three prominent poets on the cover of a book would definitely appeal to the interests of a black readership and add to that publication's credibility.

Anthologists also assisted in shaping the contours of black poetry by publishing a common group of poets and certain kinds of poems. The editors seemed less interested in anthologizing poems focusing on na-

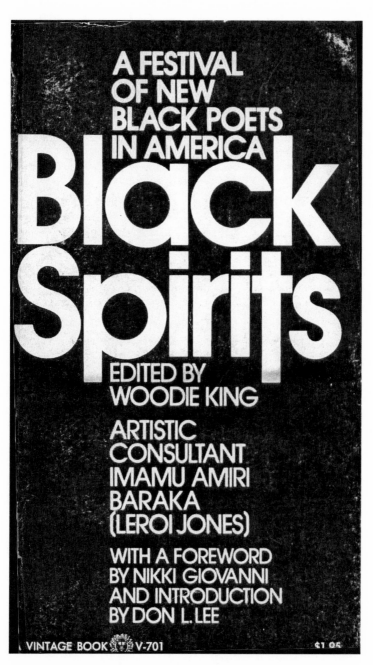

A FESTIVAL
OF NEW
BLACK POETS
IN AMERICA

Black Spirits

EDITED BY
WOODIE KING

ARTISTIC
CONSULTANT
IMAMU AMIRI
BARAKA
(LEROI JONES)

WITH A FOREWORD
BY NIKKI GIOVANNI
AND INTRODUCTION
BY DON L. LEE

VINTAGE BOOK V-701 $1.95

Paperback cover of Woodie King's anthology *Black Spirits,* showcasing the names of Amiri Baraka, Nikki Giovanni, and Don L. Lee (Haki Madhubuti).

ture and forms of experimental poetry. Poems offering critiques of antiblack racism, poems paying tribute to black political figures and musicians, and poems celebrating various aspects of African American culture appeared far more regularly in the anthologies. Featuring these kinds of poems may have left the movement open to charges from some critics that poets of the era did not produce a diverse array of African American poetry. Nonetheless, the publication of a select group of writers and certain types of poems contributed to the view of a politicized movement among poets who were seeking to appeal to an African American readership. Popularizing a group of poets and their style of poetry required that anthologists publish them over and over again. Moreover, the appearance of a core group of writers in various anthologies advanced the idea that they were contributors to a common endeavor.

That anthologists published a fairly overlapping group of black poets did not mean that all the anthologies were the same. In order to distinguish their collections among the several other anthologies being published, some editors found ways to diversify their texts and offer creative arrangements of the selected works. June Jordan's *soulscript: Afro-American Poetry* (1970), Lindsay Patterson's *A Rock against the Wind: Black Love Poems* (1973), and Arnold Adoff's *My Black Me: A Beginning Book of Black Poetry* serve as notable examples. Consistent with a recurring technique presented in poetry during the era, even the title of Jordan's anthology is written in lower-case. The title *soulscript* and the lower-case presentation of the term alert readers to the African American and poetic ethos utilized by the editor June Jordan and her book's contents.

Jordan's collection is designed thematically and thus exposes the commonalities among a range of black poets, including Langston Hughes, Jean Toomer, Gwendolyn Brooks, and Amiri Baraka. Jordan introduces each of the seven sections of the collection with a short poem that describes the kinds of poems that appear in that segment. The opening section, "tomorrow words today," includes poems by poets between the ages of fifteen and twenty-one, including two emerging writers, Gayl Jones and Julia Alvarez. Today, both Jones and Alvarez are more widely known as critically acclaimed novelists; their contributions to *soulscript* mark one of the few times that their poetry has appeared in an anthology of poetry. Jordan's book may have given the two writers their first national exposure. It is a testament to Jordan's commitment to publishing "new" writers that she included young and emergent poets in *soulscript* and that she also opened the collection with their writings.

The second section of Jordan's book, "all about the always first," focuses on "poems to the parents, the children, / the brothers and the sisters."[18] The third section, "hero hymns and heroines," contains tribute poems (35). Next, "corners on the curving sky," the fourth section, addresses "philosophy; / they reveal the corners where we organize what we know" (57). The selections in the fifth section, "saying the person," are first-person or "special I-Am" poems (83). The sixth section, "black eyes on a fallowland," features poems that bear witness to the struggles that black people face in America (101). Finally, in the seventh section, "attitudes of soul," Jordan announces, "Let these last poems sure commune / our impulse to the hourly / flourishing of soul" (117). Organizing her book thematically as opposed to chronologically allows Jordan to demonstrate the idea that black poets from across the twentieth century addressed similar topics in their writings. Despite the generational differences between Jean Toomer and Sonia Sanchez, or between Countee Cullen and Larry Neal, their writings nonetheless appear in the same sections in Jordan's anthology. Ultimately, *soulscript* advanced the black arts enterprise of publishing a common group of African American poets.

Lindsay Patterson's *A Rock against the Wind: Black Love Poems* represents another unique collection that features black arts writings. Although many black poets were primarily known for their fiery poetry, the selections printed in Patterson's collection reveal that African American poets had a tradition of writing about love as well. Like Jordan's book, Patterson's anthology is divided into sections and includes poems by a range of poets who published across the twentieth century. The collection includes poems by older and established poets Langston Hughes, Claude McKay, Georgia Douglass Johnson, Helen Johnson, and Paul Laurence Dunbar, as well as poems by New Black Poets, including Sonia Sanchez, Nikki Giovanni, Haki Madhubuti, June Jordan, Etheridge Knight, Quincy Troupe, and Carolyn Rodgers. Patterson arranges the poems in the collection into ten categories: "The Joys of Love," "A Hymn to Black Men and Women," To Be a Woman," "Advice/Wisdom," "Love Is Hell," "Revenge, Regret, Rejection," "Seduction," "Reflections of Love Lost," "Love and Death," and "For Love to Survive." *A Rock against the Wind* may have been an anomaly among African American anthologies in terms of its focus. Even so, Patterson's book provides an example of how the organizing principles of an anthology could bring attention to a less visible interest among African American poets in writing about love and relationships.

Although some poets have been criticized for being dismissive or

unaware of earlier generations of black writers, anthologists actually evidenced broad conceptions of what constituted African American literature. Henderson's *Understanding the New Black Poetry,* Jordan's *soulscript,*
Patterson's *A Rock against the Wind,* and Arnold Adoff's *The Poetry of
Black America,* among others, all include elder African American writers.
Anthologists reprinted the poems of older generations of writers in
contemporary collections and kept those writers in print and exposed a
new generation of readers to their writings. Moreover, anthologists pinpointed the connections between previous generations of writers and
emergent poets. The process of anthologizing poetry served to social-
ize poets and poems among a range of African American categories and
topics, and the appearance of varied poets in anthologies revealed a diversity of black voices.

Editors who anthologized emergent poets also reprinted poems by
such historically significant poets as Phillis Wheatley, Claude McKay,
Countee Cullen, and Langston Hughes. Thus, editors produced an expanded view of the black poetic tradition and also differentiated their
own views of poetry from those of some of the leading poets of the
era. Even though younger militant poets may have distanced themselves
from the Eurocentric style present in the writings of Wheatley, editors
ensured that her poems remained in circulation during the late 1960s
and early 1970s. Anthologists included Wheatley's poems in such collections as *An Introduction to Black Literature in America from 1746 to the Present* (1968), *Black American Literature: Poetry* (1969), *3000 Years of Black Poetry* (1970), *The Black Poets* (1971), and *Black Writers of America* (1972).

Admittedly, many editors included a relatively small sampling of
Wheatley's work, and the editors who published her poetry tended to be
elder writers and critics such as Dudley Randall and Darwin Turner.
Nonetheless, the regular appearance of Wheatley's writings in anthologies that also featured the New Black Poetry disrupts unqualified claims
that participants in the Black Arts Movement had a total disregard for
Wheatley's poetry. For instance, Henry Louis Gates Jr. holds that black
arts figures were a "more hostile group" to Wheatley than the whites
who interrogated her in 1772.[19] The stylistic and political ideologies that
informed the poetry of Amiri Baraka, Haki Madhubuti, Jayne Cortez,
and Sonia Sanchez may have been at odds with the writings of Phillis
Wheatley. However, Darwin Turner, Dudley Randall, William H. Robinson, Richard Long, and Eugenia Collier, among others, chose to reprint
her poems in their anthologies, revealing that not all black arts figures
were as hostile to Wheatley as Gates suggests.

Anthologists of the era further established Paul Laurence Dunbar's place in the canon of African American literature by frequently reprinting his poems "We Wear the Mask" and "Sympathy." Interestingly, these two poems do not contain specific racialized words. Their regular appearance in racialized sites or African American contexts, however, increased the likelihood that the poems would be interpreted as addressing black interests. In addition, the publication of Dunbar's "dialect" poems corresponded to the African American vernacular English presented in the writings of several modern black poets. On the one hand, the appearance of Dunbar's work in collections that featured contemporary black poetry exposed readers to the long-standing practice among African American poets of utilizing black vernacular in their writings. At the same time, the appearance of poems by Dunbar, Haki Madhubuti, and Carolyn Rodgers in common publishing venues exposed readers to diverse representations of African American vernacular speech.

Anthologizing the poetry of Claude McKay, Jean Toomer, and Countee Cullen in collections that also included poems by contemporary poets allowed editors to underscore the relationship between the New Negro Movement and the New Black Poetry. No poet from previous generations appeared as regularly as Langston Hughes. The publication of Hughes and other historically significant poets together with contemporary African American poets was an important and rare undertaking for mass-market anthologies. The setup of such collections revealed that the black arts enterprise was not a spontaneous movement, but rather the extension of an established and viable literary tradition. During the 1960s and early 1970s, Langston Hughes, Paul Laurence Dunbar, and even Phillis Wheatley were as likely to appear on the table of contents pages of African American anthologies as were Amiri Baraka, Nikki Giovanni, and Haki Madhubuti. As a result, anthologists demonstrated that the reclamation of an older generation of poets was an integral step in the presentation of New Black Poetry.

As an editor, publisher, and poet, Dudley Randall was an essential connector for varied aspects of black poetry. On the one hand, Randall's poems appeared in several anthologies of the era, including *Kaleidoscope* (1967), *Black Voices* (1968), *Black Poetry* (1969), *Black American Literature* (1970), *The Black Poets* (1971), *New Black Voices* (1972), *Understanding the New Black Poetry* (1973), and *Giant Talk: An Anthology of Third World Writings* (1975). At the same time, Randall facilitated—as an editor or publisher—the production of a number of notable anthologies, including *For Malcolm* (1967), *Black Poetry* (1969), *The Black Poets*

(1971), *Jump Bad* (1971), and *A Broadside Treasury* (1971). As an elder poet and editor, Randall demonstrated commitment to publishing both older and younger writers, and the anthologies that he edited and published include a diverse array of poets.

Even when Randall published his work with a large mainstream press, as was the case with his anthology *The Black Poets,* he maintained a strong interest in making readers aware of African American publishing institutions. At the end of the collection, Randall includes a listing that contains publishers of black poetry, periodicals that published African American poetry, volumes of poetry, and audio and video recordings of poets reading their work. Although *The Black Poets* was published by a white-owned press, Randall's presentation of contact information for publishers and periodicals of black poetry directed readers to various African American sites. In other words, Randall utilized a white publishing institution as a platform to alert readers to the existence of a network of black literary spaces.

The anthologies Randall edited, coedited, published, and appeared in served as sites for the display of a chorus of black poetic voices. Randall's involvement with the publication of a variety of poets and African American literary art was a testament to his wide-ranging roles as an editor, publisher, and advocate for black verse. Randall's collections and, more broadly, African American anthologies containing poetry could be utilized to promote emergent poets and simultaneously make contemporary readers aware of literary and expressive forms that preceded the Black Arts Movement, such as the blues and spirituals. Anthologists such as Dudley Randall, Stephen Henderson, and June Jordan published the work of both younger and older generations of writers, providing a broad and diverse view of African American poetry. The publication of several anthologies featuring black poetry during the era confirmed Randall's belief "that in the house of poetry there are many mansions" and that "we can enjoy different poets for the variety and uniqueness of their poetry, not because they are all of a sameness."[20] Showcasing a range of poets in common sites further instilled the sense of solidarity among African American poets of the time period.

Anthologizing Nikki Giovanni and Inscribing Signature Poems

Taken together, anthologists of black verse served as vital facilitators for the presentation of a large body of poetry. Nonetheless, editorial work is, by definition, selective and a form of commodification. In comparison to the number of poems that appeared in individual volumes of poetry and the poets who published in magazines, anthologies presented a relatively condensed view of the African American poems composed during the 1960s and 1970s. By favoring certain types of poetic styles and particular poets over various others, the editorial organizing enacted by anthologists prompted distinct ideas about what constituted black poetry. To the extent that anthologies are more regularly available to readerships across time than individual volumes of poetry, collections often shape initial encounters between poets and wide audiences. In addition, more so than any individual volume of poetry, anthologists constructed ideas about how a group of poets appear in relation to each other and to a tradition of African American and American literature.

Even though editors published a range of emergent writers, they seemed to have a special affinity for Nikki Giovanni. Between 1968 and 1974, Giovanni's poems were published in over twenty anthologies. Although anthologists tended to publish more male than female poets, the frequency with which Giovanni's poems appeared made her a notable exception. The widespread circulation of Giovanni's poetry was especially remarkable considering she was not closely associated with activist and artistic organizations or high-profile writers, as was the case with Amiri Baraka and Haki Madhubuti. Baraka, for example, was often promoted as the movement's leading figure and in fact had a distinguished literary reputation before the Black Arts Movement, which helped explain why editors favored his work for their collections. Madhubuti's close ties to Dudley Randall's Broadside Press, Hoyt Fuller's *Negro Digest/Black World,* and Chicago's OBAC group, not to mention the endorsements he received from his mentor Gwendolyn Brooks, all helped account for why a range of editors would include Madhubuti in anthologies. Giovanni, on the other hand, had relatively few direct ties to activist and artistic organizations. Nonetheless, editors routinely selected her work for inclusion.

The frequency with which certain poets were anthologized reveals how editors could influence the value placed on particular poets by devoting more space to the publication of their poems. For example, a larger number of poems by Nikki Giovanni, Amiri Baraka, and Haki Madhubuti appeared in anthologies than the number of poems by Johari Amini, Askia Toure, and Larry Neal, even though all these writers were considered militant black poets. The frequent appearance of Giovanni's poems in collections confirmed and extended her prominence in the discourse. Editors shaped and were influenced by conceptions of Giovanni as a leading poet; they consistently selected her poetry for inclusion. As a result, Giovanni became a fixture in anthologies of African American verse.

In addition to influencing the value and visibility placed on Giovanni and a few other select poets by regularly anthologizing their work, editors also helped determine what might be seen as these poets' representative or signature poems by repeatedly reprinting poets' select pieces in various collections. Giovanni's "Nikki-Rosa," which appeared in approximately fourteen collections between 1969 and 1974, seemed to be a preferred selection of editors. The poem initially appeared in Giovanni's second volume of poetry, *Black Judgment* (1968), published by Broadside Press. The poem catalogs negative and positive "childhood remembrances" such as living in a house "with no inside toilet" and experiencing "how happy you were to have your mother all to yourself." It contains such striking observations as "though you're poor it isn't poverty that concerns you," and "I really hope no white person ever has cause to write about me because they never understand Black love is Black wealth."[21] The poem's exploration of conflicting childhood memories, rejection of white biographers, and appraisal of "Black love" may have all contributed to its wide appeal. Editors' continuous reprinting of the poem established "Nikki-Rosa" as Giovanni's signature poem. Actually, a number of Giovanni's poems, including "For Saundra," "My Poem," and "The True Import of Present Dialogue: Black vs. Negro," express the nationalist sensibilities often promoted by nationalist activists and militant black poets. Accordingly, to a slightly lesser degree than "Nikki-Rosa," those three poems are among Giovanni's most anthologized pieces as well.

The regular publication of a few select poems by a poet in various anthologies amounts to a kind of communal affirmation of what presumably constitutes the poet's representative work. The establishment of a signature poem signals a collective and continuing interest, if not commitment, on the part of an audience in keeping a poet's particular ideas visible. A poem's steady inclusion in collections both reflects and generates the poem's popular value; a widely anthologized poem apparently circulates among a larger audience and subsequent anthologists. Moreover, the recurring appearance of a poem in anthologies inscribes that particular verse more deeply onto the pages of literary history and thus secures a more definite place for the poem and poet within a discourse. The wide circulation of "Nikki-Rosa" may have given Giovanni a special edge over fellow emergent poets without signature poems.

Sonia Sanchez and Carolyn Rodgers were comparably popular women poets to Giovanni, writings by all three often appearing in the same anthologies. Yet no single poem by Sanchez or Rodgers enjoyed the active circulation of Giovanni's "Nikki-Rosa." Sanchez and Rodgers certainly received widespread coverage during the era; however, anthologists were not as consistent in their common selection of a particular poem by those two poets as they were with Giovanni's poem. Giovanni's signature poem distinguished her from other notable women poets. More broadly, since Giovanni had a signature and recognizable poem, she was in relatively rare company among all poets. Indeed, when poets are anthologized over a long period of time, they are often represented by a relatively select sampling of their work. Signature poems operate as placeholders for authors' positions within literary history. Poets without widely received signature poems are often left outside of canons.

In addition to Giovanni's "Nikki-Rosa," editors regularly published Etheridge Knight's "The Idea of Ancestry" and "It Was a Funky Deal"; Haki Madhubuti's "But He Was Cool"; and Amiri Baraka's "Black Art," "A Poem for Black Hearts," and "Preface to a Twenty Volume Suicide Note." Similar to "Nikki-Rosa," Knight's "The Idea of Ancestry" and Baraka's "Preface to a Twenty Volume Suicide Note" display distinct autobiographical elements. On the one hand, poets' signature poems often overshadow their less published verse. At the same time, however, signature poems function to provide a more distinct image of the writer's poetic sensibilities and perhaps the writer's persona. The broad circulation of Baraka's "A Poem for Black Hearts," which pays tribute to Malcolm X as well as his "Black Art," confirms the poet's reputation as a strong proponent of black radical views. The title of Giovanni's "Nikki-Rosa" carries her first name, and the content of the poem is seemingly autobiographical, thus suggesting how the increased circulation of this signature poem assisted in amplifying a view of the poet's life. Indeed, "Nikki-Rosa" embeds and projects an image of Nikki Giovanni. "Nikki-Rosa" remains one of Giovanni's most unforgettable poems in large part because anthologists continually remembered to include the poem in their collections.

Although "Nikki-Rosa" apparently testifies to Giovanni's personal childhood experiences, the poem reverberates in the larger discourse of African American poetry. The poem's affirmation of African American life and culture and its contempt for white interpretations of black life parallel several other widely circulating poems during the time period. Similar to "Nikki-Rosa," Sterling Brown's "Strong Men," Lance Jeffers's "My Blackness Is the Beauty of This Land," and Mari Evans's "I Am a Black Woman" and "Vive Noir" reflect images that project black people and culture as containing much strength. To varying degrees, the defiance of white culture expressed in Langston Hughes's "I, Too, Sing America" and Amiri Baraka's "Black Art," among others, appears in Giovanni's poem as well. And certainly Giovanni's rejection of white bi-ographers/critics relates directly to the sentiments expressed by Hoyt Fuller, Haki Madhubuti, and other artists and commentators who were interested in formulating a black aesthetic. The relationship between Giovanni's poem and multiple ideas in black culture may have ac-counted for "Nikki-Rosa"'s popular appeal among anthologists.

The efforts of numerous editors to anthologize select groups of poets and poems attests to the defining role of editorial work in the process of keeping particular poems circulating among readers. An-thologies served as visible platforms for showcasing emergent writers such as Nikki Giovanni, Sonia Sanchez, and Haki Madhubuti. Anthologies also served as powerful sites of recovery and renewal, providing el-der writers with opportunities to present new and older works. The fre-quent publication of Gwendolyn Brooks's and Margaret Walker's poems in anthologies of the era solidified these two poets' stature in lit-erary history, especially among African American readerships. Although Brooks and Walker had achieved recognition for their poetry in previ-ous decades, anthologies of the 1960s and 1970s extended the circula-tion of their poems and greatly influenced what became the poets' sig-nature poems.

Walker first gained national attention for her poetry during the 1940s with the publication of her volume of poetry *For My People* (1942). The volume's title poem, "For My People," articulates a collective call to African Americans everywhere, including those "singing their slave songs repeatedly," those "walking blindly spreading joy, losing time / being lazy, sleeping when hungry, shouting when / burdened," those "noting struggles with adversity and making a call for change," and those "blundering and groping and floundering in the dark of churches and schools and clubs and societies, associations and councils and com-mittees and conventions, distressed and disturbed and deceived and de-voured by money-hungry glory-craving leeches." In the last stanza, the narrator calls on "my people" to "Let a new earth rise. Let another world be born. Let a bloody peace be written in the sky," to "Let the martial songs be written, let the dirges disappear. Let a race of men now rise and take control."

Critic Melba Boyd explains that Walker's poem, "with its terse imagery, riveting, rhythmical phrasing, and thematic embrace of the black masses, anticipates the aesthetics of the Black Arts Movement."[22] Consequently, during the 1960s and 1970s, editors seemed particularly fond of including Walker's poem in their collections. The poem appeared in more than twenty-five collections between 1968 and 1974, making it one of the most anthologized African American poems of the era. The frequent publication of "For My People" made the poem a mainstay in black arts discourse decades after the poem's initial appearance. Anthologies established "For My People" as Walker's most recognizable poem.

Walker's "For My People" corresponded, at various levels, to strong interests among poets and editors celebrating black culture. On the one hand, Walker's poem related to previous generations of poets such as Paul Laurence Dunbar and Langston Hughes. At the same time, the poem's characterizations of African American culture and its affirmation of black people relate to the poetry of Haki Madhubuti, Nikki Giovanni, Henry Dumas, and Sonia Sanchez, to mention only a few. The recurring phrase "for my people" in Walker's poem definitely connected to the distinct nationalist ethos so prevalent during the 1960s. The appearance of "For My People" in so many anthologies is not surprising, since the poem was quite compatible with the communal spirit expressed by emergent black poets.

During the same time period that Walker's "For My People" circulated, Gwendolyn Brooks's "We Real Cool" appeared in at least sixteen anthologies, providing the poem with renewed interest among readers. Brooks's poem actually corresponds to at least two recurrent themes in contemporary black poetry, namely the representation of hip young men and the implication that coolness—for better and worse—is a noteworthy feature of their cultural identity. Giovanni's "Beautiful Black Men," Calvin Hernton's "Jitterbugging in the Streets," Bobb Hamilton's "Brother Harlem Bedford Watts Tells Mr. Charlie Where It's At," and Larry Neal's "Don't Say Goodbye to the Pork-Pie Hat," to name a few, all focus on cool black men and the resonance of African American fashionable cultural expressions. Most notably, Madhubuti's "But He Was Cool" echoes Brooks's poem by highlighting the negative consequences of coolness. In his poem, Madhubuti describes a "supercool / ultrablack" man who wears tailor-made dashikis but who is unfortunately too cool to comprehend the rising heat of black radicalism. Editors frequently anthologized "We Real Cool" and in the process highlighted Brooks's connections to the concerns of a younger generation. As they had done with Giovanni's "Nikki-Rosa" and Walker's "For My People," anthologists established "We Real Cool" as Brooks's signature poem.

Anthologists collectively established tribute poems as a kind of signature mode of poetry during the era. Tribute poems celebrating the lives and legacies of Malcolm X, Frederick Douglass, John Coltrane, Billie Holiday, and Harriet Tubman were especially prevalent. The frequent appearance in anthologies of poems paying tribute to black historical figures allowed editors to advance the objective among African Americans of recovering a usable past. That is, tribute poems extol the virtues of black historical figures and provided current readers with examples of how they might lead their lives. Furthermore, the tribute poems offer striking and positive images of black people and culture in general. As mentioned earlier, Robert Hayden's "Frederick Douglass" was one of the most anthologized poems of the 1960s and 1970s. Editors also, to a lesser degree, included tributes to Frederick Douglass by Paul Laurence Dunbar and Langston Hughes. The anthologies contain tribute poems lauding historical figures composed by past and current poets and thus display an apparent shared interest among generations of writers in celebrating black heroes in verse.

The methods and regularity with which African American poetry was anthologized make us more aware of the defining role of editorial work in the production of black arts poetry and the increased visibility of poets. Anthologies showcased and consolidated the major trends and figures in African American poetry of the era by repeatedly publishing a common group of poems and poets. Collections such as *For Malcolm* and *Black Fire* underscored the poets' preoccupations with nationalist and black musical sensibilities, while anthologies such as *The Black Poets* and *Understanding the New Black Poetry* oriented readers to the existence of long-standing traditions of black poetry and related expressive forms. Anthologies made the poetry of Amiri Baraka, Nikki Giovanni, and Margaret Walker widely available to readers, and the editors of these collections assisted in establishing these poets' signature poems. Because of their influential authority in designating literary value and keeping a select group of poems and poets in print, anthologies operated as central forces in the formulation of a canon of black poetry.

3 • Understanding the Production of Black Arts Texts

In an article in *Black World* explaining the making of *The Black Book*, Toni Morrison points out that "black people from all over helped with it, called about things to put in it." Morrison, who at the time was a senior editor at Random House, where the book was published, further reveals that African Americans contributed to constructing the book at all levels. Even the production man and the printer for the book were black.[1] For her *Black World* readership, Morrison clearly sought to underscore the African American dimensions of the book, while downplaying its publication by a white-owned company. The design and promotion of *The Black Book* as a distinctly black artistic composition indicate that the publication directly appealed to African Americans and their interests—core principles in black arts discourse.

The production of publications that highlighted black cultural ideas and appealed to African American interests projected a sense of interconnectivity among black arts texts. The repeated display of popular black words and images on publications and the recurrent uses of culturally distinct sounds on recordings suggested that the writers and their compositions were connected to an interrelated set of core values and objectives. In short, the aesthetics of the writers' literary products, not only the contents of their writings, indicated their participation in a presumably unified movement. The front cover of the paperback edition of Orde Coombs's anthology *We Speak as Liberators: Young Black Poets* (1970), for instance, draws on the linguistic and visual discourse of black struggles for freedom in the process of presenting poets as a coalition of liberation advocates.

The cover of Coombs's book contains red, black, and green stripes in a manner that invokes the pan-African flag and the flag of Marcus

Garvey's Universal Negro Improvement Association and African Communities League (UNIA). At the top of the cover, the words "WE SPEAK AS LIBERATORS" appear in black lettering on a red background. In the middle, the words "YOUNG BLACK POETS" appear in white lettering on a black background, and toward the bottom, Coombs's name is shown in black lettering with a green background. Audiences cognizant of black nationalist discourses could easily identify the pan-African aesthetic expressed by the color scheme of Coombs's book cover, and readers interested in black freedom struggles would certainly take interest in poets who, as the book title suggests, comprised a collective of liberators. The front cover of *We Speak as Liberators,* like so many books featuring poetry published during the time period, displays black nationalist ideas, linking the contributors—a group of poets—to a decidedly political agenda.

The frequent publication of anthologies and volumes of poetry with packaging that corresponded to black nationalist discourses seemed to manifest prevailing pronouncements concerning the aesthetic and spiritual kinship between the Black Arts Movement and Black Power, as articulated by Larry Neal and various other writers. The fusion of words and images on the front covers of publications featuring African American verse rendered these important sites for the illustrative articulation of the politicized agendas of black poets. A drawing of the continent of Africa appears beneath the title *think black!* on the cover of Haki Madhubuti's volume of poetry. The declarative directive to "think black," paired with an outlined image of Africa, encourages the book's presumably African American audience to embrace a pan-African perspective. More important, the book's visual display showcases the author's apparent connection to the sensibilities of Black Power ideology and thus promotes the view of the poet as a political activist. At the same time, promoting the idea of Madhubuti as a political activist contributes to solidifying his credibility as a "serious" black poet.

Amiri Baraka's reputation as the leading and most controversial figure among this cadre of poets was also definitely linked to the aesthetics of his books. Most notably, the cover of *Black Magic Poetry, 1961–1967* (1969) is arguably one of the most salient examples of a volume of poetry visually projecting the idea of blacks enacting violence against whites. The cover contains a white voodoo doll with blond hair and blue eyes, needles stuck through its head, chest, and legs. Pairing the image with the words "black magic" sends a controversial message: a black poet will resort to voodoo to inflict pain on white enemies. The dramatic cover design of *Black Magic Poetry* contributed to Baraka's reputation as a militant figure willing to confront his adversaries by any means necessary. Such dynamic combinations of words and images on the covers of publications could certainly heighten reader interest in the artistic compositions of black poets.

But then, the aesthetics of poets' publications did more than simply heighten reader interest. For one, the appearance and sound of their literary products suggested that the poets were participating in an active cultural network that included poets, editors, publishers, artists, activists, musicians, and communities of general African American readerships. In this regard, individual publications seemed to represent elements of a larger black artistic enterprise. The distinguishing nature of the literary products also revealed that the poets and their supporters were trying to appeal to groups beyond select audiences of poetry readers. The goal of expanding readership prompted experimental or at least alternative approaches to the presentation and circulation of poetry—hence the production of audio recordings of poets reading their works and the packaging of poems in the discourses of social and political movements.

These alternative and expanded approaches to transmitting verse advanced the objective of presenting poets as multifaceted artists, militant activists, and advocates for black pride and liberation. Redefining, or more accurately diversifying, what it meant to be poets often provided select writers with several benefits, which will be elaborated on in subsequent sections. For now, suffice it to say that the presentation of distinguishing identities and expanded capabilities could give individual writers a competitive edge in the field of poetry, which, as always, has contained large numbers of poets and limited publishing venues. An examination of the aesthetics of black literary products reveals how different approaches in the packaging and presentation of verse assisted in giving select poets notable advantages, including increased publishing opportunities and wider appeal among audiences.

Projecting Verbal-Visual Ideas

Some leading poets collaborated with artists to produce books that utilized blends of words and images, or the interplay of verbal-visual ideas, throughout the publications, not simply on the covers. Nikki Giovanni's book *ego-tripping and Other Poems for Young Readers* (1973), which includes

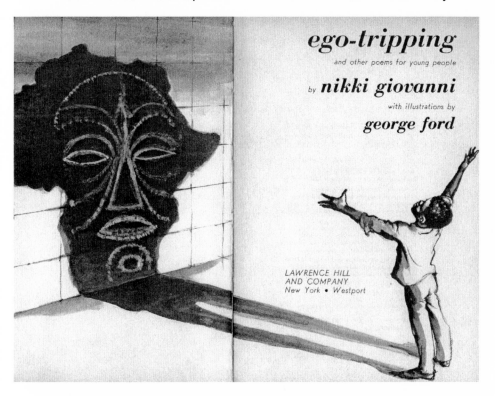

Page from Nikki Giovanni's *ego-tripping,* with illustrations by George Ford. Courtesy of the artist.

drawings by George Ford, reveals how a combination of words and images could enhance the implications of a poet's compositions. More important, *ego-tripping* expanded Giovanni's opportunity to reach a broader audience. Indeed, her book could stimulate young readers and satisfy the interests of parents who sought to expose their children to positive black images. Ford's illustrations in the volume definitely affirm African American and African cultures and project an underlining black nationalist ethos that espouses racial pride. Giovanni and Ford's collaboration demonstrates the possibility of taking ideas associated with black arts discourse and orienting those ideas to young readers.

On the title page of the book, an image of a young black boy appears, his arms spread wide as he faces a wall. His shadow casts the image of an African mask. Another illustration, which accompanies the poem "for the masai warriors," shows a group of fashionably dressed

for the masai warriors
(of don miller)

remembering my father's drum
remembering the leopard's screetch
if i could weave an ancient rope
and tie myself to history
i'd spring like daylight out of night
into the future of our land
i'd sprint across the grassy plain
and make a nation for the gods
where i could be the man

30 jan. 73

7

Page from Nikki Giovanni's *ego-tripping,* with illustrations by George Ford. Courtesy of the artist.

adolescent African American boys staring admiringly at a photograph of Africans, presumably the warriors mentioned in the title. One of the boys, who is apparently moved by the image of the Africans, leaps excitedly into the air.[2] In the poem, the speaker mentions drawing inspiration from Africa and considers making "a nation for the gods / where I could be the man" (7). The image that accompanies "for the masai warriors," as well as the image on the title page, encourages young readers, especially young black boys, to take pride in Africa. In fact, the book's images present boys displaying fascination while gazing at images relating to Africa; these kinds of drawings provide a clear model for young black readers of what it might mean to appreciate a distant yet related black culture and group of people.

Several of the poems in Giovanni's book contain prominent illustrations of black women and young girls. An illustration of a regal-looking black woman sitting in an Egyptian-style canoe accompanies the poem "ego-tripping," which begins, "I was born in the congo / I walked to the fertile crescent and built the sphinx" (2–3). Two drawings of African women appear toward the top of the page; their images are outlined within the continent of Africa. One of the women smiles while looking down toward the woman in the canoe; the other one looks in the direction of the title "ego-tripping" on the adjacent page, as if she is reading. Viewers have a side view of the woman in the canoe, as she stares in the direction that she travels. Incidentally, her gaze is at eye level with Giovanni's line "I am a beautiful woman" (3). The vibrant and self-assured images of the black women augment Giovanni's poetic statements regarding the attributes of an extraordinary, supernatural woman.

The images on the subsequent page of the poem present a woman's outstretched hands, which are adorned with bracelets. Apparently, she has recently released the bird that soars at the top of the adjoining page. Viewers who first see the bird discover its significance as they read through to the poem's closing lines: "I mean . . . I . . . can fly / like a bird in the sky" (4–5). The illustration of the flying bird provides a concrete vision of Giovanni's concluding simile, and taken together, the images of the regal black women and the soaring bird offer visual manifestations of the shape-shifting, godlike speaker of the poem, who describes her amazing qualities. The images that accompany "ego-tripping" and "for the masai warriors," the title page, and the book's cover, which shows two black children wearing the attire of pharaohs as they ride aboard an Egyptian-style vessel, all serve to orient young readers toward an appreciation of Africa. The larger body of Giovanni's poems hardly qualified her as a pan-Africanist; however, Ford's images give Africa a prominent place in *ego-tripping* and thus visibly extend the scope of black pride that appears in Giovanni's poems. Ford's artwork, in these instances, situates Giovanni's work more firmly within the movement of black writers and activists who encouraged African Americans to take pride in Africa.

Ford's images of young black girls provide vibrant complements to Giovanni's poems focusing on black girls and childhood memories. In "poem for flora," Giovanni describes a young girl who is considered "colored and ugly with short / straightened hair" until she gains a valuable lesson in Sunday school. After listening to various biblical stories, what she really remembers is that "Sheba was Black and comely," and so she decides, "I want to be / like that" (9). The accompanying illustration shows a young black girl standing in the foreground with a larger image in the background of a black woman with braided hair and a piece of jewelry, perhaps from a crown, on her forehead. The image conveys the promising future possibility of the young girl becoming a queenlike figure such as Sheba. Similar to "poem for flora," the illustrations that accompany "nikki-rosa" and "knoxville, tennessee" present images of cheerful black girls. All in all, Ford's drawings, combined with Giovanni's words, offer captivating, if not empowering, verbal-visual ideas for young readers in general and black girls in particular.

Giovanni's volume constitutes a fairly unique literary work in the field of African American poetry by popular black writers. For one, few poets produced volumes directed at adolescents. Although Broadside Press published Sonia Sanchez's *It's a New Day: Poems for Young Brothas and Sistuhs* (1971), the publisher Lawrence Hill had the resources to present *ego-tripping* in higher-quality and larger quantities, ensuring added literary value and greater visibility for Giovanni and her volume. The initial appearance of *ego-tripping* in hardcover, for instance, was a rarity among volumes of poetry and reflected the publisher's willingness to invest in a poet whose sales were likely to produce worthwhile returns. Giovanni's volume is also unique among volumes of poetry published by African American writers during the 1970s, as a paperback edition of *ego-tripping* remains in print today. The ongoing circulation of *ego-tripping* contributes to Giovanni's social and literary value, not to mention her royalties, and suggests that her volume continues to appeal to generations of adolescent readers, a rare distinction among black arts era literary works.

The use of illustrations, of course, is the most distinguishing feature of *ego-tripping,* for the display of Ford's images transforms a collection of poems into a more dynamic verbal-visual text. The verbal-visual feature of the book increased Giovanni's ability to effectively appeal to a young black readership, a typically unexplored target demographic for established poets during the time period, and the design of *ego-tripping* also demonstrates the possibility of utilizing illustrations to convey poetic ideas to readers in visually stimulating ways. The covers of volumes of poetry by African American writers, especially those writers associated with black arts, frequently showcase nationalist iconography and ideas. But illustrations were rarely interspersed throughout volumes of poetry, especially to the degree that they were in *ego-tripping.* Giovanni's book contains more than fifteen of Ford's images, which further distinguishes this presentation of poems by an already widely popular poet.

Mari Evans's volume *I Am a Black Woman* (1970), published by

William Morrow, utilizes photographic images throughout the book, which serves to illuminate the overall effect of the poet's words. Evans's volume contains images of black women juxtaposed with the poems as a way of suggesting that the lines of verse represent the women's thoughts. Similarly, Amiri Baraka and Fundi's (also known as Billy Abernathy) collaborative effort *In Our Terribleness: Some Elements and Meaning in Black Style* (1970) blends poetic phrasing and photographic images. Many of Baraka's poems in the book focus on the idea of hip, streetwise black men, while Fundi's photos present suave-looking African American men posing for the camera or coolly strolling along in their urban setting. One image shows a young black boy holding his fist up, gazing off to the side with a serious look, which appears somewhat humorous considering his age. The words beneath the photo read, "Dont ever fuck with me. An emblem of breath. Can you dig a fist, so beautiful??"[3] Baraka's words appear to correspond to the thoughts of the boy in the photo and create a connective display of verbal-visual ideas—the kind of display of verbal-visual ideas that occurs throughout the book.

Taken together, *In Our Terribleness, I Am a Black Woman,* and *ego-tripping* offered alternative, mixed-media approaches to how poets could present their literary art. The publication of these alternative volumes assisted in furthering the larger implicit and sometimes overt mission of new black poets to modify the landscape of literature and appeal to a wider, more diverse readership. In the case of *ego-tripping* in particular, the volume's design as a children's book allowed Giovanni to reach a younger and ultimately broader audience in comparison to the majority of volumes published by African American poets during the time. The addition of a children's book to Giovanni's growing repertoire of publications helps to explain her expansive popularity among a broad range of readers beyond the conventional realms of black arts literature and even American poetry. The appearance of Ford's illustrations throughout *ego-tripping* was an integral, if not required, element for Giovanni's volume to effectively appeal to its target audience. The images could usefully assist young, developing readers in envisioning the content of the poet's words. In short, Ford's illustrations serve to frame Giovanni's poems.

Whereas illustrations function to illuminate the poems in *ego-tripping,* Middleton Harris's *The Black Book* (1974) offers a different possibility for juxtaposing poetic verses with visuals. Harris's publication contains an eclectic mix of materials—newspaper clippings, song lyrics, descriptions of cultural practices, and visual images—pertaining to African American culture and history. The assorted collection of texts gives Harris's book the look and feel of a scrapbook. Most notably for the purposes of the current discussion, the publication adjoins photographs with excerpts from the writings of Langston Hughes, Robert Hayden, Gwendolyn Brooks, and Henry Dumas. The juxtaposition of words and images in *The Black Book* provides a clear example of how an editor utilized poetry as part of a mixed-media approach to amplify and sharpen ideas about African American history and culture. The poetry excerpts in the book operate as crucial framing devices.

One of the most disturbing images in the book shows four black men hanging dead from a tree. The image has no caption, but readers can presume that the photograph is of a lynching. An excerpt from Langston Hughes appears above the photo: "I've been a victim / The Belgians cut off my hands / in the Congo. / They lynched me in Texas."[4] Hughes's words give voice to the dead men in the image, and the photograph in turn illustrates the poet's statement. Taken together, the contents of the page visually and linguistically present a horrific scene of antiblack racism. Readers are inclined to exercise both prose and visual literacy in order to absorb the implications of the text.

A more calming image toward the end of the book shows two black men wearing white clothing as they stand in a body of water that comes up above their knees. The two men are bowing their heads, and one of the men holds the other man's arm. More than likely, they are participating in a baptism. Above the photograph, words from a poem by Gwendolyn Brooks read, "Believe me, I loved you all / Believe me, I knew you, though faintly, / And I loved, I loved you all" (193). Her words seem to give voice to preceding generations of African Americans. The baptism photograph and the pictures on the subsequent pages present images of black people from earlier generations, as revealed by the tattered appearance of the photographs, as well as by the age and attire of the people pictured. The images do not include captions. The positioning of endearing words (i.e., "I loved you all") at the opening of the sequence of images suggests that these past generations of African Americans are expressing their devotion to current readers and viewers. In particular, Brooks's words are utilized to establish a familial bond between the black people in the images and the presumed black people reading the book.

Excerpts from the writings of Henry Dumas, a frequently anthologized black poet of the era, appear more than works by any other writer in *The Black Book*. Notably, Morrison, as an editor at Random House at the time, was assisting Eugene Redmond in the publication of Dumas's works. Having access and the publishing rights to his poetry perhaps increased the chances that Dumas's words would appear so frequently throughout the book. One photograph presents a scene from the movie *Honey* (1930), where actress Lillian Roth is shown wearing an evening gown and holding her hands above her head; she is in the midst of a performance. A large group of black people stand behind her. The men wear the attire of ranch hands; the women are dressed as house servants, and they wear handkerchiefs on their heads. An excerpt from Dumas appears at the top of the page: "One of the greatest roles / ever created by Western man / has been the role of 'Negro.' / One of the greatest actors to play the role has been / the 'Nigger'" (167). Dumas's words operate as a biting critique of the minstrel roles performed by African Americans. The next page displays a scene from the musical comedy *A Day at the Races* (1937) and a scene from *Old Kentucky* (1935); both images present black people dancing. Framed by Dumas's words on the previous page, the images on the subsequent pages accentuate the idea of black people playing buffoonish roles. The combination of photographs and words encourages audiences to look negatively upon African Americans who perform simply to entertain whites.

Dumas's words are also juxtaposed with photographs to inspire positive ideas concerning some black personalities. An eye-catching headshot of Lucille Armstrong appears below Dumas's words, "I want you to leap high in the sky / with me until we see / yellow trees and the blue gulf" (175). The photographs on the following pages show groups of black women entertainers, including the Hot Chocolates performing at the Cotton Club in 1936, the Brown Buddies in 1930, and a female chorus. The photographs also show a dance scene from *Harlem Madness* in 1930 and a sharply dressed couple performing a vaudeville act (176–77). These photographs of dignified and elegant-looking African American entertainers rebuff the preceding images of supposed black minstrels. Dumas's words propose that the figures in the photographs are encouraging their black audiences to "leap high in the sky" and join them.

The Black Book closes with the theme of group ascension as the words and images urge readers forward. The final page of the book presents a photograph of an elder black man wearing a worn and dingy suit, as he stares directly at the camera/viewer. Dumas's words appear above the photo: "We have a journey / to take and little time; / we have ships to name / and crews" (198). The words imply that the elderly black man in the photo, and presumably those like him, are encouraging readers to advance a larger mission. Despite the man's shabby appearance, Dumas's adjoining words suggest that the man encourages his allies and mates onward with a sense of urgency. That sense of urgency appears again on the back cover of the book. "I am *The Black Book*," readers are informed. "Between my top and my bottom, my right and my / left, I hold what I have seen, what I have done, and what I have thought." The speaker, the presumable book, closes by adopting and representing from Dumas's words: "I am not complete here; there is much more, / but there is no more time and no more space . . . and I have journeys to take, / ships to name, and crews." The last page and the back cover of the book cast the excerpt from Dumas's writing as a clarion call for an impending journey of African Americans and thus give the poem's lines a prominence and visibility that they did not have in the actual volume of poetry where they first appeared.

The presentation of poetic excerpts as photographic captions and framing devices in *The Black Book* represents yet another innovative possibility for the use of black poetry. Images had often been used to highlight the words of poets; however, in the case of Harris's publication, the positioning of the poetic excerpts reveals that verse could assist in defining the apparent meaning of images. *The Black Book* demonstrates the prospect of interspersing African American verse throughout a publication that is hardly primarily about poetry and thus places poets such as Brooks, Hughes, and Dumas into contact with readers who may not have otherwise encountered the writers' volumes of poetry. In this regard, Harris's book coincided with the larger objective of increasing the potential readership for African American verse, even though *The Black Book,* with its scrapbook-like features, constituted a unique publishing platform. And though unique, Harris's publication and a volume such as Giovanni's *ego-tripping* represent important examples of how photographic and illustrative images might invigorate the implications of black poetry and expand its readership. Although the use of images was important, poets and their supporters devised other mixed-media means of broadening the reach of their literary art. In particular, they began to more fully realize the opportunities available to them by producing audio recordings.

Dealing in Sound

In the foreword to Larry Neal's volume of poetry *Black Boogaloo*, Amiri Baraka suggests that black writers move beyond the page and produce projects associated with "the post 'literary' world."[5] He asks writers to distance themselves from conventional practices associated with being "literary." According to Baraka, the word "literary sound like somethin' else . . . sound like it ain't sound. And sound is what we deal in . . . in the real world" (i). The concept of dealing in sound might serve as a useful point of departure for considering the ways that black poets used audio recordings in order to further expand and diversify their literary art, as well as their audiences. The production of audio recordings gave select poets and musicians important opportunities to participate in the transmission of African American verse. Among other notable results, these practices and processes of dealing in sound further highlighted the relationships between black poetry and black music and helped solidify the view of the Black Arts Movement as an engaging mixed-media enterprise.

Audio recordings of poets reading their poems actually represent a relatively small number of works produced by black writers. Despite Baraka's recommendation that writers move beyond the "post 'literary' world," print-based poetry continued to dominate African American literary culture. Thus, more so than serving as an alternative to print volumes, the recordings provided select groups of poets with additional mediums to expand the range of their approaches to producing poetry. The albums and cassettes of poets reading their works confirmed that the poets were both writers and performers, both authors and recording artists. These expanded capabilities associated with producing audio recordings represent some of the important technological developments taking place among black poets that so far have gained little scholarly attention.

For some time now, literary scholars have highlighted the dynamic possibilities concerning the performance of black poetry and its relationship to music. There has been little, if any, scholarly attention focusing on the technological significance of the poets' activities. Yet their use of recording devices and their work with instrumentalists contributed to the spirit of innovation so central to the claim that the movement among black poets represented something *new*. The achievement of something new partially relied on poets' engagement with audio production. Their performances and recordings of verse assisted in expanding the distinct sonic presence of black poetry in literary history.

Among those poets who worked with musicians, Jayne Cortez produced an especially impressive body of work. "Perhaps no black poet whose works began to appear in print after World War II," writes Aldon Nielsen, "has recorded as many jazz texts as has Jayne Cortez. Indeed,

Cortez has recorded nearly all of her published poems in jazz arrangements."[6] On her first album, *Celebrations and Solitudes* (1974), Cortez performs her poetry with the accompaniment of Richard Davis, who offers improvisations on bass. The collaboration between the two artists creates renewed versions of Cortez's poems. The rhythmic and patterned phrasing that Davis provides on "I Am New York City" gives the poem a flowing, moving tempo. Characteristic of her readings throughout the album, Cortez shifts her tone and pitch as she reads and slightly pauses after speaking lines of the poem for more dramatic effect.

On "How Long Has Trane Been Gone," Cortez voices anger and frustration with audiences, club owners, disc jockeys, and African Americans who have neglected to fully appreciate the work of John Coltrane and other black musicians. "You takin—they givin," she says, "You livin—they creating starving dying." Cortez modulates her voice and conveys varying degrees of anger. Throughout the readings, Davis assists Cortez in raising the intensity of her message by adding phrasing and pitches and increasing his tempo on bass to accent her tone and speed of reading. At the same time, Davis's more experimental playing—a mode of playing associated with free jazz—adds a level of abstraction to the overall delivery of Cortez's poems. The complementary phrasing of the bass shapes the surrealist sound that the duo achieves.

Cortez and Davis's collaboration constitutes an important sonic realization of the convergence of poetry and music, the combination of which had long been present in African American and American literary discourses. Blues musicians and their musical forms had been central, for instance, to the writings of Langston Hughes as early as the 1920s. The Beat writers of the 1950s had found jazz musicians especially inspiring, and black arts writers had highlighted the significance of African American music, especially the New Black Music, in both verse and critical prose during the 1960s and early 1970s. Given this backdrop, Cortez's *Celebrations and Solitudes* can easily be read as a continuation of the long-standing interactions between poetry and jazz. Yet in retrospect, Cortez's album was also a signal moment for a woman staking a claim for herself as a jazz poet, a designation often attributed to male literary artists. Thus, the inscription of Cortez's poetic voice onto the sonic discourse of jazz and poetry was a continuation but also a modification of the typical collaborations between musicians and poets.

Giovanni's foray into audio production also represented a modification of the transmission of black poetry. Her first album, *Truth Is On Its Way,* which appeared in 1971, achieves the fairly unique task of blending gospel and poetry, an especially unusual task since leading black poets tended to align their work with jazz. Whereas gospel music was hardly ever highlighted in black arts discourse, Giovanni's album was nonetheless a remarkable commercial success. Six months after *Truth Is On Its Way* was released, the album had sold one hundred thousand copies.[7] The fusion of Giovanni's poetry with the choir is not as dynamic and interactive as the exchange between Cortez and Davis, as Giovanni's reading functions as more of a voice-over to the choir. Still, Giovanni's work could appeal to the sensibilities of audiences rooted in black church music traditions.

Many of the selections on Giovanni's album, such as "Great Pax Whitey," "Alabama Poem," and "All I Gotta Do," open with singing and an organ playing; then the music lowers as Giovanni begins reading. The pairing of her poem "Nikki-Rosa" with the gospel tune "It Is Well" creates a remarkable combination. Giovanni's sentiment in "Nikki-Rosa" that she did not have a troubled childhood and that "black love is black wealth" relates to the recurring line in the gospel song declaring, "it is well in my soul." Actually, the pairing of Giovanni's poem with "It Is Well" highlights the spirit of tranquility integral to both pieces.

The presentation of "ego-tripping" constitutes another instance of how the use of black church music enhances the implications of Giovanni's poem. The recording begins with a group of people providing rhythmic clapping, soulful shouts, tambourine playing, and a recurrent drumbeat. A woman in the background shouts, "Right on! soul sister" just before Giovanni begins to read. The congregants shout "yeah," "whew," "hey," and "right on" at various intervals as Giovanni reads. The accompanying shouts and soul clapping resemble the call-and-response practices of African American church services and performances and thus serve to highlight the proximity of Giovanni and her poem to such realms of expressive culture.

Based on the amount of time the choir performs on the album, *Truth Is On Its Way* could be viewed as a gospel album that features a poet reading her work as opposed to a recording of poetry that happens to include gospel. As a result, for audiences interested in gospel music and poetry (in that order), *Truth Is On Its Way* represents a more significant work than the absence of criticism suggests. Collaborating with a gospel choir allowed Giovanni to locate her work firmly within a tradition and site where large numbers of African Americans reside: the black church. Giovanni's album might not reflect the more dominant strains of militancy represented in black poetry and free jazz; nonetheless, *Truth Is On Its Way* does tap into an expansive reservoir of black expressive culture and appeals to large number of listeners. The gospel music on Giovanni's album serves the purpose of transporting poetry to broader African American Christian audiences—a group that leading black artists regularly criticized because they felt that traditional African American religious practices were counterproductive to radical forms of liberation. Giovanni's ability to meet gospel music and, by extension, black Christian audiences on their own terms enabled her to make a rare and profitable connection. Moreover, her decision to deal in the sounds of black religious music contributed to her rising popularity. The convergence of gospel music and poetry on *Truth Is On Its Way* extended the possibility that Giovanni's literary art and her voice would reach audiences beyond the conventional discourses of poetry.

Not surprisingly, some of the most dynamic recordings of black poetry were produced by the era's leading artist, Amiri Baraka. Similar to Cortez, Baraka utilized free jazz as a vehicle for transmitting verse. Based on his writings on jazz, as well as his alliances with avant-garde musicians, Baraka served as a vital connector between the developments taking place in poetry and jazz. Interestingly, the appearance of "Black Art" on an album in 1965, before its initial printing in *Liberator* in 1966, reveals Baraka's cutting-edge commitment to utilizing audio production as a means of transmitting verse.

The audio version of "Black Art" is a dynamic interplay between a poet and a group of instrumentalists. Throughout Baraka's reading of the poem, the musicians—Sonny Murray on drums, Don Cherry on trumpet, Henry Grimes and Lewis Worrell on bass, and Albert Ayler on tenor saxophone—produce lively responses, which intensify the poet's message.[8] When Baraka raises his voice and says, "We want poems that kill," the musicians increase the volume and force of their playing.[9] The exchanges between Baraka and tenor saxophonist Albert Ayler are especially pronounced on the recording. After Baraka makes statements such as "fuck poems" and "setting fire and death to whities ass," Ayler projects deep and quick-moving phrasings on his horn. Later, when Baraka speaks in a more composed manner to point out a "Negro leader . . . negotiating cooly for his people," Ayler provides soft, low, long notes, thus producing a kind of calming effect. However, as soon as Baraka interrupts the calmness by shouting "Aggh!!!," Ayler responds in kind with a high-pitched squeal on his horn. Finally, when the poet demands, "We want a black poem," Ayler follows up with a trill on his instrument. Next Baraka says, "And a Black World," to which Ayler responds with a trill in a slightly higher octave. Finally, when Baraka says, "Let the world be a Black Poem," Ayler trills yet again, this time in the octave in which he began. Ayler's trilling, squealing responses intensify the implications of Baraka's words and give the poem distinguishing sonic attributes to complement its powerful message.

The dynamic audio rendition of "Black Art" provides a useful model for what could result from a vibrant collaboration between a militant poet and avant-garde musicians. The recording also orients literary audiences to elements of jazz while at the same time exposing jazz listeners to black verse. Thus, Baraka's partnership with the musicians creates an important crossroads for a diverse group of listeners. What Baraka's performance with Ayler, Murray, and company indicated to fellow and emergent poets was that there were indeed new opportunities for producing poetry beyond the page just waiting to be explored. So in addition to serving as a distinguishing audio rendition, the "Black Art" recording revealed the expanding possibilities of African American poetry.

Similar to "Black Art," the audio version of Baraka's "It's Nation Time" merges music and verse in a dramatic fashion. But with this poem, Baraka moves even further into explorations of sonic possibilities. The track begins with African drumming and a slow tempo. Then Baraka announces that "it's nation time," which signals a drummer to disrupt the calmness with a drumroll as Baraka begins reading the poem. He reads at a rapid pace, suggesting a sense of urgency. As Baraka shifts from reading words to wordless phrasings, the drummer begins to play more emphatically, as if responding to Baraka's call. Baraka in turn responds to the drummer's increasing pace and emphatic playing. Baraka shouts and makes percussive sounds with his mouth. As he continues shouting and wailing, a saxophone joins in and responds to Baraka with screams and screeches on his instrument. The interactions between Baraka's voice and the instrumentalists are even more energetic than on "Black Art," and it's certainly more dynamic than a conventional poetry reading. In fact, rather than being similar to typical literary presentations, Baraka's methods of delivery on "It's Nation Time" are actually more akin to the performance styles of James Brown.

Listening to Baraka's performance on the album reveals that he was innovating his modes of delivery to become a distinctly interactive performer attuned to black musical discourses. In retrospect, the engaging and entertaining reading style that Baraka is known for today was developed and honed during the late 1960s and early 1970s. The attention to newness and stylistic innovation so central to discussions of African American poetry during the era, as well as the declaration that artists should actively embrace and emulate the achievements of black music, gave Baraka and various other artists opportunities and incentives to collaborate with musicians and adjust their methods of presentation to reflect stronger connections to jazz and R&B. The prevalence of militant nationalist discourse prompted writers to view themselves as artist-activists, and in a similar fashion, their interest in music inclined writers to develop their capabilities as poet-performers. Indeed, Baraka's recordings are notable testaments to the possibilities for poets adopting the fiery and entertaining delivery styles of soul singers and jazz musicians.

Poets' forays into audio recordings did not diminish the primacy of print-based verse. Magazines, anthologies, and volumes of poetry remained the dominant venues for the presentation of African American poetry. Nonetheless, those poets who chose to deal in sound, as it were, and produce audio recordings established resonant connections to discourses of music, making it possible for them to diversify the presentation of their literary art and extend the reach of their poetry. The development of diverse repertoires of literary works that could appeal to both reading and listening audiences was especially important to the burgeoning careers of Baraka, Cortez, and Giovanni. After her first album, Cortez went on to make audio recordings and collaborations with jazz musicians a defining feature of her creative output. Baraka and Giovanni still reap the benefits of being known as dynamic performers of poetry; over the last decades, they have been continually called on to present their work to large and diverse audiences.

Beyond the musical and performance implications, the poets' audio productions and interactions with instrumentalists amounted to signal moments in the developing technological and literary histories of poetry. The collaborations with poets and musicians shaped the distinct sounds of black verse, and these sounds were inscribed in literary and cultural discourses through the use of recording devices. Without embracing the technologies of musical production, poets would have been far less successful in establishing distinct sonic qualities for their poetry, and they could hardly have done as well in nurturing a broad and modern listening audience for African American verse. The utilization of recording devices and the pursuit of collaborations with musicians highlighted or further legitimatized the possibilities of using auditory approaches for producing literary art. These approaches also expanded the methods by which poets could deliver their poetry. The technical processes of dealing in sound, then, provided additional opportunities for innovating the nature of black poetry.

Building a Brand: The Broadside Imprint

During the late 1960s and early 1970s, Broadside Press functioned as the most influential publisher of African American poetry. Even without the resources and wide distribution capabilities of large, well-funded publishing institutions, Broadside Press symbolized the promise of black self-determination in publishing. But more than just a symbol, Broadside Press published the movement's most notable figures and several lesser-known poets. Literary critic James Sullivan explains that "literature always appears under the name not only of an author, but also of a racially marked publishing institution whose mission always inflects the work."[10] Writers who published under the Broadside imprint became linked to a press whose mission was to produce inexpensive, creatively designed literary products that celebrated black culture. Under the leadership of its founder, Dudley Randall, Broadside Press secured a visible role in the circulation of African American poetry in general.

Several literary historians, including Melba Boyd, James Smethurst, James Sullivan, and Julius Thompson, have charted the history of Broadside Press and remarked on its significance as a publisher of black verse.[11] Their writings further validate the important contributions that Randall and Broadside Press made to the promotion of African American poetry and the formation of a movement among a wide-ranging group of writers. On the one hand, Randall demonstrated a commitment to veteran poets. As James Smethurst notes, "The first wave of Broadside writers," such as Robert Hayden, Melvin Tolson, Margaret Walker, and Gwendolyn Brooks, "were all veterans of the cultural and political milieu of the Popular Front in the Midwest."[12] Further, explains Smethurst, twelve of the press's first eighteen broadsides were authored by writers born before 1918 (236). On the other hand, Broadside Press also demonstrated its commitment to "new" black poets. As Melba Boyd documents in her biography of Randall, leading poets Haki Madhubuti, Nikki Giovanni, Sonia Sanchez, and Etheridge Knight benefited greatly from the publishing opportunities made possible by Broadside Press. Overall, Broadside Press published more than two hundred poets and became one of the most respected and recognizable *brands* in the production of African American poetry.[13]

Thinking of Broadside Press as a brand name means considering how the placement of the company's name or imprint on its products, such as books, broadsides, and tape recordings, gave those products added significance. A consideration of the Broadside brand also means recognizing how leading poets assisted in increasing the overall value and prominence of the press. The appearance of "Broadside Press" on volumes of poetry linked those publications and their authors to a network of African American writers and cultural practices, and consequently, the success of Broadside as a brand was the result of a convergence of writers, literary institutions, readers/consumers, and publishing practices. According to Randall, Broadside Press was "one of the institutions that black people are creating by trial and error and out of necessity in our reaching for self-determination and independence."[14] Indeed, during the Black Power era, an African American–owned press could accommodate the nationalist agenda of literary artists seeking to create and promote their own institutions. In addition to Randall's Broadside Press, Haki Madhubuti's Third Press, Amiri Baraka's Jihad Press, Joe Goncalves's The Journal of Black Poetry Press, and other African American–owned presses allowed poets to publish their works through black channels of publication. "The founding of small African American presses such as Broadside and Third World," writes Sullivan, "made it possible to publish work identified with African American cultural nationalism without that level of irony added to the text by reliance on white cultural institutions" ("Killing John Cabot," 568). Publishing books under a black imprint gave black poets added credibility. Poets who used African American presses as mediums for publication could visibly link their publishing practices with nationalist and grassroots agendas.

Through its distinct methods of transmitting black poetry, Broadside Press created a sense of community among writers and readers. As James Sullivan explains in his book *On the Walls and in the Streets,* the acts of "producing, selling, and buying" Broadside literary products constituted "elements of a material political practice, acts of solidarity with a specific cause."[15] To publish under the Broadside imprint, sell its products, or buy from the publisher was to participate in a decidedly black literary network. Despite any apparent ideological, stylistic, or generational differences among such poets as Robert Hayden, Margaret Walker, Gwendolyn Brooks, Nikki Giovanni, Amiri Baraka, Haki Madhubuti, and Audre Lorde, all these writers and dozens more published their works in some form or another under the Broadside imprint. Thus, the press served as a connector among an eclectic grouping of African American poets, many of whom aligned themselves with black arts activities and some of whom did not. Randall published a distinguished and diverse group of writers, and he thus increased the cultural capital of Broadside Press as an imprint that appealed to the varied interests of African American readerships.

The very name "Broadside Press" signaled readers and potential consumers to the company's roots and routes to grassroots publishing. "Since broadsides," writes Randall, "were the company's sole product, I gave it the name Broadside Press."[16] Although the company went on to produce volumes of poetry, anthologies, criticism, and recordings, the name "broadside" linked the press to its humble beginnings. Whereas relatively few readers will get the chance to see or own an actual broadside from Randall's press, our knowledge that the company produced inexpensive texts using a single-sheet format supports the perception of Broadside Press as an institution that operated for the people, so to speak. Certainly the phrase "Broadside Press" constitutes a ubiquitous bibliographic code in black arts discourse, appearing in literary journals, on works cited pages, and on permissions and acknowledgments pages, not to mention on the company's many products. The pervasiveness of the Broadside imprint meant that its authors and products were rarely viewed in isolation. The imprint linked authors and literary products to an apparent enterprise of African American publishing practices. The design of the press's volumes of poetry effectively projected the view that the authors were part of a network that catered to black interests.

The titles, cover designs, and formats of the press's products constituted interactions among poets, visual artists, literary critics, and a publishing company. *Think Black!* by Haki Madhubuti, *Impressions of African Art Forms* by Margaret Danner, *Black Man Listen* by Marvin X, *We a BaddDDD* by Sonia Sanchez, *Home Is Where the Soul Is* by Jon Eckels, and *Jump Bad* edited by Gwendolyn Brooks all foreground nationalist sensibilities and African American verbal styles. The front covers contain images suggestive of African American or African-related cultural symbols, while the back covers of volumes of poetry by Madhubuti, Sanchez, Brooks, and Giovanni, to name a few, contain photos of the writers. In many of the author photos, the poets sport afros or natural hairdos, and some wear dashikis and African jewelry. Presenting the poets wearing clothes and hairdos associated with popular African

American styles and cultural practices further indicated the ostensible social and political allegiances of the authors and the press. More specifically, the front and back covers of Broadside books situated the authors more firmly in black nationalist discourse.

Broadside Press publications often include introductions by poets and literary critics to extol the values of a particular writer's work. These introductions operate as ornaments to the volumes of poetry that could influence how readers might interpret the poet and poems. In the introduction to Lance Jeffers's *When I Know the Power of My Black Hand,* Eugene Redmond writes, "We are blessed and exalted by Lance Jeffers' refusal to simplify the Black Experience. . . . As an Afro-American poet of the front rank, his intellectual passion is expectedly wide-ranging and intense."[17] Redmond's comments reflect a recurring practice among writers and critics of foregrounding poets' cultural identity and ability to represent "the Black Experience" in their works. As a result, the authors of volumes of poetry were praised based on their poetic skills, as well as on the extent to which their writings served the interests of African Americans.

In the introduction to Sonia Sanchez's *Homecoming,* also published by Broadside Press, Don Lee informs readers that "the poems/poetry in this first book of poems are not those of a first book poet. The poet is skilled/confident to the point of oversay."[18] Directing his words to black readers, Lee explains that Sanchez's poems will strengthen an approach to confronting real-world challenges. Sanchez's "poetry helps u face yr/self," he writes. "Then, actually, u will be able to move thru/out the world and face otherpeople as a true blackperson" (7). Although contemporary scholars would question Lee's essentialist notions of "true" black people, what remains important for the discussion here is that he supports claims for the value of Sanchez's poetry by explaining how her poems positively relate to the lived experiences of African Americans. Thus, Lee bases his view of Sanchez on the notion that she is committed to the well-being of African Americans, as she "wants us to/live" (8).

Similar to the valuations of Jeffers and Sanchez by Redmond and Lee, respectively, Gwendolyn Brooks notes in the introduction to Don Lee's *Don't Cry, Scream,* "At the hub of the new wordway is Don Lee. Around a black audience he puts warm healing arms."[19] Here, Brooks, like so many writers extolling the virtues of black poets, emphasizes Lee's commitment to African American audiences: "Don Lee has no patience with black writers who do not direct their blackness toward black audiences" (9). Brooks's appraisal indicates that a clear-cut devotion to African American audiences is an admirable quality—a quality beyond the poet's actual writing that nonetheless contributes to how he should be perceived. The claims in the introductions concerning the commitments of the poets to distinct audiences were further substantiated by their appearance under the Broadside imprint. Surely, readers would likely deduce, poets publishing with a black press were committed to black audiences.

Broadside Press further highlighted the relationship of poets to a larger African American artistic discourse by including the press's catalog in individual volumes of poetry. The appearance of a catalog in a single volume provided publicity for the other authors and literary products offered by the press. Just as important, however, the catalog of Broadside poets and literary products revealed that an individual poet was actually participating in an extensive, ongoing cultural enterprise. The catalog indicated that the poets were located within "a specifically African American context," to use James Sullivan's phrasing ("Killing John Cabot," 560). And those literary products produced under the Broadside Press imprint and accompanied by the company's catalog, then, "had to be read as culturally specific rather than universal" (560). The extensive list of poets and publications confirmed that the Broadside imprint was an active facilitator in the publication of black literary products. The seemingly extraliterary components of Broadside's volumes of poetry—the front and back covers, the introductions, and the catalog—represent integral elements in the overall design and function of the company's books.

The increasing visibility and success of poets who published with Broadside Press generated more exposure and legitimacy for the imprint. *Negro Digest/Black World* frequently reviewed and mentioned books produced by Randall's press, providing publicity for the company at the national level. In the Detroit "News" section regarding upcoming events and publications in the 1968 issue of the *Journal of Black Poetry*, Ahmed Alhamisi identifies books that have been and will be published by Broadside Press. Alhamisi informs readers interested in purchasing Etheridge Knight's *Poems from Prison* or Randall's *Cities Burning* that the books "should be at all Black book stores," confirming the press's relationship to African American cultural sites and institutions.[20] The extensive and favorable coverage that Broadside Press received made the imprint more widely known in African American literary history than most of the poets it published, notwithstanding a few exceptions, such as Nikki Giovanni and Haki Madhubuti.

Actually, Giovanni's and Madhubuti's overall achievements can partly be attributed to their connections with the Broadside imprint. Both writers initially self-published volumes of their poetry; however, Randall provided them with the publishing venue to distribute their volumes on a larger scale. Two years after publishing Madhubuti's *Think Black* in 1967, Broadside Press had brought twenty-five thousand copies of the book into print and had printed the seventh edition of *Black Pride*.[21] The publishing opportunities offered by Broadside Press, observes Melba Boyd, assisted in taking Madhubuti "to center stage on the black literary scene" (175). Randall's press was also an inspiration for Madhubuti's cofounding Third World Press with poets Johari Amini and Carolyn Rodgers in 1967.[22] While Madhubuti benefited from the publishing opportunities made available by Broadside Press, his achievements also increased the success and visibility of the imprint. His success as one of the press's best-selling authors brought impressive financial gains to the company and made poets aware that the imprint could effectively facilitate the publishing careers of aspirant militant writers.

Like Madhubuti, Giovanni benefited from the publishing opportunities provided by Broadside Press and simultaneously contributed to the imprint's reputation as a publisher of leading black poets. Broadside became the distributor of Giovanni's *Black Judgement* in 1968 and published her *Re: Creation* in 1970, the same year that she began publishing with the more established New York publisher William Morrow. Broadside Press was a crucial step in Giovanni's journey from self-publishing to publishing with a large commercial press. Moreover, Broadside validated Giovanni's early association with a network of African American poets and the developing black arts enterprise. Giovanni's success as a poet, on the other hand, generated additional profits for Broadside Press and further solidified the status of Randall's company as a publisher of choice for aspirant black poets.

With a roster of at least two hundred poets that also included Margaret Danner, Audre Lorde, Lance Jeffers, Keorapetse William Kgositsile, Marvin X, and Margaret Walker, the centrality of the Broadside imprint to the transmission of black poetry was comparable to the position of *Negro Digest/Black World*. Like Hoyt Fuller, Dudley Randall coordinated a highly visible publishing institution that featured an intergenerational grouping of poets. Also like Fuller, Dudley Randall enacted editorial practices that were vital to the formation and operations of black arts discourse. Broadside Press published some of the era's leading figures and produced one of the movement's most well-known anthologies, *For Malcolm*. In the process of publishing broadsides, volumes of poetry, anthologies, tape recordings, and a series of poetry criticism books, the widespread appearance of the Broadside Press imprint demonstrated that a black-owned institution could adequately serve multiple interests of poets and readerships. In a *Black World* article in 1975, Carole Parks observed in an annotated directory of African American publishers that Broadside Press "is presently considered the primary outlet for Black poetry, in paper and cloth as well."[23]

Ten years after the publication of Randall's first broadsides, his press had secured a reputation as a principal cultural institution in the production of African American verse. The press embodied key values of black arts discourse by promoting self-determination, extending a nationalist agenda, and directly appealing to black readerships. Moreover, Randall's imprint transformed those values into literary products and publishing opportunities for new and veteran poets. The press brought substantial numbers of writers into print and confirmed their relationship to a larger network of African American artistic and cultural activities. Along with *Negro Digest/Black World* and the large number of anthologies featuring African American verse, Broadside Press served as an essential connector between poets and extensive readerships.

4 • All Aboard the Malcolm-Coltrane Express

A survey of the hundreds of poems published in literary magazines and anthologies, as well as the varied and large number of poems appearing in individual volumes of poetry, would reveal an aesthetically diverse and expansive picture of African American poetry published during the 1960s and 1970s. The poems that readers are regularly exposed to in anthologies and magazines containing black poetry actually constitute a relatively small sampling of the literary art produced during the era. In fact, reviewing all of Amiri Baraka's and Nikki Giovanni's poems published in their individual volumes of poetry as opposed to their anthologized poems reveals that most readers have always been presented with a limited view of the writings of these widely known poets. Thus, describing all the features of black arts era poetry would be an overwhelming task, a task that is definitely beyond the scope of this project. Given the overall focus on modes of transmission and socialization in this study, the principal interest is in explaining how the widespread and repeated publication of particular kinds of poems gave a more definite shape to an overall view of African American poetry.

Certainly, black poets always constituted a group with divergent interests and modes of writing. However, the convergence of a diverse group of writers along the same routes suggested that they were exercising a form of poetic solidarity. Their decisions to concentrate on similar themes and techniques, in fact, were integral to the view of interconnectivity that characterized their artistic enterprise. The interrelated approaches taken by black poets during the 1960s and 1970s reveal how they established a more definite shape for their movement. Tribute poems and elegies devoted to African American political leaders, activists, writers, and musicians were especially prevalent during the time period.

Memorializing deceased historical figures as black exemplars, poets expressed their political and cultural allegiances, and they also provided audiences with ideas about those elements that were most worthy of emulation. Taken together, the tribute poems reveal the preoccupation among a large number of poets with constructing positive African American images. "Image is a term which we are using more and more in the black community," wrote Carolyn Gerald, "because we are discovering that the image we have of ourselves controls what we are capable of doing."[1] The presentation of affirmative portrayals was done "to destroy the zero and negative image-myths of ourselves by turning them inside out" (Gerald, "Black Writer and His Role," 354). In his poem "A Different Image," Dudley Randall writes that the 1960s required "this task: / create / a different image; / re-animate / the mask."[2] Accordingly, tribute poems enabled writers to "re-animate the mask" or to counter negative images by producing more positive portrayals of African Americans.

Members of the older generations of poets such as Paul Laurence Dunbar, Langston Hughes, Gwendolyn Brooks, and Robert Hayden, to name a few, had published tributes and elegies prior to the 1960s. However, the proliferation of texts during the black arts era made these poems even more widely available. The militant tone of the tributes and elegies were also a distinguishing factor. In the process of paying homage to jazz musicians, for instance, poets accentuated the rebellious, nationalist, and transformative spirits of the music. In his poem "Jazz Is My Religion," Ted Joans celebrates an "Afroamerican" musical form that was created "as a weapon to battle our blues!"[3] In his poem "Elvin Jones: Jazz Drummer," Etheridge Knight explains that Max Roach "has fire and steel in his hands," and through his playing, the drummer "calls us all."[4] Sarah Webster Fabio advances this chorus of jazz homage in her poem "Tribute to Duke" by praising Duke Ellington for his contributions to the music. She writes, "Way back then, Man, / you were doing / your thing. / Blowing minds with / riffs capping / whimsical whiffs of / lush melody—/ changing minds / with moods and / modulations, / changing minds, / changing faces, / changing tunes, / changing changes."[5]

Paying tribute to activists and musicians enabled poets to convey to their readership their positions on the varied possibilities of liberation, self-determination, and black history. "In the work of poets to give us back our heroes and to provide us with new ones," explains Carolyn Gerald, musicians and political activists represented the "two types of black men" most often celebrated during the time period.[6] Malcolm X and John Coltrane, consequently, were the figures who most often re-curred in African American verse. The frequency with which these two men were alluded to in black poetry suggest that writers had arrived at a tacit agreement about the value of making these extraordinary cultural figures the subject of their poems. Apparently, poets had gotten on board a kind of Malcolm-Coltrane express, utilizing the two men as ve-hicles for transmitting ideas about the movement's commitment to rad-ical politics and creativity.

Elegizing St. Malcolm

Next to Martin Luther King Jr., Malcolm X stands as one of the most widely known and memorialized African Americans of the twentieth century. In fact, in African American discourse, the only martyr cele-brated more frequently than Martin Luther King Jr. and Malcolm X is Jesus Christ. Various poems, books, paintings, songs, history programs, documentaries, course syllabi, plays, movies, clothing, album covers, Web pages, and a U.S. stamp have all, in some way, served to memorial-ize the life of Malcolm. The different methods and media utilized to in-voke memories of the leader reveal that groups of people have sought to remember Malcolm X by any and all means available. The figure of Malcolm appeared "more than any man any time anywhere" in 1960s literature, Carolyn Gerald observes.[7] Even Malcolm's name provided for a striking visual referent in American letters. Julia Fields's poem "When That Which Is Perfect Is Come" contains a line that reads, "As long as / ◉ / Get / My X."[8] On the printed page, the X is printed in a larger font than the other letters in the poem. In addition to noting var-ious textual concerns relating to the poem, Aldon Nielsen observes, "The advent of the X in Field's post-Malcolm poem signifies for us in ways that were unavailable before Malcolm X" (27). Just as Americans could no longer see the numbers "9-11" in quite the same way after Sep-tember 10, 2001, the sign X came to connote new and distinctive mean-ings in the post-Malcolm era.

Malcolm gained national attention during the 1960s for his fiery speeches, his radical stances against antiblack racism, his black national-ist views, and ultimately his tragic death. Moreover, Malcolm won the hearts and imaginations of creative artists of the 1960s and 1970s, as his style, appearance, and ideology became prevalent points of reference throughout the discourse. The numerous elegies to Malcolm reveal that poets made the slain leader a central figure in African American literary history in general. In her poem "Saint Malcolm," Johari Amini closes by noting that Malcolm's "word cauterizes our infection / unifying blackness."[9] The title of Amini's poem indicates the reverence bestowed upon the leader, and the closing suggests how he inspired black nationality.

Malcolm came to represent a significant element in the aesthetics of black poetry and the formation of the Black Arts Movement. Literary histories, in fact, trace the movement's origins to late February and early March 1965, when Amiri Baraka moved uptown to Harlem and cofounded the Black Arts Repertory Theater/School. "When Malcolm was murdered," explains Baraka, "we felt that was the final open declaration of war on black people and we resolved to fight. The Harlem move was our open commitment to this idea."[10] Although African American writers were involved in organizing themselves and composing militant art before Malcolm X's death, Baraka's move to Harlem and the subsequent African American literary and cultural activism after that point are significant, especially considering the fact that the Black Arts Repertory Theater/School that Baraka and others founded gave the movement its name. In view of reflections by Baraka, the death of Malcolm provided impetus for the birth of the Black Arts Movement. Even a cursory survey of black arts era writings reveals the extent to which Malcolm figures prominently in the discourse.

Well-known anthologies such as *Black Fire,* edited by Amiri Baraka and Larry Neal, *The Black Poets,* edited by Dudley Randall, and *Understanding the New Black Poetry,* edited by Stephen Henderson, all contain poems, essays, or references in their introductions and afterwords that memorialize Malcolm X. Abraham Chapman's edited collections *Black Voices* (1968) and *New Black Voices* (1972) include, respectively, an excerpt from Malcolm X's autobiography and his coauthored "Statement of the Basic Aims and Objectives of the Organization of Afro-American Unity." On the pages of literary magazines, such as *Negro Digest/Black World, Freedomways,* and the *Journal of Black Poetry,* writers often mentioned and invoked memories of Malcolm X, and images of the leader appeared in these and several other black arts publications, such as *Liberator.*

Allusions to Malcolm X also appeared in creative and critical prose of the era. In John A. Williams's 1967 novel *The Man Who Cried I Am,* "Minister Q of the Black Muslims" is clearly inspired by Malcolm X. The narrator in John Oliver Killens's 1971 novel *The Cotillion* makes reference to Malcolm throughout his story, often equating Malcolm with a deity. At a point when no human knows what people are thinking, the narrator observes in passing that only God and Malcolm know.[11] At one point in a 1920s scene in Ishmael Reed's *Mumbo Jumbo,* a character predicts the coming of a Malcolm X figure: "Maybe I won't be around but someone is coming. I feel it stirring. He might even have the red hair of a conjure man but he won't be 1. No, he will get it across. And he will be known as the man who 'got it across.'"[12] The character in Reed's novel is apparently alluding to a younger Malcolm X, who had his hair conked and was known as "Detroit Red."

Keorapetse William Kgositsile comments in his essay "Brother Malcolm and the Black Revolution" on the various and multiple mentions of the slain leader and observes that Malcolm "is too many things to too many people."[13] Actually, the idea that Malcolm is "too many things" perhaps helps make him such a useful site of inspiration for such a large number of poets. As discussed in chapter 2, *For Malcolm,* edited by Dudley Randall and Margaret Burroughs, published under Broadside Press, represents one of the most notable African American anthologies of the era. Randall and Burroughs's anthology demonstrates how Malcolm could serve as a poetic muse and a unifying force for a diverse range of poets. Given the visibility of *For Malcolm,* as well as its inclusion of so many prominent writers, aspirant poets would have certainly been inclined to consider Malcolm as a subject for their works as well.

Invoking the idea of Malcolm in their poems enabled poets to project a range of black nationalist aesthetics in their works. By focusing on Malcolm, poets covered issues such as black solidarity, liberation, and the development of radical identities. In her "Poems for Malcolm," Carolyn Rodgers closes with the request, "I want us to be a Black Nationhood Poem / for El Hajj Malik El Shabazz [Malcolm X]."[14] Here Rodgers calls on fellow poets and general readers to develop a nationality in the name of Malcolm. Similarly, in her poem "How Long Has Trane Been Gone," Jayne Cortez imagines a day when black people will reside in "The State of Malcolm X."[15] Similarly, James Emanuel writes in his poem "For Malcolm, U.S.A." that "Malcolm was / My native land."[16] By envisioning Malcolm as a basis on which black people might establish a nation, these three poets further extend Malcolm's black nationalist ideology. They go beyond declaring the leader a chief proponent of black nationalism; they suggest that he is the very embodiment of the ideology.

The process of memorializing the slain leader led some black poets to "become" types of Malcolm. In his poem "Malcolm X—An Autobiography," Larry Neal adopts the persona of Malcolm and charts the leader's life experiences. "I sprang out of the Midwestern plains / the bleak Michigan landscape, the black blues of Kansas / City, these kiss-me-nights; / out of the bleak Michigan landscape wearing the slave name / Malcolm Little," Neal writes, alluding to Malcolm's adolescent years.[17] Later Neal discusses Malcolm's experiences in the Northeast, when the leader was known as a conk-haired street hustler: "I am Big Red, tiger, vicious, Big Red, bad nigger, will kill." Neal alludes to key biographical details and articulates Malcolm's deep understanding and appreciation of black expressive culture. For instance, as he discusses Malcolm's time in Harlem even before he converted to Islam, Neal reveals the leader's developing radical consciousness: "I hear Billie sing, no good man, and dig Prez, wearing the Zoot / suit of life," and "I understand the mystery of the Signifying Monkey" (316).

The Malcolm that Neal envisions bears a striking resemblance to the unnamed narrator of Ralph Ellison's *Invisible Man*. Like Ellison's protagonist, the main figure of Neal's poem is drawn to the complex ideas embedded in black music and African American expressivities in general. Neal's Malcolm "digs" Lester 'Prez' Young, the saxophonist, wearing a Zoot suit with his stylish hat titled to the right hip angle, in ways similar to Ellison's main character digging a group of young men in Harlem wearing Zoot suits. According to Ellison, these stylish figures were "the saviors, the true leaders, the bearers of something precious."[18] Interestingly, part of what made Malcolm X such a dynamic leader and cultural *bearer of something precious* related to the fact that he had once been Detroit Red, one of those stylish "transitory" Harlemite cats like those described in *Invisible Man*. Neal's poem closes with Malcolm in jail, as he recognizes his father's connection to the "ghost of Garvey" and begins to adhere to the teachings of the Honorable Elijah Muhammad, the leader of the Nation of Islam. Notably, Neal's "autobiography" focuses less on Malcolm X's more prominent stature as a 1960s black radical leader and instead showcases a younger Malcolm and his streetwise, hustler persona. As a result, Neal's memorial expresses the idea that we can learn from the street hustler Malcolm as well as the minister. For Neal, the hip, hustling Malcolm stood as an important model for the radical potential of black style.[19]

While Neal takes on the first-person voice of the slain in his poem, a number of other poets emulated Malcolm in their public personas. Naming and renaming already carried particular resonance among African Americans and writers long before the presence of Malcolm X on the national scene. However, his name changes from Little to X and then to Shabazz definitely helped popularize the notion of a black nationalist transformation in name and attitude. During the 1960s and 1970s, a range of poets changed their names: Johari Amini (Jewell Latimore), Ebon (Thomas Dooley), Haki Madhubuti (Don Lee), Marvin X (Marvin Jackmon), Kalamu ya Salaam (Val Ferdinand III), and Askia Muhammad Toure (Ronald Snellings). Apparently, black artists had something to gain by figuratively becoming like Malcolm in their public personas. For one, writers could celebrate or memorialize the life of Malcolm X and thus make known their own commitments to black radical views. Doing so could make them credible to their African American audiences with similar interests. Additionally, since Malcolm X had developed a considerable following, writers who aligned themselves with Malcolm could tap into an already established audience interested in Malcolm and black nationalist ideology. Finally, by taking on a Malcolm X–like persona, poets fashioned themselves in line with a proven and respected model. Thus, by incorporating Malcolm's views and delivery styles into their works, poets gave the slain leader a prominent afterlife in African American literary history.

Part of what made Amiri Baraka, Sonia Sanchez, and Haki Madhubuti three of the most popular writers of the era had to do with the degree to which they echoed Malcolm in their works and public personas. As writer and editor Joe Goncalves observed in 1966, "If you want to grasp the importance of Malcolm X compare the late writings of Sonia Sanchez or Imamu [Amiri] Baraka with their early, pre-Malcolm works."[20] Certainly, Baraka's public persona was akin to Malcolm's. As mentioned above, Baraka credits Malcolm's vision and death as being central to the organizing efforts that gave rise to the Black Arts Movement. But further, there were other distinct connections between Baraka and Malcolm. Not only did the two men go through name changes and adopt black militant views, but both Malcolm X and Amiri Baraka were charismatic speakers who stood as highly visible spokespersons for black nationalism and black arts, respectively. Given how he was represented on the covers of African American literary magazines, how fellow black writers respected him, and how he positioned himself against a white establishment, Amiri Baraka became, metaphorically speaking, a kind of Malcolm X among poets.

Novelist Charles Johnson, for instance, explains, "One of the most powerful literary voices that reached our constantly ringing ears [during the 1960s–70s] was Amiri Baraka's."[21] Johnson observes, "I must admit that no other speaker moved me quite so thoroughly. Flanked by guards wearing dashikis (this in 1969), Baraka read poetry . . . [and] carried away the breath of the young, impressionable audience with him" (23–24). Few American poets produced the kind of work that would require their having bodyguards during readings. That Baraka was flanked by guards during his readings projected the Malcolm-like image of a black speaker requiring a small security detail for his radical views.

In his poem "It Was a Funky Deal," Etheridge Knight further advances the mystique of Baraka and his links to Malcolm. Referring to the slain leader in his poem, Knight writes, "You reached the wild guys / Like me. You and Bird [saxophonist Charlie Parker]. (And that / Lil LeRoi cat.)"[22] So at the end of his Malcolm poem, Knight acknowledges Parker and Baraka as major influences, placing Baraka once again in esteemed company. Now, I do not want to overestimate the centrality of Malcolm X's influence alone on black cultural workers of the era. Indeed, the climate of the 1960s and early 1970s was such that a number of models existed for aspiring black radicals. Still, the figure of Malcolm X appears to be an indelible mark on the black arts personae of Amiri Baraka. The idea of Malcolm certainly emerged regularly in Baraka's poems.

In "A Poem for Black Hearts," first published in *Negro Digest* in 1965, Amiri Baraka (then LeRoi Jones) memorializes the slain leader in the poem by relying on a rhythmic pattern: "For Malcolm's eyes," "For Malcolm's words," "For Malcolm's hands," "For Malcolm's heart," and later "For Malcolm's pleas for your dignity, black men." The repetitive phrasing gives the poem a chantlike mood, which allows the piece to function as a funeral song for Malcolm. The opening lines, "For Malcolm's eyes, when they broke / the face of some dumb white man," set a combative tone toward whites that characterizes much of the militant black poetry of the era. Toward the end of the poem, Baraka writes, "For Great Malcolm a prince of the earth, let nothing in us rest / until we avenge ourselves for his death . . . let us never breathe a pure breath if / we fail."[23] Here, as he directly addresses a black audience, Baraka memorializes Malcolm and at the same time makes a call to other "black hearts" to commit themselves to radical action.

The focus on self-determination in many of Baraka's poems corresponds to the nationalist ideology and militancy expressed by Malcolm X. That Baraka's "Black Art" was initially directed to an audience in Harlem in 1965 is especially notable given Malcolm's connections to Harlem. The anger and intensity of Baraka's poem seem to figuratively and literally *stand in* where the slain political leader had left off. The black nationalist aesthetics and by-any-means-necessary approach of "It's Nation Time," "Black People!," "Black Art," and several other poems by Baraka all demonstrate varying degrees of the nationalist philosophy popularized by Malcolm. As a result, Baraka's poems re-present traces of the slain leader's ideology and intensify the poet's Malcolm-esque aura.

Like Baraka, Sonia Sanchez sought to infuse her writing with a Malcolm aura as well. In an interview with Houston Baker, Sanchez explains, "Our poems were almost direct results of how (Malcolm) presented things . . . always a strong line at the end—the kick at the end that people would repeat, repeat, and repeat, always a finely tuned phrase or line that people could remember."[24] Here Sanchez identifies a technique of Malcolm's speeches adopted by poets seeking to sound like the fiery and eloquent speaker. For Sanchez, "the kick" refers to a short, witty, and forceful statement regarding black liberation or nationalist concerns. Sanchez was widely known for producing poems that had "the kick" in them. In her poem "blk/rhetoric," she writes, "who's gonna make all / that beautiful blk/rhetoric / mean something." Structurally, starting with a short question allows her to engage her audience immediately in the poem. In addition, Sanchez's question functions to get her audience thinking about "what next?" or future actions. Thus, like Malcolm's speeches, Sanchez's poem relies on the distinct delivery style of employing nationalist content and directly addressing the audience in order to develop meaning. In short, she provides a "kick" that people could "repeat, repeat, and repeat."

During the 1960s, Sanchez established herself as an eloquent speaker, and her nationalist poems often rely on repetition and quick, forceful questions in order to achieve effects. In her poem "Malcolm," Sanchez attempts to become a voice of or for the leader as she writes that Malcolm "said, 'Fuck you white / man. we have been / curled too long. nothing / is sacred now.'"[25] Since Malcolm X was known to avoid using profanity, it becomes clear that Sanchez is using "poetic license" in order to put words in the mouth of the slain leader. Sanchez's critique of whites and encouragement of African Americans carried more credibility as she drew on the Malcolm brand. In addition, her use of derogatory words accentuates the idea that Malcolm responded defiantly to white adversaries.

Like Sanchez and Baraka, Madhubuti too aligned himself with the figure and sensibilities of Malcolm. Madhubuti dedicated his volume of poetry *Black Pride* (1968) to "brothers" Malcolm X, Langston Hughes, and John Coltrane, who were "All innovators in their own way." He expresses a connection to creative figures and a prominent political figure. The titles of Madhubuti's first three volumes of poetry, for instance— *Think Black!* (1966), *Black Pride* (1968), and *Don't Cry, Scream* (1969)—are parallel to the nationalist worldview expressed by Malcolm X and Black Power proponents. And like those militant figures, Madhubuti often utilizes streetwise language in order to appeal to his audiences and deliver provocative messages.

In his poem "But He was Cool or: he even stopped for green lights," Madhubuti satirizes a "cool-cool ultracool" black man who is out of touch with the heated political realities of most African Americans. In "a poem to complement other poems," Madhubuti humorously observes that a black man "standing on the corner, thought him was / cool. him still / standing there. it's winter time, him cool." While his critiques of coolness share qualities with Gwendolyn Brooks's poem "We Real Cool," Madhubuti's sentiments also invoke memories of points made by Malcolm X about some groups of black people being out of touch with the circumstances of African Americans.

Humor and delivery style distinguish Malcolm's critiques. In one speech, as he critiqued tactics of the Civil Rights Movement, Malcolm said, "That's your problem: you do too much singing. You need to stop singing and start swinging." At another point, Malcolm recalled a magazine article he read while in prison; he interrupted or improvised his own narrative and said, "And don't look surprised when I say I was in prison, you still in prison. That's what America means: prison." The strategic pauses and improvisations, voice inflections, signifying, and rhythms in Malcolm X's speeches, as well as the humorous and direct appeals to African American audiences, are elements of a long tradition of black sermonizing and verbal play.

In addition, Malcolm often expressed ideas about the need for black transformation and self-determination, as he noted in his "Ballot or the Bullet" speech: "We have to change our own mind. . . . We've got to change our own minds about each other. We have to see each other with new eyes."[26] Similar to Malcolm, Madhubuti made transformation a recurring theme in his poems "a poem to complement other poems," "But He Was Cool," and "Change." Overall, the connections between Malcolm's ideology and the poetics of Baraka, Sanchez, and Madhubuti link all of these figures to the larger nationalist ethos central to black poetry during the era. Sanchez, Baraka, and Madhubuti, of course, were only three among a larger chorus of writers who gained a broader readership by paying homage to Malcolm. Given the respect audiences had for Malcolm, poets who chose to transmute his ideology and delivery style to their poetry had much to gain in regards to a tried and proven approach for appealing to African American audiences and projecting distinct black radical principles.

The affirmations of Malcolm were not without limitations. In the process of celebrating Malcolm, poets and commentators often present narrow definitions of black masculinity. Recall, for instance, Ossie Davis's remarks: "Malcolm was our manhood, our living, black manhood! This was his meaning to his people."[27] Several poets—male and female—viewed Malcolm's confrontational rhetoric and militant persona as the ideal conception of manhood and rarely advocated for more diverse representations of the slain leader and black men in general. Thus, even as writers and audiences concentrated on achieving black self-determination and higher degrees of liberation, they often left limited definitions of black manhood underexplored. As literary critic Phillip Harper observes, uncritical celebrations of black manhood encourage "the unexamined acceptance and promulgation of conventional masculinity's most deeply problematic features, in the name of racial progress."[28] Of course, the motive to celebrate and elevate black leaders and make them compatible with the interests of large audiences requires simplification. By and large, poets were more concerned with constructing popular views of Malcolm as opposed to decidedly diverse and complex interpretations.

Just as some of the poems fell into limited and predictable patterns while celebrating Malcolm, some offered new possibilities. In particular, one of the most provocative poems on the slain Muslim leader was Welton Smith's "malcolm." The shifting modes, forceful tone, and length of Smith's poem make the piece especially notable. The poem initially appeared in *Black Fire* (1968), and sections of the poem were reprinted in Dudley Randall's *The Black Poets* (1971) and Arnold Adoff's *Poetry of Black America* (1973). Smith's poem contains six sections: "malcolm," "the Nigga Section," "interlude," "Special Section for the Niggas on the Lower Eastside or: Invert the Divisor or Multiply," another "interlude," and "The Beast Section." The narrator shifts the presumed audience based on the varied segments of the poem. In the first section, the speaker appears to communicate directly with Malcolm, lamenting the leader's death and routinely informing Malcolm that "you knew" or prophetically understood the signs being given during various stages of the minister's life.

The tone is serene, befitting a mourning individual who communes with a lost loved one. Conversely, "The Nigga Section" expresses strong rage directed at those African Americans who actually killed Malcolm: "slimy obscene creatures. insane / creations of a beast. / you have murdered a man. you / have devoured me."[29] The term *beast* refers to white people and reveals that even as the speaker criticizes the black assassins, he links their origins to Caucasians. Still, the brunt of the condemnation remains on the African American killers as the tone of the section becomes angrier: "you rotten motherfuckin bastards / murder yourselves again and again / and call it life" and "spread your gigantic ass from / one end of america to the other / and peeped from under your legs / and grinned a gigantic white grin / and called all the beasts / to fuck you hard in the ass / you have fucked your fat black mothers / you have murdered malcolm" (286). The speaker draws on the tradition of the dozens and street language to articulate a strong sense of anger and frenzy toward Malcolm's assassins. The section concludes with the message to the murderers that "I hope you are smothered / in the fall of a huge yellow moon." These lines are notably poetic, in a formal sense, as opposed to the raw tone and obscene wording presented in the rest of the section, and offer slight closure and a calming transition to the next section.

The first "interlude" is markedly tranquil in comparison to "The Nigga Section." In this section, the speaker expresses his regrets directly to his "Friend," presumably Malcolm, that they never spent more quality time together. "Friend / we never danced together as men / in a public park Friend we never / spent long mornings fishing or laughed / laughed falling all down in the dirt holding / our stomachs laughing" (287). The peaceful and remorseful mood of this section illustrates an individual voicing regrets about failing to develop a closer companionship with a friend. The next segment, "Special Section for the Niggas on the Lower Eastside," directs attention to bourgeois African Americans who "are deranged imitators / of white boys acting out a / fucked-up notion of the mystique / of black suffering." Unlike the "uptown" African Americans who "believe they are niggas," the ostensibly uppity African Americans have "jive-ass explanation[s] / for being niggas." The speaker criticizes these bourgeois African Americans as "slobbering punks lapping in the / ass of a beast," "frauds," and "jive revolutionaries / who will never tear this house down / you are too terrified of cold / too lazy too build another house."

As in "The Nigga Section," the speaker harshly criticizes African

Americans for their embrace of white culture, presumably an act that makes them complicit in their own demise. Near the close of the section, the speaker rhythmically condemns the "jive mercenary frauds" for

selling nappy hair for a party invitation
selling black   for a part in a play
selling black   for a ride in a rolls
selling black for a quick fuck
selling black   for two lines on page 6,000 in the new york
times
selling babies in Birmingham for a smile in the den

These biting accusations are framed within a cadence, providing the harsh statements with a visible musicality or streetwise verbal play. The repeated focus on "selling black," of course, suggests a link to the historic exchange of African Americans during slavery. The section closes with a command to the bourgeois African Americans to "turn white you jive motherfucker and ram the bomb up your ass" (289). Returning again to the image of violence and sodomy, as in "The Nigga Section," the speaker recommends a self-inflicted assault using a nuclear bomb.

The next "interlude" section is dominated by a series of "screams," or recurring bursts of piercing and sonic fury. The speaker

screams
screams
malcolm
does not hear my screams
screams
betty
does not hear my screams
screams scraping my eyes
screams from the guns. (289)

Throughout the section, the speaker screams and laments the culture of violence that permeates America and the world by alluding to Malcolm and others who have met tragic ends, such as Martin Luther King Jr. and John Kennedy. Apparently, the screams are everywhere: "screams in the laughter of children / screams in the black faces" and later "screams in my head screams / screams six feet death" (290). The intense and recurrent auditory image of screams raises the readers' ears to the pained and unsettling sound that emerges in such turbulent times. It is fitting perhaps that unlike the other sections, this "interlude" appears not to have a specific intended audience, since the sounds of the piercing screams can be heard and go unheard by anyone.

Finally, the closing segment, "The Beast Section," directed at white America, is notably calm and seemingly indifferent. The speaker observes:

> I don't think it important
> to say you murdered malcolm
> or that you didn't murder malcolm
> I find you vital and powerful
> I am aware that you use me
> but doesn't everyone
> I am comfortable in your house
> I am comfortable in your language
> I know your mind   I have an interest
> in your security. (290)

The speaker's disinterested temperament is especially striking given his rage-filled invectives and persistent screams in the previous sections of the poem. But here, the speaker seems resigned or relaxed. The cool-toned acknowledgments that he is comfortable in a white space and language and that he knows the white mind allow him to move effortlessly while drawing little attention. The supposed audience of whites seems unacquainted with the depths of the speaker's rage as expressed in the preceding segments; that audience remains unaware of how threatening their humble servant is. The speaker only wants "to sit quietly / and read books and earn / my right to exist." As a final gesture of his generosity, the speaker informs the audience that "i've made you a fantastic dish / you must try it, if not now / very soon." Given the speaker's prior anger, one wonders if the food is actually poisoned.

The range of modalities from rage to coolness, the shifts in audience, the graphic language, and the piercing sonic images make Welton Smith's work one of the most dynamic Malcolm elegies and one of the most explosive, multivocal poems of the black arts era. Larry Neal and Stanley Crouch both liken the force of Welton Smith's "malcolm" to the more radical elements of free jazz. According to Neal, the scatological language of the poem represents a "burst of tension-releasing images. Heard aloud, this poem takes on the characteristics of a contemporary saxophone solo by a John Coltrane or an Albert Ayler."[30] In a review of the anthology *Black Fire,* Crouch devotes special attention to Smith's "malcolm." Crouch notes that the poem "rises to a level of RAGE" and draws on a long tradition of black verbal practices as Smith "takes the strongest rip-off language from the street, couples it with the dozens, turns it rhythmically so that it sails above mere conversation, orchestrates it melodically into a heavy, long, growling Blues strophe and sets the whole thing up with such dynamics that you are reminded of one of those fantastic solos Max Roach took in the fifties with Sonny Rollins."

Crouch notes that "emotionally, in terms of force, it's the closest thing to Coltrane's long CHASIN THE TRANE solo that I've ever read."[31] More recently, in her book *Gender and the Poetics of Excess: Moments of Brocade,* Karen Ford provides an extensive analysis of Smith's "malcolm," explaining that the poem "fulfills the aspirations of Black Arts excesses and yet also registers deep ambivalence about that rhetorical strategy."[32] In other words, the poem embodies features of militant black poetry and at the same time critiques or extends the discourse. Editor and literary critic Cary Nelson includes Smith's "malcolm" in his *Anthology of Modern American Poetry* (2000), observing that the poem's "tonal shifts help make it one of the most memorable and one of the more inventive poems to come out of the Black Arts movement."[33] Even if Smith's poem is the most memorable, he was certainly writing out of a larger discourse, one voice among a large chorus paying tribute to the slain leader.

The chorus of poetic voices cemented a place for Malcolm in the literary history of black poetry. The slain leader was a ubiquitous subject of poems, but he was also presented as a model for how militant writers should display commitments to black communities. With their elegies for Malcolm, poets were mourning his absence, celebrating his life, and raising him as an exemplar for black radicalism. Making Malcolm central to their poems and public personas was more than simply a selfless act on the part of poets, however. Malcolm was a widely known and widely respected figure, and making him central to their works thus heightened the possibility that they might resonate with the more popular tenets of black arts discourse in particular and black nationalist discourse in general. While Malcolm was one of the most popular celebrated personages among poets, he was hardly the only subject of tribute. Poets focused on a wide range of African American artists and political figures in their writings. Still, Malcolm's assassination in 1965, as well as his black militant views, guaranteed that he would become a martyr figure and guiding inspiration for the writers' artistic enterprise.

The untimely death of Coltrane in 1967 determined that he too would become a revered and inspirational force in the writings of black poets.

Chasing Trane

In New York City on November 2, 1961, Jimmy Garrison and Elvin Jones embarked on a daring sonic voyage. They chased a steaming, screaming locomotive into the outer reaches of the cosmos. With quick patience on bass and dynamic repercussions on drums, Garrison and Jones, respectively, followed saxophonist John Coltrane's lead as he raced along with wild and brilliant phrasings on a fifteen-minute-plus solo. "The melody not only wasn't written," said Coltrane, "but it wasn't even conceived before we played it. We set the tempo and in we went." The result of their collective composition was a song aptly entitled "Chasin' the Trane."[34] Jones and Garrison, of course, were only two among many creative artists to dramatically follow Coltrane.

Similar to Malcolm, Coltrane became a prominent, pervasive subject in black poetry of the 1960s and 1970s. Shortly after Trane's death in 1967, poets began to represent the musician as a revered creative figure and significant poetic muse. Many poets even promoted a saintly view of the late saxophonist. When the seemingly nonreligious narrator of Carolyn Rodgers's poem "Jesus Was Crucified" is asked if she prays, she responds, "sorta when I hear Coltrane."[35] Rodgers, like so many poets, would continually celebrate Trane as a tremendous guiding artistic force.

The timing of the musician's death was actually a crucial factor in why he became such an important figure of poetic exploration. Coltrane had died just as groups of writers were developing their movement and searching for ideal models. Trane had produced an incredible body of wide-ranging ideas—ideas that could and would be interpreted as distinctly black. As a recently deceased exemplar of artistic excellence, the saxophonist represented a common source of mourning and prideful reflection for black artists. Memorializing the loss and accomplishments of remarkable black figures was integral to the objectives of poets who wanted to channel and influence the larger, shared concerns of African Americans.

Altogether, the numerous elegies focusing on Coltrane enabled poets to celebrate his achievements and decode the racial implications of his life and music. Whereas Malcolm's words were available through his speeches and coauthored autobiography with Alex Haley, Coltrane presented a new and exciting challenge for poets interested in assessing his message. Trane's statements were primarily wordless; therefore, representing his ideas required poets to delve into the discourses of music in order to produce convincing poetic interpretations of what the saxophonist was sharing with his audiences. The process of elegizing Coltrane led poets to draw on the jazz lexicon and structural patterns and allude to musicians and songs, embedding their writings with what several scholars have referred to as a "jazz aesthetic."[36]

According to William Harris, jazz aesthetics relate to issues of "transformation," as in "the conversion of white poetic and social ideas into black ones" and the conversion of musical ideas into literary ones. The display of jazz aesthetics is certainly not exclusive to African American literary art; however, it is important to note that the phrase "jazz aesthetics" has specific routes in black arts discourse, as the term "grows out of the way critics used *aesthetic* in the expression *Black Aesthetic,*" explains Harris.[37] The appearance of jazz aesthetics in the writings of such leading poets as Amiri Baraka, Sonia Sanchez, Larry Neal, Jayne Cortez, and Haki Madhubuti reveals the connections between the New Black Poetry and what was known as the New Black Music, or free jazz.

According to musicologist John Szwed, 1959 marked an important year in the emergence of this experimental movement in jazz, as three influential albums were released: John Coltrane's *Giant Steps,* Miles Davis's *Kind of Blue,* and Ornette Coleman's *The Shape of Jazz to Come.*[38] In 1960, Coleman's album *Free Jazz: A Collective Improvisation* included a double quartet and an innovative sound that gave even more shape to the developing movement among musicians. Free jazz, as the movement was called, was characterized by "modal playing" and unconventional approaches to tonality, melody, and rhythm, which gave the music unconstrained or *free* structures. The movement's leading figures, Sun Ra, Albert Ayler, Ornette Coleman, and John Coltrane, ultimately inspired a break with standard forms in ways that corresponded well to the spirit of radicalism so prevalent during the 1960s. Certainly, advocates of black power and empowerment took notice. In *Black Nationalism and the Revolution in Music* (1970), Frank Kofsky explains that "the same milieu which gave rise to Malcolm had also generated the most vital forms of contemporaneous jazz."[39] Free jazz musicians did not gather the financial profits or popular followings of Motown artists and other major R&B singers, yet the experimental musicians, with their quest for something new, appealed to the sensibilities of New Black Poets.

Although free jazz began taking shape across the country, John Szwed explains, "it was on the Lower East Side of Manhattan that the music first found itself, among the new community of musicians who settled there in the early 1960s."[40] Consequently, the music was being played in the places where Baraka, A.B. Spellman, Larry Neal, and other black arts poets gathered. At 27 Cooper Square in the Village, Baraka's home was a gathering place for musicians and artists in 1964; saxophonist Archie Shepp also lived in the same building. Larry Neal explained that "there was this community of people circling around Archie and LeRoi, really getting various ideas about the role of art in the struggle."[41] The legendary Five Spot jazz club was nearby and allowed the writers to catch groups that included Coltrane, Thelonius Monk, Cecil Taylor, and Ornette Coleman.[42]

Coltrane was one of several musicians, including Sun Ra, Betty Carter, Albert Ayler, and Archie Shepp, who participated in a benefit concert for the Black Arts Repertory Theatre/School in March of 1965. Baraka described Coltrane's contributions and the larger implications of his music in the liner notes for *New Wave in Jazz*, the live recording of the benefit concert. "*TRANE* is now a scope of feeling," wrote Baraka. "A more fixed traveler, whose wildest onslaughts are now gorgeous artifacts not even deaf people should miss."[43] Coltrane's performance at the black arts benefit signaled to the writers that the saxophonist was indeed sympathetic to their interests. Actually, since the concert was a black arts event, Trane could be viewed in some respects as a contributor to the movement.

Trane was hardly known as a militant nationalist, at least not in any conventional sense, yet his music was regularly interpreted as displaying elements of radical consequence. "Jazz musicians like Coltrane," observes William Harris, "have routinely revised popular white tunes into black compositions by criticizing popular white songs; their listeners can identify the original song but sense that it has been altered to fit a different perspective."[44] Coltrane's varied renditions of "My Favorite Things" stand as the most outstanding example in this regard; he constantly revised his performance of the song, infusing the stylistics of free jazz into the piece. Trane's disruption of conventional forms was certainly appealing to a group of black artists who sought to rupture established Eurocentric forms. A brief examination of Coltrane poems by Michael Harper, Jayne Cortez, Sonia Sanchez, Askia Toure, A. B. Spellman, Keorapetse William Kgositsile, Haki Madhubuti, and Quincy Troupe reveals the ways that poets incorporated jazz aesthetics into their works in their pursuit of Trane. Focusing on these kinds of poems illuminates a ubiquitous mode of African American verse, namely, celebrations of black music and elegies for musicians.

Michael Harper's poem "Dear John, Dear Coltrane" begins with the words "a love supreme, a love supreme," lines from Coltrane's well-known 1964 suite *A Love Supreme*. Readers familiar with the sound of Coltrane's famous phrasing can, presumably, *hear* Trane as they read Harper's poem. At different intervals throughout the poem, Harper interjects the phrase "a love supreme" as he briefly charts the life experiences of Coltrane. Harper starts with Coltrane's birth in Hamlet, North Carolina, notes his career as a musician, and closes the poem by mentioning the struggles that Coltrane had near the end of his life with a "diseased liver."[45] The poem is written as if Harper is communicating directly with Coltrane. As a result, Harper provides the audience with the opportunity to overhear a personal conversation between a poet and the musician, as he appears to commune directly with Coltrane. "Dear John, Dear Coltrane" raises the possibility that poets can converse with the dead. Whereas Harper is not typically considered a black arts poet, his poems on Trane and other jazz figures situate his work firmly within the discourse.

Jayne Cortez's "How Long Has Trane Been Gone" establishes a connection to the black community by addressing her audience directly. Cortez is also interested in an audience that may not have adequately appreciated the sacrifices made by black musicians. Cortez explains: "You takin—they givin / You livin—they / creating starving dying / trying to make a better tomorrow / Giving you & your children a history / But what do you care about / History—Black History / and John Coltrane." In the process of remembering Coltrane, Cortez encourages her audience to understand and appreciate their history—black history. By exhorting her audience to embrace consciousness and black culture, Cortez assumes the position of poet as political agitator, a familiar role among black creative artists.

At intervals in her poem, Cortez repeats the phrase "How long how long has that Trane been gone." Using this rhymed phrasing allows her to present a musicality in her poem, celebrate Trane, and at the same time voice her frustrations and regrets that "some / of you / have yet to hear him [Trane] play."[46] Cortez plays on the word "Trane" as she blends the idea that her audience has missed an automotive train with the notion that they did not fully grasp the importance of Coltrane. Cortez extends her remembrance of Trane and envisions a day when

African Americans will inhabit places such as Charlie Parker City, Billie Holiday Street, James Brown Park, and "The State of Malcolm X" (16). Apparently, Cortez's play on Trane and trains led her from memories of disappointment to prophecies of worlds where black people will have greater degrees of self-determination.

Poets often went a step further in paying tribute to Coltrane and suggested that the musician inspired African American audiences to positive, if not revolutionary, action. Toward the end of Sonia Sanchez's "a/coltrane/poem," she explains, "yeh. john coltrane. / my favorite things is u. showen us life. / liven. / a love supreme. / for each / other / if we just / lisssssssSSSTEN."[47] Sanchez interprets Coltrane's music as providing messages to African Americans about the necessary steps for living more fulfilling lives. Like Sanchez, several poets project the view of Coltrane as a kind of spiritual being and guide. In his poem "Juju," Askia Toure refers to Coltrane as "a Black Priest-prophet" and closes noting that the saxophonist is "Not gone, for I can see, can hear him still: my Heart / my Soul my All vibrating—Trane!"[48] In the closing lines of his poem "Did John Coltrane's Music Kill Him," poet and music critic A .B. Spellman writes, "o john death will / not contain you death / will not contain you."[49] Similarly, in his poem "Acknowledgment," taken from a title section of Coltrane's album *Love Supreme*, Keorapetse William Kgositsile writes, "John Coltrane, they say / he died, the hasty fools," and he concludes, "how could he die / if you have ears!"[50] As these poems suggest, in the process of situating Coltrane within the contexts of their works, poets pinpointed the ability of the musician to transcend death and thus influence the living, "if we just lisssssssSSSTEN."

Listening closely to Coltrane led several poets to follow the musician's lead and experiment with sound, most notably by utilizing screams and wordless phrasings. A major technique utilized by Coltrane and other free jazz saxophonists was the application of a shrilling and forceful projection from their instruments during their solos. In short, it sounded as if the musicians were making their horns scream and wail. Trane's scream, as well as the saxophone screaming of musicians Albert Ayler, Ornette Coleman, and John Gilmore of Sun Ra's group, was a hallmark of the New Black Music. "If you even put a toe into mid-60's Coltrane," writes Ben Ratliff in the *New York Times,* "you have to come to grips with the scream."[51] A number of poems focusing on Coltrane emulate the actual sound of the saxophonist made in his songs. Haki Madhubuti and Baraka, to name only two, transmuted Trane's signature screaming techniques in dramatic fashion on the page. The poets interpreted Trane's scream as a radical call to action and a disruption of the seemingly typical Eurocentric serenity of art. The process of emulating Trane's scream gave poets reason to alter the way words were presented on the page, not to mention how they were presented out loud.

In his poem "Don't Cry, Scream," Madhubuti speaks of Trane as an inspiration and seeks to represent the "SCREAMMMM" of the saxophonist in his poem. Rather than weep about the pain of loss, Madhubuti writes, "I didn't cry / I just / Scream-eeeeeeeeeeeeeee-ed / SCREAM-EEEEEEEEEEEEEEEEE-ED."[52] In order to provide a more faithful rendering of the sounds that Coltrane made, Madhubutui adds multiple e's to the words "scream" and "screech." He also capitalizes words to represent an increased volume. The "SCREAMMMM" of Madhubuti's poem correlates to the "sCReeeEEECHHHHHH" that Sanchez presents throughout her "a/coltrane/poem" and reveals that for Madhubuti and Sanchez emulating Trane meant disrupting conventional forms of typography. Presenting elements of free jazz in their poems meant that they would alter, in spectacular fashion, approaches to writing words. Further, by representing jazz in their work, they assumed the role of poet-performers.

In the field of Coltrane poems, Quincy Troupe's poem "Ode to John Coltrane" constitutes one of the most vivid examples of a poet using the musician as a point of reference for drawing connections between varied elements of African American cultural history. Thematically, Troupe's tribute to Trane covers black musical, literary, and speculative histories and African American spiritual or sacred traditions. Troupe begins the poem by noting that "With soaring fingers of flame / you descended from Black Olympus / too blow about truth and pain; yeah, / just to tell a story about Black existence." He writes that Trane was "Hurtling thru spacelanes of jazz / a Black Phoenix of Third World redemption," and later in the poem, Troupe refers to the musician as "John the Baptist."[53] First, by speaking of Trane descending from Black Olympus, Troupe invokes the saxophonist as emerging from mythic African American origins. Thus, Troupe's poem memorializes Trane, but the poem also suggests that Trane is part of a black mythology. Referring to Coltrane as "a Black Phoenix" who traveled through "spacelanes," Troupe associates the musician with African American science fiction or a black sense of speculative cosmology. In Troupe's poem, Trane is supernatural. At the same time, labeling him John the Baptist allows Troupe to situate the musician in biblical history.

As a result, then, Troupe presents a mythical, cosmic, and religious idea of Coltrane. The exaggerations used to describe Trane do not weaken Troupe's credibility as a narrator so much as reveal his poetic skills and creativity in honoring the musician.

Over the course of the poem, Troupe charts black musical history by mentioning several songs Coltrane composed or songs that the saxophonist appeared on, including "Kulu Se Mama," "Ole," "Ascension," "A Love Supreme," "Kind of Blue," "Round Midnight," and "Equinox." Also, he mentions other musicians whom Trane was influenced by or played with, such as Lester Young, Charlie Parker, Miles Davis, and Eric Dolphy. The appearance of the songs and musicians in the poem solidifies the speaker's authority as a jazz poet. In addition to providing musical history, Troupe constructs a narrative that highlights Coltrane's centrality to African American social histories. According to Troupe, "Those who were familiar with your [Trane's] agony. / Those who were familiar with your pain" would relate (234). In addition, those who "chased america's illusions" and who were "garbed in the evil mantle of white doom" would feel a connection with the overall expressions and implications of Coltrane's work.[54] Ultimately, Troupe's poem suggests that Coltrane's music serves as the soundtrack for the larger experience of a group of people seeking to achieve self-determination and confront antiblack racism in America.

From a technical standpoint, "Ode to John Coltrane" reads like a prayer, as Troupe employs African American stylistics in order to convey his ideas. For one, the recurring use of "you" to refer to Coltrane allows Troupe to imply that he is communicating directly to the deceased musician. As was the case with Harper's "Dear John, Dear Coltrane," the larger effect is that readers are actually overhearing Troupe talking to the seemingly supreme being Coltrane in the poem. Applying exclamation marks to emphasize certain words such as "style," "James Brown," "Coltrane," and "you" in the poem, Troupe figuratively adjusts the volume and pitch of the poem on particular notes. In addition, he uses the word "yeah" throughout the poem as a way of instilling a conversational tone. At various points toward the beginning of the poem, Troupe utilizes a chanting style to describe Coltrane's achievements and actions. Troupe writes, "*Trane Trane runaway train smashing all known dimensions / Trane Trane runaway train smashing all known dimensions*" (230). That he italicizes the words suggests that they are sung or spoken differently than the nonitalicized words.

Similar to Cortez's poem on Coltrane, Troupe's sentences play on the idea of Trane and a train, giving readers the image of Coltrane as a locomotive. Moreover, as Shirley Anne Williams explains, the word "train" is a "mascon" in African American discourse communities. Mentioning a train carried importance on multiple levels, especially since locomotives represented literal and figurative historical significance for black people because of the Underground Railroad, south-north African American migrations, and religious and secular music relying on "Gospel Trains" and "Soul Trains." Therefore, as Williams observes, "It is the stored energy of this mascon which enables Afro-American poets to play so lovingly and meaningful with John Coltrane's name and they capture something of his function as an artist in their use of his nickname, Trane."[55] Troupe's play on "Trane" and "train" connects him to a larger network of interrelated black verbal practices that draw on the significance of locomotives as vessels of freedom. Much like the music of the saxophonist whom the poem seeks to memorialize, Troupe's "Ode to Coltrane" reflects multiple African American thematic and technical modalities in dramatic fashion.

Taken together, the multiple appearances of Malcolm and Coltrane poems is indicative of the larger practice among editors of publishing verse on African American historical figures and musicians. Collections such as *Black Fire, For Malcolm, Understanding the New Black Poetry,* and *The Black Poets* and magazines such as *Liberator, Negro Digest/Black World,* and the *Journal of Black Poetry* featured poems that celebrated the revolutionary potential of music and presented past and modern African American leaders and activists as models for how to achieve liberation. The recurrent publication of tributes and elegies solidified the place of these kinds of poems in the canon of African American poetry. This recurrent publication was mediated, as always, by anthologists and magazine editors. The widespread publication of tributes and elegies should be viewed as an active collaboration between poets and editors. The editors ensured that these particular types of poems would have wide circulation. These processes of socialization were integral to the formation of black arts discourse, as well as how African American poetry was viewed then and now.

Amiri Baraka's "A Poem for Black Hearts," for instance, appeared in several anthologies, including *For Malcolm, Understanding the New Black Poetry, Dark Symphony,* and *The Black Poets,* making this elegy for Malcolm one of Baraka's most anthologized pieces. Anthologists also seemed to favor Malcolm poems by Gwendolyn Brooks, Etheridge Knight, Larry Neal, and Margaret Walker, reprinting their tributes to the leader in several collections as well. Similarly, poems focusing on Coltrane and various other musicians seemed to be regular fixtures in publications featuring African American poetry. The receptiveness of anthologists and magazine editors to verse displaying jazz aesthetics seemed to guarantee publishing venues for poets who highlighted black musicians in their works. In the process, editors determined that poems paying tribute to the radical impulses of black music and the militant spirit of black historical figures would become central features of the discourse.

5 • The Poets, Critics, and Theorists Are One

Although black arts discourse gave rise to a wide range of criticism, commentary, and theoretical formulations, the critical contributions of the writers have sometimes been described in rather narrow terms. For example, Henry Louis Gates Jr. addresses what he perceives as the weaknesses of black aesthetic theories in his book *Figures in Black* by focusing on the writings of three academic critics: Stephen Henderson, Addison Gayle, and Houston Baker. According to Gates, the theory of poetry that Henderson provided is based on insufficient, "sometimes jumbled broad categories."[1] Despite the flaws inherent in Henderson's research, explains Gates, the theories of African American literature offered by Houston Baker and Addison Gayle are even weaker.[2] In Gates's view, the critical writings of Henderson, Gayle, and Baker represent "the best and most sophisticated work of the black aesthetic critics."[3] Gates's conception of whose work constitutes "the best and most sophisticated" probably rests on academic evaluative standards. Yet within black arts discourse, Henderson, Gayle, and Baker are certainly not in a league of their own. In addition, their efforts to promote black aesthetic theorizing were not as pervasive during the era as the efforts of, say, Hoyt Fuller and Larry Neal.

Focusing primarily on the work of three academic critics actually delimits the broader implications of black arts critical discourse. For now, the concern is less about providing a comprehensive treatment of the merits and shortcomings of black aesthetic theories. Besides, Houston Baker and Henry Louis Gates Jr. have already provided fairly extensive exchanges on this subject.[4] Instead, keeping with this study's overall focus, the goal is to concentrate on how poets utilized critical discourse to shape the formation of a movement. Indeed, a particularly notable feature of the Black Arts Movement relates to the degree to which poets actively participated in the assessment and critical appreciation of African American literary art. Poets published hundreds of reviews and commentary focusing on black poetry. They published essays that highlighted the connections between black music and literature, and they were at the forefront in the critical conversations regarding theories of "black aesthetics." Rarely have poets been so visibly involved in the publication of criticism and theoretical formulations.

Several leading poets of the time period blurred the lines between genres and modes of writing. Beyond Amiri Baraka's reputation as a principal poet of the movement, he was an ethnomusicologist long before the term was widely used. Baraka's *Blues People* (1963) and *Black Music* (1968) highlighted the interrelated rhythms of black music and experience. Carolyn Rodgers's series of essays on poetics published in *Negro Digest/Black World* offered a useful and influential framework for new black poetry and anticipated Stephen Henderson's anthology *Understanding the New Black Poetry*. Rodgers also identified "signifying" as a major technique practiced by black writers, a subject that Henry Louis Gates Jr. would address in his book *The Signifying Monkey* (1990). Sarah Webster Fabio's essay "Tripping with Black Writing" was quite experimental, if not daring, in its blend of poetic rhythms and critical delineation, and it revealed how a poet might jazz up the typically stiff prose of academic writing.

Few studies devoted to African American poetry have been as extensive as Eugene Redmond's thoroughly researched book *Drumvoices: The Mission of Afro-American Poetry* (1976). Covering over one hundred African American poets, from Phillis Wheatley, Lucy Terry, and Jupiter Hammon through Gwendolyn Brooks, Amiri Baraka, and Jayne Cortez of the 1970s, Redmond's *Drumvoices* constitutes a landmark study in the effort to historicize African American writing. Finally, in regards to criticism and theoretical formulations, Larry Neal's work holds a special place in black arts discourse. Neal's signature piece, in fact, is not one of his poems, but rather his essay "The Black Arts Movement." It was Neal, by the way, who stated in his often quoted afterword to *Black Fire* that "the artist and the political activist are one." Consequently, considering the active involvement of creative writers in shaping critical discourse, it might also be accurate to say of several writers associated with the black arts enterprise that poets, critics, and theorists were one. That is not to say that the writers were of one accord. Yet their use of overlapping terms and points of reference, as well as their tendency to address interrelated issues, reveals that despite their differences, the writers often contributed to a common conversation concerning artistic composition, black people, and political agency.

An examination of critical writings and commentary on African American poetry shows the degree to which black poets took on leading roles in framing their movement. As I demonstrate in this chapter, Larry Neal's writings anticipated and projected the defining principles of black arts discourse. Poets such as Nikki Giovanni, Carolyn Rodgers, and Eugene Redmond offered invaluable frameworks for understanding African American verse, and poets also took vanguard positions in black aesthetic theorizing. Ultimately, the writers went well beyond conventional roles of poets by actively participating in the formulation of critical models for appreciating literary art and expressive culture in general.

The Roles of Larry Neal

The style, content, and aims of Larry Neal's articles contributed to popularizing the idea that what he and his fellow artists were involved in was, in fact, a movement. As a cofounding member of the Black Arts Repertory Theatre/School, coeditor of *Black Fire,* and contributing poet and essayist to central black arts publications, Larry Neal produced and promoted black arts writings and black aesthetic theorizing in a decisive manner. "Neal found himself," observes literary critic Kimberley Benston, "continually at the heart of the most critical activity in the determination of a productive *intelligentsia:* the lively embodiment of an evolving communal consciousness."[5] Beginning with short articles he published in *Liberator* in the mid-1960s, Larry Neal became an active and widely read participant-observer of the developing cultural movement.

Neal's *Liberator* articles reveal his interest in emphasizing the significance of making connections between issues of black self-determination and African American artistic culture. In an article entitled "The Cultural Front," published in *Liberator* in June 1965, Neal provides a short description of a symposium in Harlem, as well as a brief report on the opening of the Black Arts Repertory Theatre/School.[6] Near the beginning of "The Cultural Front," Neal tells his African American audience that those who were contemplating freedom struggles should consider this: "The political liberation of the Black Man is directly tied to his cultural liberation" (26). In this brief statement, Neal appeals to those readers associated with black activist and radical discourses, and he expresses the necessity of connecting politics and art, an idea that would become commonplace in discussions of literature. Neal took it for granted that his audience would know what he meant by "political liberation," "cultural liberation," and "the Black Man." To support his initial assertion, Neal explains that popular cultural figures Malcolm X, Marcus Garvey, and Black Muslims all realized that an understanding of black artistic and expressive culture was central to any attempt to develop a comprehensive analysis of the political conditions of African Americans. Suggesting that respected black nationalist leaders valued the importance of artistry and expressive culture allowed Neal to establish more credibility for his propositions that artists should take activism seriously and that political activists should recognize the viability of artistic productions as a means of mobilizing large numbers of African Americans.

Neal also notes that during the era, Amiri Baraka came closest to describing the souls and aspirations of black folks by using music as a major point of reference in his book *Blues People.* By associating Baraka with Malcolm X and Marcus Garvey, Neal provides Baraka with high praise and suggests the favorable possibility of writers modeling themselves on political figures. Neal's appraisal of Baraka in "The Cultural Front" anticipates, if not promotes, the idea of Baraka as the epitome of a black artist/activist and as a leading figure in the Black Arts Movement. The linkages between black politics and expressive culture, the appeal to an African American readership, the reverence for Malcolm X and Amiri Baraka, and the focus on black music displayed by Neal in "The Cultural Front" are ideas that would permeate the movement. Later in *Liberator,* Larry Neal published a series of articles on "the black writer's role," where he focused on Richard Wright, Ralph Ellison, James Baldwin, and the question of black writers' responsibilities to "our own people." In retrospect, it appears Larry Neal's major role would be that of articulating, and in many ways influencing, the aims of black arts poets and discourse.

In "The Black Arts Movement," Neal's most widely circulated essay, he explains the objectives of black artists: "We advocate a cultural revolution in art and ideas. The cultural values inherent in western history must either be radicalized or destroyed. . . . What is needed is a whole new system of ideas."[7] From here, Neal goes on to explain the development of a black aesthetic that formed the basis of what black arts writers were seeking to do with their literary art. Keeping in line with the fact that he was writing for a publication on drama, Neal spends much of his essay discussing the Black Arts Theatre. He identifies Baraka as the movement's leading figure and favorably assesses his artistic vision and productions. "In drama," Neal writes, "LeRoi Jones represents the most advanced aspects of the movement. He is its prime mover and chief designer" (33). That Neal's article appeared in the *Drama Review,* a white-owned journal with a wide and diverse readership, helped ensure the visibility that it gained for the movement's objectives and principal figure, LeRoi Jones. Like "The Black Arts Movement," Neal's essays "And Shine Swam On," "Any Day Now," and "New Space/The Growth of Black Consciousness in the Sixties" return to and expound on the issues he raises in "The Cultural Front."

The far-reaching circulation of Neal's essays was, indeed, quite impressive. His article "And Shine Swam On" appeared as the afterword to *Black Fire,* one of the most frequently referenced anthologies in black arts discourse. "The Black Arts Movement" was initially published in a special issue of the *Drama Review* in 1968 and was subsequently published in anthologies such as *The Black American Writer* (1969), *Black Literature in America* (1970), *Cavalcade: Negro American Writing from 1760 to Present* (1971), and *The Black Aesthetic* (1971). The essay remains in print even today. Neal's "Any Day Now: Black Art and Black Liberation" and "Ellison's Zoot Suit: Politics as Ritual" appeared, respectively, in *Ebony* in 1969 and in *Black World* in 1970. The publication of Neal's essays in these sites ensured that Neal's views would reach large, diverse groups of readers interested in black arts. The publication history of the above essays suggests that Neal, more so than academic critics Addison Gayle, Stephen Henderson, and Houston Baker, exposed a wide audience of fellow writers and general readers to the major objectives, features, and figures of the Black Arts Movement as the movement was taking shape.

Larry Neal's essays were published as widely as his poems. He was as much a black arts commentator as he was a black arts poet, and his sensibilities as a poet seemed to influence the stylized presentation of his prose. His "Any Day Now," which addresses his familiar theme about the correlation between the political and the cultural freedoms of black people, displays resonating black vernacular expressive qualities, giving the piece a vibrant, distinctive edge. For Neal, black arts discourse was not academic discourse produced for a specialized scholarly audience. Instead, he delivered his ideas in a hip prose style for a presumably hip and general black readership. Throughout the essay, he utilizes vernacular phrasings such as "can you dig it," "sho nuff," "soul," "right on," and "Black freedom" and employs communal pronouns such as "we" and "us," thus revealing a familial bond with his intended audience, in this case, the readers of *Ebony* magazine.

As he did in "The Black Arts Movement," published a year earlier, Neal highlights the connections between Black Power and radical efforts of black arts writers. However, in "Any Day Now," Neal goes a step further and explains that the movement among black artists actually preceded the Black Power Movement. Furthermore, Neal describes the concerns that black artists had with developing a black aesthetic, and he also utilizes elements of this African American value system and black style as a way of delivering his message. To support his underlying claims about the involvement of black people in the production of various forms of knowledge, Neal mentions dozens of black political figures, creative intellectuals, writers, musicians, and even folk heroes like Shine and Stagalee in his essay. He compares the creations and practices of singers and musicians James Brown, Aretha Franklin, John Coltrane, and Bessie Smith to the work of poets Amiri Baraka, Sonia Sanchez, Carolyn Rodgers, and Haki Madhubuti. As a result, he could suggest that the New Black Poets were as engaging as popular musicians.

Throughout the piece, Neal testifies about the active linkages across the expansive landscape of black culture. He pinpoints the intraracial connections between varied forms of African American expressive culture by presenting lines from black poetry, blues and R&B song lyrics, and riffs on black sermons. In effect, he highlights the close proximity between modes of black expression across various genres. Taken as a whole, Neal's approach to showcasing the intraconnectivity of different cultural forms confirms the centrality of poetry to multiple modes of black expression. But Neal's essay is more than a descriptive historical account, as Neal also made time to speculate about new, unrealized possibilities.

To illustrate the idea of a radicalized black religion, Neal presents a eulogy for Charlie Parker, the great bebop saxophonist: "*The text of my sermon is the Life and Death of Charlie Parker. People loved him and called him Bird.*" Neal goes on to preach, "*And after my sermon, Brother Sun Ra will perform some songs about the nature of the universe; and after that we will have some words from the Self-Defense Committee.*"[8] Here, Neal connects fields of knowledge, including bebop, free jazz, and Black Power ideology, together with black church and sermonic traditions. Neal is doing more than simply code switching between so-called black and white modes of expression. Instead, he is impressively demonstrating his deft abilities at synthesizing varied African American modalities of thought and expression in order to illuminate his overall message about the expansive viability of black artistic culture.

Neal returns to the sermon form to close his essay. The italics throughout the sermon section suggest that the words are to be spoken or at least read and performed differently than the words in standard font. In the closing sermonizing paragraphs, Neal declares, *"Black people you are Art. You are the poem"* (62). He goes on to write, *"Black Liberation to you Baby. Hey Now! Black Liberation for the ditty-bopping hip ones; for all of the righteous sinners and hustlers; for Chaka Zulu and Honky Tonk Bud, the hip cat's stud."* For the next five closing paragraphs, he calls for *"Black Liberation"* for African American people, mythic figures, and organizations, including Sugar Ray Robinson, the Signifying Monkey, Jack Johnson, High John the Conqueror, Jack and Jill, Elks, and Masons. Neal's text is informative, entertaining, and communal. The exhaustive references to notable African Americans, organizations, and black folklore figures dispersed throughout the essay display and tap into a vast matrix of African American knowledge and expressive culture. Neal's "Any Day Now" provides an impressive view of black arts criticism and artistic cultural production in action. Indeed, "Any Day Now" is Neal's most spectacular piece of black arts commentary.

Larry Neal was certainly not the only black arts poet to produce stylistically daring prose pieces. Amiri Baraka, Carolyn Rodgers, and Sarah Webster Fabio also composed essays that relied on unconventional syntax in the presentation of their ideas. Of course, few essays circulated as widely in black arts discourse as did Neal's. Neal's "Any Day Now" may have lacked the formality of standard academic writing; however, his essay was designed to communicate with a range of African Americans in ways that academic style essays are underequipped to achieve. "Any Day Now" appeared in *Ebony,* one of the largest venues directed at a black readership, and thus allowed Neal to spread the gospel of black arts discourse far beyond the more limited range of literary journals. Among other things, Neal's article assisted in the popularization of the New Black Poetry among readers who may not have been as familiar with the enterprises of hip, militant poets.

One of Neal's major achievements as an essayist was his ability to produce a body of work that addresses a variety of black and general audiences. "The Black Arts Movement," "Any Day Now," and "New Space/The Growth of Black Consciousness in the Sixties" explain and define the aims of the developing cultural movement and identify some of the movement's principal figures for African American and general readerships. To be sure, "The Black Arts Movement" continues to circulate as an oft-cited point of reference for students and scholars investigating the movement. Neal codified the letter and spirit of the movement in such widely circulated articles that his ideas and descriptions represent a major window into understanding the movement, especially for African American and general readers.

On the other hand, Neal's *Liberator* articles, as well as "And Shine Swam On" and "Ellison's Zoot Suit: Politics as Ritual," appeal more specifically to African American writers, encouraging them to adopt black arts principles in their work. "New constructs will have to be developed. We will have to alter our concepts of what art is, of what it is supposed to 'do,'" Neal informs his readers, many of whom he presumes to be fellow black writers, in the afterword to *Black Fire*.[9] In "Ellison's Zoot Suit," Neal discourages black writers from only describing themselves in "purely negative terms." According to Neal, "We are not simply, in *all* areas of our sensibilities, merely a set of black reactions to white oppression."[10] Neal concludes, "What I think we have to do is understand our roles as synthesizers; the creators of new and exciting visions out of the accumulated weight of our Western experience" (50). Here, Neal does more than preach to the choir about a subject with which they all agree. He actually challenges his fellow writers to move beyond narrow conceptions of nationalism and presentations of black culture. In these essays, Neal addresses black writers, identifies their mistakes (including mistakes he has made), and proposes directions that they must take in order to achieve a more liberating future.

Neal's direct appeals to fellow artists and activists reveal his interest in helping give shape to the operations of the Black Arts Movement, and his appeals to general audiences confirm his desire to frame how the movement might be viewed. He was particularly interested in communicating the idea that the movement's participants were making connections to black music and fusing art and politics. Neal's widely circulated essays ensured that he was a major influence in the production of the movement. Neal also exemplifies the multiple roles of a black arts writer as poet-critic-theorist. Unlike most poets, who must wait for academic critics to define their places in literary history, Larry Neal, for one, was describing the objectives and principal aims of black poets as their movement took shape. Not simply as a poet but as a critic and theorist, Neal was composing a blueprint for black arts poetry.

Classifying Black Arts Poetry

Whereas Larry Neal produced the most widely circulated essays on black arts principles, he was certainly not the only poet actively contributing to the critical discourse and commentary on poetry. Black poets were involved in a number of writing activities beyond composing and publishing poems. Amiri Baraka, Askia Toure, Haki Madhubuti, Carolyn Rodgers, Sarah Webster Fabio, and several other poet-critics also made useful contributions to the understanding of African American artistic productions and cultural activism during the time period. Like Neal, these writers often addressed themselves to their fellow black writers, seeking to establish common objectives and solidify shared interests. The journalistic writings of poets Joe Goncalves of the *Journal of Black Poetry* and David Llorens of *Negro Digest/Black World* frequently focused on the activism of poets. And June Jordan, Gwendolyn Brooks, Dudley Randall, and other poet-anthologists did editorial work that created venues for the publication of poetry. These anthologists provided introductions and biographical information that operated to pinpoint trends and leading figures in African American poetry. Similarly, the poets who provided introductions and blurbs for volumes of poetry published by Broadside Press and Third World Press contributed to the body of commentary promoting the value of African American poets and verse.

Poets often reviewed volumes of poetry themselves, rather than wait on evaluations from academic scholars and book reviewers for mainstream publications. Sterling Plumpp, Nikki Giovanni, Dudley Randall, Johari Amini, Julia Fields, Carolyn Rodgers, and Haki Madhubuti, all of whom were broadly published poets, wrote the majority of the hundreds of reviews that appeared in *Negro Digest/Black World* during the era.[11] The poetry of the reviewers was often more widely known than the poems being reviewed. The status of reviewers such as Giovanni, Madhubuti, and Randall, in particular, seemed to suggest that highly regarded poets could and should write about the work of lesser-known poets. In retrospect, the record of reviews in *Negro Digest/Black World* indicates a network of poets actively reading and evaluating each other's work.[12] Leading poets were, in this popular venue, at the forefront as composers and reviewers of poetry.

Along with their work as reviewers, poets made contributions to the interpretation of African American poetry as essayists. The poetry section of Addison Gayle's *The Black Aesthetic* includes essays by Sarah

Webster Fabio, James Emanuel, Dudley Randall, Haki Madhubuti, and Keorapeste William Kgositsile. Of all the essays on poetry by a poet, however, Carolyn Rodgers's essay "Black Poetry—Where It's At" may have been one of the most cited. "Black Poetry" was the first in a series of articles that Rodgers published in *Negro Digest/Black World*.[13] Literary critic Darwin Turner refers to Rodgers's "Black Poetry—Where It's At" as "the best essay on the work of new black poets."[14] Turner does not elaborate on why he considers Rodgers's essay the best, but what makes Rodgers's essay particularly impressive and meaningful in regards to literary criticism on black verse is that the article focuses on the literary art of emergent poets and utilizes African American verbal styles as an approach for categorizing the writings. Her article is a pioneering essay on black poetry and poetics, and her explanations of signifying and the relationships between poetry and music served as a precursor to studies in African American literature and culture by scholars such as Stephen Henderson, Houston Baker, and Henry Louis Gates Jr.

Rodgers's essay appeared under the subheading "A Black Perspective" in the September issue of *Negro Digest,* the month of the publication's annual poetry editions. Also, her essay followed an article on the black aesthetic by Amiri Baraka.[15] The byline for Rodgers in the article states, "One of the new poets takes a look at the poetry of her peers and delivers some provocative and insightful opinions."[16] These seemingly minor issues concerning how and where "Black Poetry—Where It's At" appeared are important in that they reveal that Rodgers was clearly a part of the early conversations about the New Black Poetry and the black aesthetic.

As the title of the article by Rodgers suggests, the essay focused on the current state of black poetry in the late 1960s. Rodgers acknowledges early in her essay that although black poets differ from each other, she would classify the New Black Poetry in several broad categories. Rodgers utilizes vernacular terms as headings for her categories, including "signifying," "teachin/rappin," "bein," "coversoff," and "shoutin." Using these culturally distinct terms allows Rodgers to indicate the viability of black words and language as tools for arranging and theorizing poetry. To explain the terms, Rodgers uses examples from New Black Poetry, including excerpts from poems by Amiri Baraka, Sonia Sanchez, Haki Madhubuti, Nikki Giovanni, Ebon, and Barbara Mahone. Unlike many academic critics, she avoids relying on white scholars, Eurocentric frameworks, and literary terms such as *onomatopoeia* and *allusion* to support her explanations of black literary art. Relying on African American frames of reference to analyze the New Black Poetry, Rodgers appeals more directly to the sensibilities of fellow black writers, literary critics, and general readers familiar with African American speaking patterns, and similar to Larry Neal, Rodgers addresses her comments directly to a presumed black readership throughout the essay.

Of the terms that Rodgers discusses, she devotes special attention to signifying because of how meaningful it was in a historical and cultural sense and also because she views signifying as a central practice in the New Black Poetry. Rodgers defines signifying as "a way of saying the truth that hurts with a laugh, a way of capping on (shutting up) someone. Getting even talking bout people's mammas & such. It's a love/hate exercise in exorcising one's hostilities" (15). To illustrate her point, Rodgers uses examples from Richard Wright's autobiography and excerpts from two poems by Nikki Giovanni and Haki Madhubuti. Rodgers writes that the most dynamic black poems of the era utilize signifying and that such poems have the ability to involve and move black people. The humor of poems that make jokes about black or white people, for instance, is entertaining to audiences grounded in a black nationalist ethos. Also, laughing at such insults allows these audiences to join poets in expressing contempt for adversaries in positions of authority. Toward the close of her essay, Rodgers states, "I trust that I have initiated here a rather complete incomplete picture of where Black poetry is at" (16). She acknowledges that some would disagree with the labels she has proposed, but her main objective, she notes, is not to let outsiders "define what we be doing" (16).

Rodgers's essay does meet the requirements of typical scholarly articles in terms of offering extensive explanations for key terms. Her article does not provide a brief summary of the historical context that led to developments in black poetry, nor does she cite scholars in the field who have covered the subject. In addition, Rodgers's use of conversational language, including contractions and the informal pronoun "we," is contrary to the ostensibly objective tone employed in essays that appear in academic journals. Despite these issues, however, it is actually the seemingly nonacademic features of her article that make "Black Poetry—Where It's At" such an accessible and groundbreaking explanation of the New Black Poetry. The shortness of the essay, its use of informal language, and the author's arrangement of the New Black Poetry into categories are rhetorically appropriate for the readership that Rodgers addressed.

Rodgers's use of vernacular terms to classify poetry is especially fascinating. Organizing poetry in this manner reveals the possibilities for basing the analysis of literature more firmly on African American frames of reference. As a result, Rodgers makes direct connections between the objects and the tools of investigation. Furthermore, Rodgers bases her criteria for arranging black verse on how she sees the poetry functioning to entertain, educate, involve, or inspire African Americans. Her concern is with what New Black Poets actually "be doing" to move their audiences to various levels of consciousness and action. Rodgers is interested in producing criticism that concentrates on the effects of poetry on distinct audiences.

While Rodgers's essay is important and groundbreaking for its interpretation of modern African American poetry, a number of factors have contributed to the lack of attention her article has received. For one, literary critics have tended to focus on a rather narrow body of male academic writers when charting the critical discourse pertaining to the Black Arts Movement, thus overlooking the significance of Rodgers's essay. Also, "Black Poetry—Where It's At" was published in *Negro Digest,* and for copyright issues, it seems, articles that appeared in that publication have seldom been reprinted over the years. Since Rodgers's essay has remained out of print for so long, the article receives little attention from critics and general readers. In addition, although Rodgers was widely known throughout black arts discourse, she, like the majority of her fellow writers, received minor attention after the 1970s, thus diminishing opportunities for serious considerations of her critical work. Finally, the critical discourse on African American literature provides relatively little attention for poetry and even less for poetry criticism. Thus, even a notable essay like Rodgers's often goes largely unnoticed.

Rodgers and several other poets contributed to the critical discourse primarily through the publication of essays and reviews, and some of them published book-length studies. Eugene Redmond, consequently, produced one of the most comprehensive works devoted to African American poetry. Redmond's *Drumvoices: The Mission of Afro-American Poetry, A Critical History* (1976) provides important biographical and interpretive information regarding a wide range of emergent poets, and just as important, Redmond's book charts the larger history of black poetry beginning with oral and musical traditions. Few studies of American and African American literature have treated the work of such a large number of African American poets. Certainly, it has been rare for a poet to take on such an ambitious critical project.

Among other attributes, what makes *Drumvoices* especially notable rests on Redmond's mission to create a far-reaching narrative concerning the development of African American verse. Sure, poets and readers may have always known that there were connections among various writers, but Redmond's work usefully highlights the presence of interconnected themes and styles across generations of black poets. *Drumvoices* impressively demonstrates that African American poetry constitutes an established tradition and not simply periodic movements in American literature, as Redmond analyzes writings by such a large number of black poets together in one study. His extensive treatment of emergent black poets also assists in solidifying these writers, and more notably their movement, within the critical discourse of literary history. In addition to examining "new" black poets, Redmond's book paints a picture that portrays his contemporary subjects as extensions of a long line of African American verse.

Taken together, Redmond's *Drumvoices,* the articles by Larry Neal and Carolyn Rodgers, and the reviews and essays by several other poets associated with black arts discourse reveal that these creative writers were at the forefront in providing commentary on and assessments of their literary art and cultural activities. Promoting fellow writers, addressing African American readerships, employing black verbal styles to categorize ideas about black literary art, and publishing articles about black poets and poetry in African American venues are defining features of the criticism and commentary produced by many of these poets. Their writings provided invaluable publicity for fellow poets and clarified the interconnected enterprises among black artists in advancing their movement.

Black Aesthetic Theorizing and Canon Formation

Contemporary examinations of the Black Arts Movement often chart the development and quality of theories regarding "the black aesthetic." Literary critics Jerry Ward, David Smith, and Tony Bolden, among others, have expanded our understanding of black arts critical discourse by explaining the benefits and shortcomings of black aesthetic theories.[17] Scholars have also been likely to examine the work of leading academic-oriented theoreticians such as Addison Gayle, Stephen Henderson, and Houston Baker. Collectively, these studies on black aesthetics provide important information regarding the most provocative theoretical framework of black arts discourse. For now, the objective is to concentrate on a less examined aspect of this subject: how black aesthetic theorizing contributed to the formation of a black arts poetry canon.

Actually, the frequent attempts to answer the question about the definitions, functions, and viabilities of black aesthetics or philosophies of African American art constitute practices that greatly influenced the production of black arts poetry and the visibility of the poets. That many of the leading voices regarding black aesthetics, such as Larry Neal, Amiri Baraka, Hoyt Fuller, Addison Gayle, and Stephen Henderson, were also anthologists or editors seems significant. Fuller, for example, could translate his vision of what a black aesthetic might look like by publishing certain kinds of poems and poets. And although Dudley Randall is hardly considered a leading black aesthetic theorist, his efforts as a publisher certainly influenced perceptions of poetry. During the Black Arts Movement, writers never arrived at a consensus concerning a black aesthetic. However, black aesthetic theorizing did operate as one of the most central features of their discourse.

During the era, discussions of black aesthetics operated in at least three major ways to shape the participation of poets in black arts discourse. First, black aesthetic theorizing provided the occasion for poets to engage in lively conversations among critics, editors, activists, and other writers about a philosophy of African American literary art. Second, the discussions of black aesthetics encouraged poets to develop a more direct relationship to African American audiences, and finally, they were encouraged to incorporate the virtues of black music into their writings. Thus, the subject of black aesthetics influenced the presentation of poetry, and the topic also created opportunities for poets to serve as theorists of literary art and expressive culture.

Early on, Hoyt Fuller set the stage for poets to have a prevalent voice in the discussion of black aesthetics. In the January 1968 issue of *Negro Digest,* Fuller explained that the periodical had developed a twenty-five-question survey and polled thirty-eight black writers. Most of the questions in the survey requested that writers identify their literary influences and values. Questions 19 and 25 were particularly relevant to the objectives of the developing black arts movement: "Do you see any future at all for the school of writers which seeks to establish 'a black aesthetic'?" and "Should black writers direct their work toward black audiences?"[18] According to Larry Neal, Fuller's question initiated the discussion of a black aesthetic that was so pervasive during the era. "Not because Hoyt sat down and wrote any theory of Black Aesthetics," explains Neal, "but because it was Hoyt who asked the question . . . 'is there a Black Aesthetic? Does there need to be one?'"[19] Among the respondents presented in the issue, Hoyt Fuller published replies from a number of emergent poets, including Carolyn Rodgers, Haki Madhubuti, Julia Fields, Sarah Webster Fabio, Etheridge Knight, and Larry Neal.

Overall, the respondents offered varied responses to the question regarding a black aesthetic. Sarah Webster Fabio offered a concise answer: "Yes. A Black Aesthetic will be necessary to create a power force which will interpret, support, and validate the reality of 'black experience.'"[20] Etheridge Knight provided a more lengthy response, affirming the need for African American writers to embrace black aesthetics: "The Black Artist must create new forms and new values, sing new songs (or purify old ones); and along with other Black Authorities, he must create a new history, new symbols, myths and legends." Knight also warned fellow black artists to "beware of the white aesthetic."[21] The longest published response concerning the viability of a black aesthetic was written by Larry Neal. Interestingly, he rejected the push for the creation of an African American philosophy of art. "There is no need to establish a 'black aesthetic,'" wrote Neal. "Rather it is important to understand that one already exists. The question is: where does it exist? And what do we do with it? Further, there is something distasteful about a formalized aesthetic."[22] The responses from Neal, Knight, and Fabio are suggestive, revealing how differently the writers viewed black aesthetics.

The diversity of responses in the *Negro Digest* issue reveals that the writers were far from being of one accord concerning the definition and value of black aesthetics. As the editors concluded, the survey demonstrates that "there exists a dramatic division among black writers," which the editors believed resulted from African Americans' "alternating desire for assimilation and separation." Despite the differences, though, many of the writers were, in some form or another, generally favorable about their "pursuit of 'a black aesthetic.'"[23] The appearance of so many writers in one magazine suggests that while they did have a range of views, they were willing to share their views on literary values in a common venue, *Negro Digest*.

In retrospect, that January 1968 issue of the magazine anticipated a discussion of aesthetics that would permeate black arts discourse. And, similar to the tone set by Hoyt Fuller, poets would serve as the discussion's most prominent contributors.

The respondents identified Amiri Baraka (then still known as LeRoi

Jones) as the "most important living black poet."[24] In addition to his stature as a leading poet, however, Baraka was also a visible theorist, as his prose pieces promoting black philosophies of art circulated widely during the era. In his essay "The Myth of a 'Negro Literature,'" initially published in his 1966 collection *Home,* Baraka wonders how African American writing could "even begin to express the emotional predicament of black Western man?" Sounding what would become a recurrent tune of black aesthetic theorizing, he explains that black writers had been prevented from proposing their "own symbols" and "own personal myths." Further, he proposes, black poets would better serve themselves and their audience by listening to Bessie Smith and Billie Holiday "than be content to imperfectly imitate the bad poetry of the ruined minds of Europe." Baraka concludes the essay by speculating that the future development of a distinct African American literature would rest on the degree to which that literature could "disengage itself from the weak, heinous elements of the culture that spawned it, and use its very existence as evidence of a more profound America."[25] In many respects, Baraka's ideas were not new. He echoed sentiments expressed by preceding generations of black writers, including Langston Hughes, Richard Wright, and Ralph Ellison. What distinguished Baraka, however, was the context in which he was writing.

In particular, the circulation routes of Baraka's essays espousing philosophies of African American art reveal that his writings are directly related to the aims and audiences of black arts discourse. His status as a leading figure of the movement gave him the credibility, as well as the access to black publishing venues, to influence large numbers of emergent creative intellectuals and poets. So, after its initial publication in 1966, "The Myth of a 'Negro Literature'" appeared in at least six different African American anthologies between 1969 and 1971, as conversations regarding black aesthetics were gaining wide attention. Baraka's manifesto "The Revolutionary Theatre," which draws on vivid rhetoric in its call for the development of a distinct African American radical art form, asserts that revolutionary art must, among other functions, "look into black skulls," teach white people "their deaths," and create "new kinds of heroes." The *Liberator* version of Baraka's essay contains an opening editorial note that explains, "This essay was originally commissioned by the *New York Times* in December 1964, but was refused, with the statement that the editors could not understand it. The *Village Voice* also refused to run this essay. It was first published in *Black Dialogue*."[26] Here, within the context of *Liberator* magazine, the rejection of Baraka's piece by the *New York Times* probably gave him and his ideas more credibility among a black readership that was frequently encouraged to free itself from white standards. At the same time, *Liberator* and *Black Dialogue* were signaling their own commitments to Baraka and his militant ideology by publishing an artist and essay that was presumably too black and revolutionary for the mainstream press to understand.

Baraka's essay appeared again in the April 1966 issue of *Negro Digest,* and in this version, the article was titled "In Search of the Revolutionary Theatre" and contained the lead note "Needed: New Heroes." Most notably from a visual standpoint, the essay includes a photograph of Baraka sitting with a small group of black people on the steps outside the Black Arts Repertory Theatre/School in Harlem. An excerpt from Baraka's essay appears near the bottom of the page: "The force we want is of 20 million spooks storming America with furious cries and unstoppable weapons. We want actual explosions and actual brutality."[27] The image of Baraka in the photograph, seated with a group of students or supporters near a large Black Arts Repertory Theatre/School flag, offers a striking and alternative visual idea concerning how a poet might engage the world beyond the page. Framing the essay with the image of Baraka at his institution in Harlem amplifies the idea that he practiced what he preached. The publication of Baraka's "The Revolutionary Theatre" in *Black Dialogue* and *Liberator* in 1965, in *Negro Digest* in 1966, and in Robert Hayden's anthology *Afro-American Literature: An Introduction* in 1971 reveals that editors were quite aware of his work as an essayist and interested in creating a larger readership for his proposals regarding the key imperatives of radical black art.

In his essay "The Black Aesthetic," published in the September 1969 issue of *Negro Digest,* Baraka directs his message more specifically to black poets, explaining the routes they might take in order to project "feelings about reality" and achieve revolution through their literary art. Similar to the modes of writing in his foreword to *Black Fire* (1968), the style of Baraka's "The Black Aesthetic" utilizes experimental or unconventional terminology and sentence structures. Using the plural pronouns "we" and "us" in reference to fellow black poets throughout the essay, Baraka writes, "Our selves are revealed in whatever we do. Our art shd be our selves as self-conscious with a commitment to revolution. Which is enlightenment." He informs poets that "the purpose of our writing is to create the nation" and thus promotes the production of black nationalist verse. Echoing the sentiments he expresses in his poem "Black Art" and his essay "The Revolutionary Theatre," Baraka suggests that black artists must redefine themselves: "We are 'poets' because someone has used that word to describe us." Thus, beyond being poets in any conventional sense, black poets must come to understand that "we are creators and destroyers-firemakers, Bomb throwers and takers of heads." In addition, their writings must be concerned with "the breakthru the break out the move New ness New forms Explorations Departures all with the responsibility to force and be change all with the commitment to Black Revolution, utilizing the collective spirit of Blackness."[28] The dynamic, original style of Baraka's essay suggests that the development of a new, radical approach to black poetry might also lead to alternative approaches to prose.

The broad circulation of his essays concentrating on theories of black art indicates that poetry was only one means through which Baraka actively participated in black arts discourse. The pervasiveness of his essays also suggests that editors contributed significantly to ensuring the high visibility of Baraka as an essayist and theorist. Thus, Baraka potentially influenced large numbers of writers and the formation of a black arts poetry canon in at least three ways. For one, he regularly directed his writings at fellow poets and offered them suggestions, if not directions, on the themes and techniques that they should adopt in their poems. Second, he served as the most highly regarded *model* for what it meant to be a "black artist." His own publishing career as a poet, playwright, and essayist, for instance, suggested that black artists should produce work across genres. And finally, Baraka's widely circulating theories concerning the look and aims of new and radical black writing may have influenced the selection criteria adopted by editors and publishers during the era. Along with the writings of his fellow poet Larry Neal, Baraka's essays were widely published and reprinted in venues commonly available to black readerships.

Baraka and Neal were among the most popular poets to participate in black aesthetic theorizing, but they were certainly not the only poets actively promoting such theories. Poets Dudley Randall, Carolyn Rodgers, Haki Madhubuti, Stanley Crouch, and Sarah Webster Fabio published essays regarding the development of distinct philosophies of African American literary art as well. Taken together, their writings, as well as the essays offered by Baraka and Neal, constitute an impressive body of theories exploring the possibilities of developing forms of black art that actively engaged the sensibilities of African Americans. As active contributors to the theoretical discourse, the poets were exerting an influence on the formation of the black arts canon, not simply as composers of verse.

Not surprisingly, several poet-essayists published their work in *Negro Digest,* where Hoyt Fuller was apparently establishing his magazine as a major forum for black aesthetic theorizing. In the September–October 1968 issue of *Negro Digest,* Haki Madhubuti, Sarah Webster Fabio, and Keorapetse William Kgositsile published essays seeking to define the objectives of contemporary black poets in a section entitled "Toward a Black Aesthetic," which was the same title as that of a previously published essay by Hoyt Fuller that appeared in the *Critic* magazine. As evidenced by the titles, Madhubuti's "Black Poetry: Which Direction?," Fabio's "Who Speaks Negro? Who Is Black?," and Kgositsile's "Paths to The Future" indicate that African American poetry was at an important transitional stage, and these poets offered insight on where black verse was going. The editors of *Negro Digest* highlighted the authority of these three poets to theorize the paths of black poetry by situating the essays under the larger heading "Toward a Black Aesthetic" and positioning the three articles as a prelude to a "portfolio of poetry," which included works by over thirty poets. It was a recurrent feature of his editorial practice that Hoyt Fuller created opportunities for poets to theorize new and ostensibly more militant directions for African American verse.

An October 1968 letter from Stanley Crouch to Hoyt Fuller reveals that Crouch was favorable to the mission of developing approaches to black aesthetics. "What we must do, and I was talking to Larry Neal about this a few days ago," writes Crouch, "is come up with an esthetic that *actually* takes in Black Speech." Later in the letter, Crouch informs Fuller that he was "going to try to have the bookstore get about forty-five copies of the Sept/Oct 1968 DIGEST. Those esthetic statements will be very useful." Crouch explains that his own essay concerning black aesthetic issues had been recently accepted for publication in Joe Goncalves's the *Journal of Black Poetry,* and notes, "If you're interested, and if he'll give up reprint rights, I'd like to have it published in DIGEST also." In closing, Crouch expresses his view to Fuller that in order to develop a body of distinct forms of black art, "we need as much as we can get in terms of ACTUAL poetry, and propositions that move that way."[29] Notably, Crouch seemed as interested in circulating his black aesthetic propositions as he was in getting his poems published. The high visibility of publishing opportunities available to poet-essayists likely made it more possible for creative intellectuals such as Stanley Crouch to view themselves as both poets and theorists in black arts discourse. In retrospect, by identifying Larry Neal, Hoyt Fuller, Joe Goncalves, the *Journal of Black Poetry,* and *Negro Digest,* Crouch's letter also confirms the existence of a broad and interconnected conversation on poetry and aesthetics.

In addition to promoting the significance of black speech in poetry, as Crouch suggests in his letter to Fuller, black aesthetic theorists regularly highlighted the importance of incorporating black music into literary art. African American musical references indeed pervade the poetry and prose of Amiri Baraka, Carolyn Rodgers, Larry Neal, and many other black arts writers. James Stewart's "The Development of the Black Revolutionary Artist," the lead essay in *Black Fire,* proposes that free jazz could serve as a model for how black writers might depart from relying too heavily on European forms and chart their own routes. Following the example of musicians John Coltrane, Ornette Coleman, Grachan Moncur, and Milford Graves, explains Stewart, black writers could "emancipate our minds from Western values and standards" and "make new definitions founded on [our] own culture—on definite black values."[30] Here, Stewart advocates using black music as a way to radicalize African American literary art and create a body of writing that would serve the needs of black people. Stewart's urging that writers make black music a central element of their poetics is a sentiment expressed throughout the discourse.

On the one hand, a reader could agree with literary critic David Smith's observation that the tendency of African American writers of the era to focus so often on musicians and other nonliterary artists "reflects a common problem among Black Aesthetic theorists in finding literary precedents for Black Arts Movement writing."[31] At the same time, however, the persistent focus on black music, especially free jazz and its musicians, allowed theorists to offer interpretations that move beyond primarily literary influences. Writers and literary critics, of course, had alluded to nonliterary forms and music prior to the 1960s. Still, black arts writers distinguished their discussions of black music with their particular fusing of concepts relating to free jazz, militant poetry, and black liberation. In addition, the widespread focus on black music in prose directly correlated to the preoccupation with black music in verse and thus further solidified links among criticism, theory, and poetry.

The frequent publication of essays that extolled black music as an ultimate model for poets seems to suggest that this aspect of black aesthetic theorizing served as both a guide and an explanation for the tremendous number of poems focusing on music. According to many of the writers, black music represented the most advanced form of African American artistic production and thus encouraged forward-thinking or radical poets to incorporate the sensibilities of black music in their literary art. At the same time, the most popular poets focused on music and, accordingly, provided evidence to theorists and critics that music-infused poetry was essential to the production of black radical writing. Demonstrating overlapping interests among the distinct and presumably revolutionary force of black musicians, poets, critics, and theorists, along with the editors and publishers who provided the platforms to transmit the writers' views to larger readerships, ensured that music would become a distinguishing feature of the black arts poetry canon. The centrality of black music in both prose and verse is perhaps not so surprising, since many of the leading poets were also the leading theorists.

By the time Addison Gayle published his anthology *The Black Aesthetic* in 1971, a number of poets had, evidently, already established themselves as important voices in the conversation regarding black aesthetics. Without suggesting that we diminish the importance of Gayle's contributions to black aesthetic theorizing, it is nonetheless essential that we recognize that examinations of black aesthetics did not begin with the publication of Gayle's collection. One of Larry Neal's contributions to the anthology, in fact, is entitled "Some Reflections on the Black Aesthetic." Many of the contributors to the collection developed their reputations as black aesthetic theorists based on their writings on the subject prior to the publication of *The Black Aesthetic*. Gayle's book served the useful task of consolidating various black aesthetic theories in book form, as opposed to initiating the conversation among writers. Hoyt Fuller's influence on the organization of Gayle's collection is especially important.

One of the first essays to employ the phrase "a black aesthetic" to refer to the mission of black arts writers, Fuller's "Towards a Black Aesthetic" was submitted to the *Critic* magazine in 1967 and first published there in 1968; the essay was later reprinted in Addison Gayle's *Black Expression* (1969), David P. Demarest and Lois S. Lamdin's *The Ghetto Reader* (1970), and eventually Gayle's *The Black Aesthetic* (1971). Fuller's explanation that a black aesthetic is "a system of isolating and evaluating artistic works of black people which reflect the special character and imperatives of black experience" served as a central framing principle for *The Black Aesthetic.* The essays by Ron Karenga, Leslie Rout, Ronald Milner, Carolyn Gerald, and Keorapetse William Kgositsile, which appeared in the collection, had been previously published in *Negro Digest,* revealing that Fuller's magazine was a useful source for Gayle to obtain materials for his collection. Finally, Fuller's practice at *Negro Digest / Black World* of including poets at the forefront of black aesthetic theorizing was a practice apparently adopted by Gayle as well. Larry Neal, Sarah Webster Fabio, Amiri Baraka, and Haki Madhubuti are a few of the poets who contributed to the book. Notably, poets authored all the essays in the poetry section of the anthology.

Although most modern literary critics concentrate their examinations of Gayle's work on his theories of black aesthetics, the current investigations of the formation of a black arts canon highlight Gayle's editorial work. Rather than only considering him a black aesthetic theorist, viewing Gayle as an anthologist supports the larger claim in this study that editors contributed significantly to establishing and maintaining the parameters of black arts discourse and circulating the writings of poets. Gayle's three anthologies *Black Expression: Essays by and about Black Americans in the Creative Arts, The Black Aesthetic,* and *Bondage, Freedom and Beyond: The Prose of Black Americans* (1971) contain the work of historically significant African American writers such as Frederick Douglass, W. E. B. Du Bois, Richard Wright, and Langston Hughes, as well as Amiri Baraka, Larry Neal, Sarah Webster Fabio, and other black poets. With the publication and reprinting of a range of creative intellectuals who promoted black nationalist principles in their works, Gayle's collections accentuate the connections between past and contemporary black writers. *The Black Aesthetic,* in particular, parallels the objectives of Amiri Baraka and Larry Neal's *Black Fire,* Stephen Henderson's *Understanding the New Black Poetry,* and Dudley Randall's *The Black Poets,* to name a few anthologies, by featuring the work of prominent black arts poets. Overall, Gayle's editorial work contributed to the larger mission in black arts discourse of developing publishing venues and a system for the valuation of African American literary art.

The contributions made by poets, the emphasis placed on black music as a model for radicalizing poetry, and the editorial work enacted to bring together a range of writers focusing on philosophies of African American art all constituted essential features of black aesthetic theorizing. These features were also central to the formation of a common discourse. The transmission of essays—many of which were written by poets—that proposed directions for the development of black radical art and artists was quite prevalent and defined the social interactions among writers and their readers. The overlap between black aesthetic theorizing and black arts poetry was especially pronounced in the works of Larry Neal and Amiri Baraka, whose prose and poetry publishing records epitomize the idea that poets and theorists are one. Moreover, the editorial work of black arts proponents such as Hoyt Fuller and Addison Gayle charted and consolidated African American writers' considerations of the definitions and functions of black aesthetics.

6 • The Revolution Will Not Be Anthologized

The publication of *The Norton Anthology of African American Literature* in 1997 marked a signal moment in the transmission of black arts era poetry. Poets associated with the movement had been steadily appearing in anthologies since the 1970s, but, more so than most other imprints, Norton could raise the value and visibility of its contributors, particularly in African American literature survey courses on college campuses. The Norton imprint, note Henry Louis Gates Jr. and Nellie McKay, "had become synonymous to our generation with canon formation" and thus offered writers a noticeable, if not definite, place in literary history.[1] The *Norton* devoted a full section to 1960s writings, entitled "The Black Arts Movement: 1960–1970." Edited by Houston Baker Jr., the section includes poems by Amiri Baraka, Nikki Giovanni, Etheridge Knight, Haki Madhubuti, Sonia Sanchez, and Carolyn Rodgers, and essays by Addison Gayle, Hoyt Fuller, Maulana Karenga, and Larry Neal. The presentation of these poets and essayists in a collection that highlights two hundred years of writing solidified the presence of black arts discourse in the tradition of African American literature. Anthologies, of course, have a way of concealing even as they reveal. Consequently, the *Norton* and its second edition, published in 2006, illustrate that the more salient features of black arts literature will not be easily anthologized.

Although convincing cases could be made for the inclusion of a number of writers in the *Norton,* the concern here is what the presentation of the current contributors suggests about the challenge of representing black arts discourse in an anthology. Actually, the notable revisions to the black arts section in the second edition confirm that the editors were inclined to reconsider their approach to representing writings and authors of the era. In the second edition, the section is re-named "The Black Arts Era, 1960–1975" and includes June Jordan, Au-dre Lorde, Lucille Clifton, Michael Harper, Ishmael Reed, and Toni Cade Bambara, all of whom are presented in the "Literature since 1970" section of the first edition. Baker includes an additional subsection en-titled "Expanding the Black Arts Movement" to his introduction of the section, which serves to explain the editorial changes. According to Baker, 1975 has "representative value" as an end date, and those writers initially presented as post–black arts "were far more 'of' the move-ment—adherents and exemplars of distinctive and distinguishing char-acteristics and structures of feeling of the Black Arts—than opponents or successors."[2] Indeed, 1970 was definitely hardly representative of the decline of the movement, and those writers initially presented as suc-cessors were clearly part of the developing discourse. But how does the change from "The Black Arts Movement: 1960–1970" to "The Black Arts Era, 1960–1975" alter perceptions of black arts? To what ends were the aforementioned writers excluded from the black arts section in the first edition and then included in the second? And what view of the contributors might emerge based on the presentation of their particular selections? These kinds of questions attempt to address how the edito-rial practices of the *Norton* influence the canon formation of black arts discourse and African American literature in general.

First, the designation "The Black Arts Era, 1960–1975" expands the possibilities for viewing the literature of that particular time period. A section on the "movement" would presumably feature writers and texts central to the cause of black arts. Focusing on an era, however, provides greater flexibility for selecting an array of canonical texts that circulated widely during that time period. For example, Martin Luther King Jr. and Malcolm X were not black arts participants, but King's "Letter from Birmingham Jail" (1964) and Malcolm X's autobiography (1965) were widely read and influential documents during the 1960s. King's essay and an excerpt from Malcolm's autobiography are reprinted in the *Norton,* along with excerpts from novels by John A. Williams, Eldridge Cleaver, and James Alan McPherson. Presenting these works under the heading "era" as opposed to "movement," as they are in the first edition, offers more latitude for viewing texts pro-duced and circulated during that period. In addition, suggesting that the black arts era extended at least to the mid-1970s is far more plausible than the earlier designation of 1970. Actually, using 1960 as a starting date obscures the fact that it was not until the mid- and late 1960s that "black arts" became a popular designation in African American literary history, based in large part on Baraka's poem "Black Art" and Neal's essay "The Black Arts Movement." Whereas 1975 might carry "representative value" as a concluding date, 1976 arguably serves as a more convincing date for the decline of "New Black Poetry," given the downfall of *Black World* and Broadside Press in that year.

The inclusion of June Jordan, Audre Lorde, Lucille Clifton, Michael Harper, Ishmael Reed, and Toni Cade Bambara in the black arts section produces a more diverse view of the era in comparison to the first edition. The initial placement of these writers outside black arts discourse was in part a result of the first 1970 ending date. Extending that date by five years necessitated the inclusion of six writers. Still, temporal markers do not entirely account for why some of the writers are presented as successors of the movement and not contributors. Ishmael Reed's poetry, for example, appeared in collections along with poems by Giovanni, Madhubuti, and Sanchez. The initial disassociation of Reed's work from these writers diminishes both the multiplicity of voices in black arts discourse and Reed's contributions as a novelist *and* poet. Similarly, although Michael Harper may not have been a vocal advocate of black nationalism in the vein of, say, Larry Neal and Amiri Baraka, his allegiance to jazz is comparable to theirs, and all three poets published verse highlighting black music in common venues.

The arrangement of selections in the first and second editions of the *Norton* delimits perceptions of the increased publishing opportunities made available to veteran writers during the black arts era. Although Robert Hayden, Gwendolyn Brooks, and Margaret Walker published works prior to the emergence of the movement, they received new and wide exposure during the 1960s. Walker's "For My People" (1942), Gwendolyn Brooks's "We Real Cool" (1960), and Hayden's "Frederick Douglass" (1962) were, along with Giovanni's "Nikki-Rosa" and Baraka's "A Poem for Black Hearts," among the most widely anthologized poems of the era. Furthermore, similar to younger black poets during the time period, Brooks, Hayden, and Walker published Malcolm X elegies, all of which appear in the *Norton*. The publishing records of these veteran poets reveal that they too were "of" the movement, and not only its predecessors. It was during the 1960s and 1970s, not the 1940s and 1950s, that Brooks, Hayden, and Walker first became widely anthologized. The circulation of poems by these elder poets placed them firmly within black arts discourse.

At the same time, Maya Angelou, Toni Morrison, and Alice Walker were not as post–black arts as the table of contents of the *Norton* implies. Angelou's *I Know Why the Caged Bird Sings,* Toni Morrison's *The Bluest Eye,* and Alice Walker's *The Third Life of Grange Copeland* were all published in 1970, during the height of the black arts era. Placing these writers, as well as Albert Murray and Clarence Major, outside the black arts section undermines the links between their works and the body of writings published during the era. If the "black arts" label were removed and the section was simply labeled "black literature produced between 1960 and 1975," the editors would perhaps be more inclined to acknowledge that Morrison, Angelou, Walker, Murray, and Major were in fact contemporaries of Amiri Baraka, Larry Neal, Sonia Sanchez, Haki Madhubuti, and Nikki Giovanni.

Finally, because of copyright and page restrictions, the *Norton,* like any anthology, must minimize the materials that it publishes by contributors. As a result, we are left with a rather limited view. The absence of poems focusing on black music and musicians by Baraka and Etheridge Knight perhaps mutes their notable contributions to jazz poetry. Further, without including poems by Larry Neal and without essays by Carolyn Rodgers, readers may develop a one-dimensional view of these multigenre creative artists. Hoyt Fuller's essay "Towards a Black Aesthetic" appears in both editions of the *Norton;* however, Fuller's most enduring contribution—his editorial work—cannot be reproduced in a single collection. Overall, then, the black arts section of the anthology usefully introduces readers to leading figures of the movement while simultaneously offering a truncated view of the publishing activities that led to the fervent circulation of African American poetry during the time period.

Despite any shortcomings, the *Norton,* which was adopted by "1,275 colleges and universities worldwide," currently stands as one of the most influential texts containing black arts era literature.[3] The consequential role that this collection plays in the canonization of 1960s and 1970s African American literature confirms the extent to which anthologies and editorial practices remain defining features in the transmission of black arts poetry. The *Norton* is actually one of several anthologies published during the last ten years that features leading black arts era writers. Jerry Ward's *Trouble the Water* (1997), Patricia Hill and colleagues' *Call and Response: The Riverside Anthology of the African American Literary Tradition* (1998), Michael Harper's *Vintage Book of African American Poetry* (2000), Keith Gilyard and Anissa Wardi's *African American Literature: Penguin Academics Series* (2004), and Arnold Rampersad and

Hilary Herbold's *The Oxford Anthology of African American Poetry* (2005) are some of the more modern collections to also contain black arts era poetry. These modern African American anthologies, similar to the *Norton,* highlight the strong presence of black arts era poetry in the larger context of African American literature. Still, the inability, so far, of a single collection to re-present the hundreds of poems and complementary essays and images published during the era suggests that the movement will not be easily anthologized.

The Decline of the Black Arts Movement

Some observers have noted that the black arts movement began to recede somewhere around the mid-1970s. According to cultural worker and poet Kalamu ya Salaam, "The decline of the Black Arts movement began in 1974 when the Black Power movement was disrupted and co-opted. Black political organizations were hounded, disrupted, and defeated by repressive government measures, such as Cointelpro and IRS probes."[4] Salaam's reasoning coincides with Larry Neal's comments that black arts and Black Power share a spiritual kinship. Salaam's suggestion that the status of black political culture largely influenced the state of African American artistic production also relates to Houston Baker's explanation of a concluding date for the black arts era in the second edition of the *Norton.* Baker notes that 1975 serves as a useful ending boundary for the era "when one considers the post–civil rights and post–Black Power events on the economic, athletic, political, expressive, cultural, and legal fronts."[5] In short, Baker's and Salaam's views suggest that the arrival of the post–Black Power era also meant the departure of black arts at least as a coherent enterprise.

Major political trends would certainly affect the resonance of literary art that was so consciously aligned with a militant movement. But is artistic production solely dependent on activism? To what degree did trends in literary discourse affect the decline of the black arts era? Salaam's and Baker's view that political developments and repressions signaled the diminishing force of black arts is partly agreeable. However, factors relating to decreased literary transmission—including fewer anthologies and the closure of major publishing institutions—also account for the diminished prominence of the black arts movement.

By the mid-1970s, anthologies of verse highlighting black militant agendas appeared infrequently. In 1976, the discontinuation of *Black*

World, the *Journal of Black Poetry,* and Broadside Press represented a major decline in the circulation of new black poetry.[6] The closure of major publishing outlets did not mean that leading poets immediately ceased presenting their work. Indeed, Amiri Baraka, Sonia Sanchez, Nikki Giovanni, Haki Madhubuti, and several other poets associated with the movement continued producing their literary art. Nonetheless, without a network of publishing venues to promote the convergence of black poetry and poets on a national scale, the movement lost considerable momentum.

The infrequent appearance of African American anthologies featuring black poetry during the late 1970s could have been a reflection of market forces and not only the breakup of Black Power groups. Publishers may have lost the interest, or better yet, the financial motivation, to continually produce anthologies of black verse. And perhaps anthologists, as Dudley Randall suggests in the introduction to *The Black Poets,* were not finding enough reasons for publishers and readers to support new collections of poetry. By the late 1970s, justifying new collections of black verse may have been more of a challenge, given that African American anthologies had saturated the market during the early years of the decade. Whatever the case, the lack of new anthologies featuring a common group of poets reduced the likelihood that observers would view the activities of poets as constituting a movement.

The termination of *Black World* was particularly detrimental for publishing opportunities among African American writers. More so than any other periodical of the era, the periodical gave African American poets and poetry a national readership. The magazine, of course, was more than an outlet for poetry. In addition to publishing verse, *Black World* presented essays and news on cultural events, and the publication was integral to the operations of black arts discourse. Further, as Melba Boyd observes, "Fuller's periodical served as the main source for announcements and provided critical space for poets and book reviews."[7] The closure of the magazine guaranteed a loss of national publicity for Broadside Press. So the downfall of *Black World* represented a striking blow for Randall's press and for other poets and small presses.

Black World had also regularly displayed photographs of poets and an array of striking images relating to African American culture. Without *Black World,* readers lost a meaningful site for visualizing black arts and artists. The photographs of black writers, which appeared most frequently and visibly on the pages of *Negro Digest/Black World,* were crucial to the popularization of the era's leading figures. The photographs of activists, African artifacts, and African American–inflected images also gave viewers ideas about the visual aspects of black aesthetics. *Black World*'s functions as a magazine, in short, gave writings of the era notable visual complements. The closure of *Black World,* then, meant that black arts discourse was losing its major venue for the display of extraliterary images.

Of course, the decline of black arts discourse was not immediate or absolute. If the demise of *Black World,* the *Journal of Black Poetry,* and Broadside Press constituted a low point for the publication of black poetry in 1976, then certainly the appearance of Eugene Redmond's *Drumvoices* that year represents an important occasion in the study of African American poetry from a critical perspective. Redmond's book traces a vast body of verse and confirms the multidirectional routes of black poetry. Redmond brings generations of poets together in one study and pinpoints their relationship to common themes and technical practices. In the process, he addresses the existence of a vibrant and extensive black poetic tradition. His book locates black arts era poetry within the continuum of literary history, and just as important, *Drumvoices* anticipates the increased scholarly attention that would be placed on African American literature in the academy in subsequent decades.

With its impressive identification of approximately a hundred African American poets and even more volumes of poetry and poems, *Drumvoices* can be read as a prototype for the kind of bibliographic studies and biocritical recovery works that would define the careers of such leading scholars as Bernard Bell, Henry Louis Gates Jr., Maryemma Graham, Nellie McKay, and Gloria Wade-Gayles. No doubt, *Drumvoices* is a book-length confirmation of what previous essayists had been suggesting and what several subsequent scholars have been continuing to validate: black poetry comprises a long-standing tradition. Similar to Larry Neal, Amiri Baraka, Carolyn Rodgers, and several other black arts poets, Redmond was an artist-critic. And so in addition to being an accomplished poet, he was a literary historian and critic whose book impressively illuminates the African and American routes of, well, African American poetry. In retrospect, *Drumvoices* was a pioneering work in the critical treatment of black literature, which would begin appearing at increasing rates in the 1980s. Interestingly, Redmond's work appeared at a crossroads in literary history—at the decline of the black arts era and at the dawn of a major professionalizing era of African American literature in the academy.

"Now that the spectacular Black Arts Movement seems to have run its course," explained Stephen Henderson in 1977, "the question of evaluation takes on crucial importance."[8] As Henderson's comments suggest, writers and literary critics were looking back on the movement by the mid- to late 1970s. To the extent, though, that leading figures and key issues of the movement did not totally disappear, it might be more accurate to say that black arts discourse shifted rather than subsided. Whatever the case, during the late 1970s and early 1980s, black arts discourse was subsumed by the larger discourse of African American literature, which was quickly becoming more firmly institutionalized in the U.S. academy. An unprecedented number of black scholars were taking faculty positions at leading colleges and universities, and academic presses and scholarly journals began to prominently shape conversations concerning black literature. In the process, recovery work, prose, and literary theory far more than verse and poetics became the primary subjects in the discourse on African American literature. As a result, the scholarship on slave narratives and novels is far more extensive than the work on poetry.

Actually, the decline of black arts poetry is often juxtaposed with the ascension of black women's novels. In the section "Literature since 1970" in the *Norton,* Barbara Christian explains that black women novelists such as Toni Morrison and Alice Walker differentiated their work from works by male writers such as Richard Wright and Amiri Baraka. "Rather than idealizing black communities, as so many writings of the 1960s had attempted to do," writes Christian, "African American women writers of the 1970s articulated the complexities of African American culture and history; at the same time, they demonstrated how black communities had also deeply internalized racist stereotypes that radically affected their definitions for and expectations of women and men."[9] According to Kalamu ya Salaam, the declining interest in black arts era writing was assisted in part by "the upsurge of interest in the feminist movement," which led "establishment presses" to focus more on the work of black women writers. Christian's and Salaam's descriptions, to some degree, overgeneralize the differences between black arts writers and seemingly "post"–black arts writers.[10] One difference, though, is that Salaam identifies the mid- to late 1970s as a major time of change in black publishing practices, while Christian, adhering to the framework offered by the first edition of the *Norton,* pinpoints 1970 as a pivotal year for the shift. Both Christian and Salaam suggest that black women writers took on a more prominent role than black men writers.

To better understand that major shift in black literary history, we would perhaps need to pay attention to genre, and not simply gender.

For the most part, novels carry more value than poetry in the marketplace and in fields of literary studies. In general, novels have the possibility of earning publishers greater financial returns, as novels have the potential of becoming best-sellers, book-of-the-month-club picks, Oprah selections, or the subject of extensive scholarly study. And because they are more likely than volumes of poetry to appear in bookstores and on reading lists in college courses, novels tend to stay in print longer. Of course, in view of the large body of both fiction and verse published each year, relatively little literature receives substantial attention.

Given the position of the novel in the marketplace and the academy, it is not so surprising that novelists would receive a different kind of reception than poets. The increased popular and critical receptions of novels by Toni Morrison and Alice Walker should not be seen as a direct move by audiences away from volumes of poetry produced by Haki Madhubuti and Amiri Baraka. What is more likely is that market forces and literary studies have, over the last decades, maintained and expanded an environment that concentrates more extensively on select novels as opposed to select volumes of poetry. Ultimately, sustaining long-term popular and critical receptions of texts requires tremendous resources—resources that were certainly not largely available for writers who sought to continue a grassroots artistic movement. Whatever the case, the popularity of a few select novelists is common. What is extraordinary was that at one point in modern history, black poets commanded such widespread attention.

The paucity of critical work on American and African American poetry in general over the past few decades further ensured that black arts poetry would receive little attention. Although Amiri Baraka, Haki Madhubuti, Sonia Sanchez, Nikki Giovanni, June Jordan, Michael Harper, Clarence Major, Kalamu ya Salaam, Jayne Cortez, and Ishmael Reed continued to compose and publish poetry well after the mid-1970s, the absence of an extensive body of research on their poetic works suggests that their activities as poets merely subsided along with the movement. On the contrary, though, these black arts poets outlived and extended the black arts era. Yet the relatively small body of scholarship on African American poetry makes the multiple connections between black arts era poetry and modern verse less apparent. For this reason, the recent book-length studies by Tony Bolden, Melba Boyd, Cheryl Clarke, Aldon Nielsen, James Smethurst, and the late Lorenzo

Thomas are all the more important. Collectively, the research by these scholars orients readers to the historical and ongoing significance of black arts literature. Ideally, this critical work will lead to a better understanding of the black arts era and to the inclusion of more of its contributors on course syllabi. However, exposing students to a wide range of black arts texts presents a serious challenge, especially since most of the volumes of poetry, anthologies, and magazines produced during that time period are out of print.

Ironically, the idea that the Black Arts Movement declined or ended actually confirms the movement's consequential nature. If the movement had an end, then presumably it also had a beginning and middle, and considerations of the movement's successes and failures imply that its participants had agendas and goals, all of which suggests that its participants did indeed have a noteworthy presence. Scholars have yet to adequately develop and characterize the presence and activities of large numbers of poets who published work during the 1940s and 1950s, as well as the 1980s and 1990s. Conversely, scholars and various commentators have frequently adapted Larry Neal's phrase "The Black Arts Movement" to describe the wide-ranging African American literary art and activism produced during the time period. The phrase "Black Arts Movement," along with the subsequent categorizing of writers, texts, activities, ideology, and artistic productions under this broadly defined concept, provides a rather large group of writers with an identifiable name and a distinct place in literary history.

The Power of Connectors

In his book *The Tipping Point,* Malcolm Gladwell identifies the factors that give rise to popular social phenomena. Among other issues, Gladwell explains that "connectors, people with a special gift for bringing the world together," are integral to the increased circulation of ideas, goods, and services.[11] The concept of connectors is useful for understanding how African American poetry reached a tipping point and gained such increased circulation and wide visibility. In many ways, this study has attempted to explain how the power of connectors—in the form of people, institutions, and practices—generated the incredible force known as the Black Arts Movement.

The connection between poetry and activism became one of the distinguishing features of the era. Leading poets composed poems that addressed African American sociopolitical causes and paid tribute to black activist figures. Poets fashioned themselves as activists in their public personas and thus projected the idea that committed poets have the responsibility to serve the interests of black communities. Poets also aligned themselves with the rhetoric and ideology of nationalism and exhibited strong ties to music. Sure, Paul Laurence Dunbar, Langston Hughes, and countless other poets had previously celebrated music and musicians in their writings. Nonetheless, the frequency with which poets collaborated with musicians and the centrality of jazz to black arts discourse expanded the possibilities for writers and their readerships. Most notably, poets took a lead from musicians and intensified the art of presentation by transforming poetry readings into performances and converting volumes of poetry into audio recordings. Taken as a whole, music and black nationalism functioned as powerful connectors for the poets.

The writers themselves, of course, embodied a sense of connectivity that significantly determined the shape of their movement. Leading figures of the era envisioned themselves as poet-activists, poet-performers, poet-critics, and multigenre artists in general, and they participated, at various stages, in the composition, distribution, and reception of poetry. In their role as poet-critics, Carolyn Rodgers, Larry Neal, Amiri Baraka, and Eugene Redmond, among others, produced some of the most important commentary on African American poetry and expressive culture during the era. The writers actively reviewed volumes of poetry by their contemporaries and were among the most frequent contributors to discussions of black aesthetics. The ubiquitous presence of poets throughout literary discourse during the 1960s and 1970s guaranteed their defining influence on the production of African American literature during the era and on subsequent generations of writers.

Whereas the black arts enterprise gave rise to publishing opportunities for hundreds of poets, the popularity attained by Haki Madhubuti, Nikki Giovanni, and especially Amiri Baraka was particularly remarkable. In many respects, these writers became icons of the New Black Poetry, similar to the way that Langston Hughes became the most iconic figure of the New Negro Movement. That is not to say that their writings were representative of the entire field of poetry produced during the time period. However, these writers in particular were the most popular poets associated with the movement. Their poetry and images circulated widely, and they were often called upon as speakers on college campuses and at cultural events across the country. Thus, they developed nationwide influence. Not coincidentally, their popularity persists even today. On the downside, interest in these three writers often overshadows the works of their contemporaries. On the other hand, Baraka, Giovanni, and Madhubuti serve as the most visible contemporary links to black arts poetry. The popular attention and critical conversations surrounding Baraka and his work have created the most vibrant opportunities for considering the ongoing influence of black arts discourse.

As demonstrated throughout this study, publishing venues and editorial practices were among the principal connectors in the far-reaching transmission of poetry during the black arts era. Magazines such as *Liberator, Negro Digest/Black World,* and the *Journal of Black Poetry,* publishers such as Broadside Press and Third World Press, and the sixty or so anthologies published during the era brought an eclectic and intergenerational mix of poets together in common sites of publication. Editors highlighted the interconnections among a diverse group of writers by publishing poems that focused on tributes to black historical figures and music, the desire for liberation, and other themes relating to a nationalist ethos. The efforts of anthologists, publishers, and magazine editors to get so many African American poets on the same pages accounts in large part for why we now see the Black Arts Movement as a movement. No doubt, it was the connective power of editorial work, combined with the interest of writers to transform themselves into poets-plus, that made their collective artistic endeavors such a decisive moment in the history of African American and American literature.

List of Anthologies Containing African American Poetry, 1967–75

1967

Hayden, Robert, ed. *Kaleidoscope: Poems by American Negro Poets*. New York: Harcourt, Brace, 1967.

Randall, Dudley, and Margaret Burroughs, eds. *For Malcolm: Poems on the Life and Death of Malcolm X*. Detroit: Broadside Press, 1967.

Schulberg, Budd, ed. *From the Ashes: Voices of Watts*. New York: New American Library, 1967.

1968

Adoff, Arnold, ed. *I Am the Darker Brother: An Anthology of Modern Poems by Americans*. New York: Collier Books, 1968.

Chapman, Abraham, ed. *Black Voices: An Anthology of Afro-American Literature*. New York: Mentor, 1968.

Emanuel, James A., and Theodore Gross, eds. *Dark Symphony*. New York: Free Press, 1968.

Jones, LeRoi, and Larry Neal, eds. *Black Fire: An Anthology of Afro-American Writing*. New York: William Morrow, 1968.

Murphy, Beatrice, ed. *Ebony Rhythm: An Anthology of Contemporary Negro Verse*. 1948. Rpt., Freeport, N.Y.: Books for Libraries Press, 1968.

Patterson, Lindsay, ed. *Introduction to Black Literature in America, from 1746 to the Present*. New York: Publishers' Co., 1968.

Shuman, Robert, ed. *Nine Black Poets*. Durham, N.C.: Moore, 1968.

Troupe, Quincy, ed. *Watts Poets: A Book of New Poetry and Essays*. Los Angeles: House of Respect, 1968.

1969

Adoff, Arnold, ed. *City in All Directions: An Anthology of Modern Poems*. New York: Macmillan, 1969.

Alhamisi, Ahmed, and Harun Kofi Wangara, eds. *Black Arts: An Anthology of Black Creations*. Detroit: Black Arts Publications, 1969.

Brown, Sterling A., Arthur P. Davis, and Ulysses Lee, eds. *The Negro Caravan*. 1941. Rpt., New York: Arno, 1969.

Lowenfels, Walter, ed. *In a Time of Revolution: Poems from Our Third World*. New York: Random House, 1969.

Major, Clarence, ed. *The New Black Poetry*. New York: International Publishers, 1969.

Randall, Dudley, ed. *Black Poetry: A Supplement to Anthologies Which Exclude Black Poets*. Detroit: Broadside Press, 1969.

Turner, Darwin, ed. *Black American Literature: Poetry*. Columbus, Ohio: Charles E. Merrill, 1969.

1970

Adams, William, ed. *Afro-American Literature: Poetry*. Boston: Houghton Mifflin, 1970.

Adoff, Arnold, ed. *Black Out Loud: An Anthology of Modern Poems by Americans*. New York: Macmillan, 1970.

Cade, Toni, ed. *The Black Woman: An Anthology*. New York: Mentor, 1970.

Chambers, Bradford, and Rebecca Moon, eds. *Right On! An Anthology of Black Literature*. New York: New American Library, 1970.

Coombs, Orde, ed. *We Speak as Liberators: Young Black Poets*. New York: Dodd, Mead, 1970.

Davis, Charles T., and Daniel Walden, eds. *On Being Black: Writings by Afro-Americans from Frederick Douglass to the Present*. New York: Fawcett, 1970.

Demarest, David P., and Lois S. Lamdin, eds. *The Ghetto Reader*. New York: Random House, 1970.

Freedman, Frances S., ed. *The Black American Experience: A New Anthology of Black Literature*. New York: Bantam Books, 1970.

Hughes, Langston, and Arna Bontemps, eds. *Poetry of the Negro, 1746–1970*. Garden City, N.Y.: Doubleday, 1970.

Jordan, June, ed. *Soulscript: Afro-American Poetry*. New York: Doubleday and Company, 1970.

Kearns, Francis E., ed. *The Black Experience: An Anthology of American Literature for the 1970's*. New York: Viking, 1970.

Kearns, Francis E., ed. *Black Identity: A Thematic Reader*. New York: Holt, Rinehart, and Winston, 1970.

Kendricks, Ralph, and Claudette Levitt, eds. *Afro-American Voices, 1770's–1970's*. New York: Oxford Book Co., 1970.

Lomax, Alan, and Raoul Abdul, eds. *3000 Years of Black Poetry*. New York: Dodd, Mead, 1970.

Miller, Adam David, ed. *Dices or Black Bones: Black Voices of the Seventies*. Boston: Houghton Mifflin Co., 1970.

Turner, Darwin, ed. *Black American Literature: Essays, Poetry, Fiction, Drama*. Columbus, Ohio: Charles E. Merrill, 1970.

1971

Baker, Houston A., ed. *Black Literature in America.* New York: McGraw-Hill Book Company, 1971.

Brooks, Gwendolyn, ed. *A Broadside Treasury.* Detroit: Broadside Press, 1971.

Brooks, Gwendolyn, ed. *Jump Bad: A New Chicago Anthology.* Detroit: Broadside Press, 1971.

Brown, Patricia, ed. *To Gwen with Love: An Anthology Dedicated to Gwendolyn Brooks.* Chicago: Johnson Publishing, 1971.

Burnett, Whit, ed. *Black Hands on a White Face: A Timepiece of Experiences in a Black and White America.* New York: Dodd, Mead, 1971.

Davis, Arthur P., and Saunders Redding, eds. *Cavalcade: Negro American Writing from 1760 to the Present.* Boston: Houghton Mifflin, 1971.

Ford, Nick Aaron, ed. *Black Insights: Significant Literature by Black Americans—1760 to the Present.* Waltham, Mass.: Ginn and Co., 1971.

Hayden, Robert. *Afro-American Literature: An Introduction.* New York: Harcourt, Brace, 1971.

Miller, Ruth, ed. *Blackamerican Literature, 1760–Present.* Beverly Hills, Calif.: Glencoe Press, 1971.

Randall, Dudley, ed. *The Black Poets: A New Anthology.* New York: Bantam Books, 1971.

Rose, Karel, ed. *Gift of the Spirit: Readings in Black Literature for Teachers.* New York: Holt, Rinehart and Winston, 1971.

Stanford, Barbara Dodds, ed. *I, Too, Sing America.* Rochelle Park, N.J.: Hayden Books, 1971.

Weisman, Leonard, and Elfreda S. Wright, eds. *Black Poetry for All Americans.* New York: Globe, 1971.

1972

Barksdale, Richard, and Keneth Kinnamon, eds. *Black Writers of America: A Comprehensive Anthology.* New York: Macmillan, 1972.

Bell, Bernard W., ed. *Modern and Contemporary Afro-American Poetry.* Boston: Allyn and Bacon, 1972.

Chapman, Abraham, ed. *New Black Voices: An Anthology of Afro-American Literature.* New York: Mentor, 1972.

King, Woodie, ed. *Black Spirits: A Festival of New Black Poets in America.* New York: Random House, 1972.

Long, Richard A., and E. W. Collier, eds. *Afro-American Writing: An Anthology of Prose and Poetry.* New York: New York University Press, 1972.

Robinson, William H., ed. *Early Black American Poets: Selections with Biographies and Critical Introductions.* New York: Macmillan, 1972.

Robinson, William H., ed. *Nommo: An Anthology of Modern Black African and Black American Literature.* New York: Macmillan, 1972.

Simmons, Gloria M., and Helene D. Hutchinson, eds. *Black Culture: Reading and Writing Black.* New York: Holt, Rinehart, and Winston, 1972.

1973

Adoff, Arnold, ed. *The Poetry of Black America: An Anthology of the Twentieth Century.* New York: Harper and Row, 1973.

Breman, Paul, ed. *You Better Believe It: Black Verse in English from Africa, the West Indies and the United States.* Baltimore: Penguin Books, 1973.

Henderson, Stephen, ed. *Understanding the New Black Poetry.* New York: William Morrow, 1973.

Patterson, Lindsay, ed. *A Rock against the Wind: Black Love Poems.* New York: Dodd, Mead, 1973.

1974

Adoff, Arnold, ed. *My Black Me: A Beginning Book of Poetry.* New York: E. P. Dutton, 1974.

Bontemps, Arna, ed. *American Negro Poetry.* Rev. ed. New York: Hill and Wang, 1974.

Exum, Pat Crutchfield, ed. *Keeping the Faith: Writings by Contemporary Black American Women.* Greenwich, Conn.: Fawcett, 1974.

Hopkins, Lee Bennet. *On Our Way: Poems of Pride and Love.* New York: Knopf, 1974.

1975

King, Woodie, ed. *The Forerunners: Black Poets in America.* Washington, D.C.: Howard University Press, 1975.

Troupe, Quincy, ed. *Giant Talk: An Anthology of Third World Writing.* New York: Random House, 1975.

Notes

Introduction

1. Larry Neal, "Cultural Front," 27.
2. Gates, "Black Creativity," 74.
3. Bornstein, *Material Modernism;* Shillingsburg, *Resisting Texts;* Schulze, *Becoming Marianne Moore;* McGann, *Textual Condition.*
4. McGann, *Textual Condition,* 15, 13. Over the past few decades, several literary texts by black authors have been "rediscovered" or unexpurgated, including books by Hannah Crafts, Zora Neale Hurston, and Richard Wright, to name a few. Also over the last decade, the Schomburg Library of Nineteenth-Century Black Women Writers has released several books by authors such as Phillis Wheatley, Pauline Hopkins, and Harriet Jacobs. Despite all of this activity on the level of technical production, at present there remains a paucity of criticism on the editorial practices and policies that inform the presentation and reprinting of black books.
5. Sullivan, *On the Walls and in the Streets,* 21.
6. Sullivan, "Killing John Cabot," 560 (subsequently cited in the text).
7. Reid, *Black Protest Poetry;* Benston, *Performing Blackness;* Nielsen, *Black Chant;* Thomas, *Extraordinary Measures;* Bolden, *Afro-Blue.*
8. Smethurst, *Black Arts Movement,* 7.
9. Llorens, "Writers Converge at Fisk University," 62.
10. Fuller, "Black Writers' Views on Literary Lions and Values," 33.
11. Pool, "Robert Hayden," 41–42; Hayden, "1949 Runagate Runagate," 44–45; Hayden, "1964 Runagate Runagate," 46–47.
12. Smitherman, "Black Power Is Black Language," 91.
13. Joans, "Let's Get Violent!" 23.
14. Giovanni, "True Import of Present Dialogue," 318 (subsequently cited in the text).
15. Hernton, "Jitterbugging in the Streets," 206.
16. Malcolm X was not the sole author of the document, but it is often attributed to him because of his leadership role with the Organization of Afro-American Unity. Malcolm X, "Statement of Basic Aims and Objectives," 557, 563.
17. Amiri Baraka, "Dutchman," in *LeRoi Jones/Amiri Baraka Reader,* 97.

18. Larry Neal, "Don't Say Goodbye to the Pork-Pie Hat," 290; Sanchez, "Liberation / poem," 337.

19. Giovanni, "For Saundra," 322.

20. Toure, "Notes from a Guerilla Diary," 220–22.

Chapter 1

1. The Editors, "A Portfolio of Poetry," *Negro Digest* (Sept.–Oct. 1968): 53.

2. Gerald, Untitled, 29.

3. Hall, "On Sale at Your Favorite Newsstand"; Abby Arthur Johnson and Ronald Maberry Johnson, *Propaganda and Aesthetics,* and "Charting A New Course"; Redmond, "Stridency and the Sword"; Thompson, "Literary and Critical Analysis."

4. Redmond, "Stridency and the Sword," 558.

5. Sanchez, "a ballad for stirling street," 16.

6. Larry Neal, "Black Contribution to American Letters: Part II," 777, 778.

7. I am not suggesting that journals such as *Liberator* and the *Journal of Black Poetry* were insignificant. Indeed, several journals made important contributions to the presentation of the New Black Poetry. However, none had the reach and resources of *Negro Digest/Black World.* Abby Arthur Johnson and Ronald Maberry Johnson, *Propaganda and Aesthetics,* 187.

8. Semmes, *Roots of Afrocentric Thought,* xi.

9. Hall, "On Sale at Your Favorite Newsstand," 191.

10. Semmes, *Roots of Afrocentric Thought,* xi.

11. Salaam, "Black Arts Movement," 73.

12. For an index of poems, poets, articles, and reviews published in *Negro Digest/Black World,* see Semmes, *Roots of Afrocentric Thought.*

13. "Question," *Black World* (Dec. 1970): 65.

14. "Perspectives," *Negro Digest* (July 1968): 49.

15. Crouch, "Howling Wolf," 60.

16. LeRoi Jones, "Who Will Survive America?" 20.

17. Evans, "A good assassination should be quiet," 24.

18. Forms of literary criticism that focus on the words of poems and ignore the surrounding visual representations perhaps underestimate the effect that images have on readers. Scanning through dozens of black arts publications has made me aware, however, that in addition to offering sites for the publication of literary works of art, the Black Arts Movement also gave rise to the presentation of a multitude of visual texts.

19. Hoyt Fuller, interoffice communication (letter) to Mr. J. H. Johnson, Oct. 1, 1970, Hoyt W. Fuller Collection, Archives Department, Robert W. Woodruff Library, Atlanta University Center.

20. Johnson returned Fuller's letter regarding the two issues with a line drawn from Fuller's request for the increase to the top of the letter with an "ok" and his signature.

21. "About the Cover," 92.

22. "Down deep, we should know," back cover.

23. Hall, "On Sale at Your Favorite Newsstand," 203.

24. Reginald Hayes, untitled press release containing note "For Release after May 1, 1970," box 19, folder 14, 2, Fuller Collection.

25. Fuller, "Editor's Notes," 4.

26. Fuller, "Editor's Notes," 4; Lee, "Blackman/an unfinished history," 22; Okai, "African," 30.

27. See, e.g., Hill-Collins, *Fighting Words,* 167–74.

28. Virginia C. Fowler, *Nikki Giovanni,* 47.

29. Giovanni, quoted in Virginia C. Fowler, *Nikki Giovanni,* 47.

30. Giovanni, "Black Poets, Poseurs, and Power," 32.

31. Hurston, *Their Eyes Were Watching God,* 219.

32. Christian, "But What Do We Think We're Doing Anyway," 499–500.

33. LeRoi Jones, "Poem for Black Hearts," 58.

34. Llorens, "One Year Ago," 67.

35. Evans, "A good assassination should be quiet," 24; Gilbert, "Mirrors," 37.

36. I am indebted to Paul Youngquist for talking through this particular phrasing with me.

37. Moreland, "a panther, named paul," 72; Sutton, "Poem for a Panther," 73.

38. Parks, "Tenth Anniversary Celebration in Detroit," 84–90.

39. Plumpp, "Decade (for Dudley Randall)," 82–83; Brooks, "For Dudley Randall," 91.

40. Madhubuti, "One-Sided Shoot-Out," 90 (subsequently cited in the text). Also see William Hampton's "Fred Hampton: Martyr," 46–48.

41. Jordan, "Poem," 63 (subsequently cited in the text).

42. Kgositsile, "Lumumba Section," 46.

43. Haki Madhubuti (Don Lee), *Negro Digest* (January 1968): 44.

44. Rivers, "Malcolm, A Thousandth Poem," 47.

45. Marvin X, "Don L. Lee Is a Poem," 59.

46. Alicia L. Johnson, "To (2) Poets," 59.

47. Raphael, "Roi," 84.

48. Knight, "Elvin Jones: Jazz Drummer," 93.

49. Fabio, "Tribute to Duke," 243–46 (in *Understanding*).

50. LeRoi Jones, "Evolver," 58.

51. Thompson, "Literary and Critical Analysis," 248.

52. "OBAC—A Year Later," 94.

53. "Chicago's OBAC," 44, 48.

54. Redmond, "Stridency and the Sword," 560.

55. Reed, "You Can't Be A Literary Magazine and Hate Writers," 20.

56. Amiri Baraka, "How Black Is *Black World?*" 13.

57. The exact reason for Johnson's ending of the publication of *Black World* remains sketchy. Some suggest that the magazine's pro-Palestine sentiments angered some of Johnson's white advertisers for *Ebony.* On the other hand, the publication was not financially profitable, and thus Johnson may have finally considered the publication too much of a financial liability. See Hall, "On Sale at Your Favorite Newsstand," 188–206.

58. Kalamu ya Salaam explains that in addition to the demise of *Black World,* the disruption of the Black Power movement and the commercialization and co-optation of black culture during the mid-1970s were among other factors that con-

tributed to the decline of black arts activity. Abby Arthur Johnson and Ronald Maberry Johnson, *Propaganda and Aesthetics,* 370; Salaam, "Black Arts Movement," 74.

59. For a complete list of the editorial advisors, see *First World* 1, no. 1 (1977): 2.

60. Smethurst, "'Pat Your Foot and Turn the Corner,'" 261.

61. Lawrence P. Neal, "LeRoi Jones' *The Slave* and *The Toilet,*" 22, 23.

62. Lawrence P. Neal, "Development of LeRoi Jones," 4.

63. Lawrence P. Neal, "Development of LeRoi Jones (part 2)," 18 (subsequently cited in the text).

64. Larry Neal, "Black Arts Movement," 33 (subsequently cited in the text).

65. Clayton Riley, "The Black Arts," *Liberator* (April 1965): 21.

66. Larry Neal, "Cultural Front," 27.

67. LeRoi Jones, "Revolutionary Theatre," 4.

68. Fuller, "Negro Writer in the U.S. Assembly at Asilomar," 43.

69. LeRoi Jones, "In Search of the Revolutionary Theatre," 20.

70. Amiri Baraka, "Toward the Creation of Political Institutions," 54.

71. See *Ebony,* Aug. 1969.

72. Llorens, "Ameer (LeRoi Jones) Baraka," 75 (subsequently cited in the text).

73. Llorens, "Poet Is Acclaimed Creator of Black Art," 72 (subsequently cited in the text).

74. Bailey, "Nikki Giovanni," 48–49 (subsequently cited in the text).

75. For more on the ways that feminism poses threats to black nationalism, see Hill-Collins *Fighting Words.*

Chapter 2

1. Randall, *Black Poetry,* back cover.

2. Randall, *Black Poets,* xxiii.

3. Nelson, "Murder in the Cathedral," 321.

4. Kinnamon, "Anthologies of African-American Literature from 1845 to 1994," 461.

5. Major, *New Black Poetry,* 12.

6. Alhamisi and Wangara, *Black Arts,* 13.

7. LeRoi Jones, "Foreword," xvii–xviii (subsequently cited in the text).

8. Randall and Burroughs, *For Malcolm,* xix (subsequently cited in the text).

9. Smethurst, *Black Arts Movement,* 223.

10. Randall, "Broadside Press," 140.

11. Redmond, *Drumvoices,* 354.

12. Larry Neal, "And Shine Swam On," 638 (subsequently cited in the text).

13. "Contributors," in Jones and Neal, *Black Fire,* 668 (subsequently cited in the text).

14. "Note to First Paperback Edition of *Black Fire,*" in Jones and Neal, *Black Fire,* xvi (subsequently cited in the text).

15. The Civil Rights Movement and the media attention it received helped create a strong interest in African American issues nationally and internationally and thus made it financially profitable for mainstream white publishers to add black-au-

thored books to their lists. As Hettie Jones, Amiri Baraka's former wife, pointed out, "Negroes were now newsworthy. A trend had been spotted. Book sales could be predicted." Hettie Jones, *How I Became Hettie Jones,* 147.

16. Henderson, *Understanding the New Black Poetry,* xi, 3 (subsequently cited in the text).

17. Barksdale and Kinnamon, *Black Writers of America,* 809.

18. Jordan, *soulscript,* 17 (subsequently cited in the text).

19. Gates, *Trials of Phillis Wheatley,* 83.

20. Randall, "Broadside Press," 144.

21. Giovanni, "Nikki-Rosa," 15–16.

22. Boyd, *Wrestling with the Muse,* 170.

Chapter 3

1. Although Toni Morrison is more widely known as a novelist, she was also an editor at Random House and assisted in the publication of writers such as Gayl Jones and Toni Cade Bambara. She also played a role in the publication of Henry Dumas's posthumously published poetry. Morrison, "Behind the Making of the Black Book," 90.

2. Giovanni, *ego-tripping,* 6–7 (subsequently cited in the text).

3. Amiri Baraka and Fundi, *In Our Terribleness,* 24.

4. Middleton Harris, *Black Book,* 55 (subsequently cited in the text).

5. LeRoi Jones, "Sound for Sounding," i (subsequently cited in the text).

6. Nielsen, *Black Chant,* 220.

7. Virginia C. Fowler, "Chronology," xxxvii.

8. Murray, *Sonny's Time Now.*

9. Amiri Baraka, "Black Art."

10. Sullivan, "Killing John Cabot," 568 (subsequently cited in the text).

11. Randall, "Broadside Press," 139–48; Boyd, *Wrestling with the Muse;* Smethurst, *Black Arts Movement;* Sullivan, *On the Walls and in the Streets;* Thompson, *Dudley Randall.*

12. Smethurst, *Black Arts Movement,* 209 (subsequently cited in the text).

13. Boyd, *Wrestling with the Muse,* 172–85. Boyd also writes that "between 1966 and 1975, Dudley Randall's Broadside Press published eighty-one books, seventy-four of which were poetry, including single collections by forty poets, and of those forty, fifteen authored two or even three titles. . . . Under the auspices of Dudley Randall, Broadside Press published eighty-six books by more than two hundred poets." *Wrestling with the Muse,* 3–4.

14. Randall, "Broadside Press," 145.

15. Sullivan, *On the Walls and in the Streets,* 45–46.

16. Randall, "Broadside Press," 139.

17. Redmond, "Planter of Trees," 9.

18. Don Lee, introduction to Sanchez, *Homecoming,* 6 (subsequently cited in the text).

19. Brooks, "Further Pioneer," 9 (subsequently cited in the text).

20. Alhamisi, "News," 87.

21. Randall, "Broadside Press," 142.

22. Smethurst, *Black Arts Movement*, 227.

23. Parks, "Black Publishers," 76.

Chapter 4

1. Gerald, "Black Writer and His Role," 349 (subsequently cited in the text).

2. Randall, "Different Image," 142.

3. Joans, "Jazz Is My Religion," 117.

4. Knight, "Elvin Jones," 93.

5. Fabio, "Tribute to Duke," 245 (in *Understanding*).

6. Gerald, Untitled, 28.

7. Gerald, Untitled, 28.

8. Julia Fields, quoted in Nielsen, *Black Chant*, 26–27 (subsequently cited in the text).

9. Amini, "Saint Malcolm," 230.

10. Amiri Baraka, *Autobiography of LeRoi Jones*, 311.

11. Killens, *Cotillion*, 25.

12. Reed, *Mumbo Jumbo*, 39.

13. Kgositsile, "Brother Malcolm and the Black Revolution," 4.

14. Rodgers, "Poems for Malcolm," 348.

15. Cortez, "How Long Has Trane Been Gone," 16.

16. Emanuel, "For Malcolm, U.S.A.," 235.

17. Larry Neal, "Malcolm X—An Autobiography," 315–17.

18. Ellison, *Invisible Man*, 441.

19. For an engaging and extended discussion of black aesthetics, as well as Ralph Ellison's tendency to keep "checking out style," see Larry Neal, "Ellison's Zoot Suit," 31–52.

20. Quoted in Abby Arthur Johnson and Ronald Maberry Johnson, *Propaganda and Aesthetics*, 185.

21. Charles Johnson, *Being and Race*, 22 (subsequently cited in the text).

22. Knight, "It Was a Funky Deal," 21.

23. Amiri Baraka, "Poem for Black Hearts," 211–12.

24. Quoted in Baker, "Our Lady," 181.

25. Sanchez, "Malcolm," 38–39.

26. Breitman, *Malcolm X Speaks*, 40.

27. Ossie Davis, "Our Shining Black Prince," xii.

28. Phillip Brian Harper, *Are We Not Men?* 1996, 68.

29. W. Smith, "malcolm," 286 (subsequently cited in the text).

30. Neal, "Black Contribution to American Letters: Part II," 771.

31. Crouch, Review of *Black Fire*, 69.

32. Ford, *Gender and the Poetics of Excess*, 182.

33. Nelson, *Anthology of Modern American Poetry*, 1062.

34. Liner notes to Coltrane's *Live at the Village Vanguard*.

35. Rodgers, *Songs of Black Bird*, 10.

36. Several critics have discussed jazz aesthetics represented in poetry. See, e.g., William J. Harris, *Poetry and Poetics of Amiri Baraka*; Feinstein, *Jazz Poetry*.

37. William J. Harris, *Poetry and Poetics of Amiri Baraka,* 13.

38. Szwed, *Jazz 101,* 211–12.

39. Kofsky, *Black Nationalism and the Revolution in Music,* 256 (subsequently cited in the text).

40. Szwed, *Jazz 101,* 225.

41. Larry Neal, "Social Background of the Black Arts Movement," 15.

42. Amiri Baraka, *Autobiography of LeRoi Jones,* 260.

43. Amiri Baraka (LeRoi Jones), *Black Music,* 197–98.

44. William J. Harris, *Poetry and Poetics of Amiri Baraka,* 13.

45. Michael Harper, "Dear John, Dear Coltrane," 238, 239.

46. Cortez, "How Long Has Trane Been Gone," 13–14, 14–15 (subsequently cited in the text).

47. Sanchez, "a/coltrane/poem," 278.

48. Toure, *Juju,* 13, 16.

49. Spellman, "Did John's Music Kill Him?" 262.

50. Kgositsile, "Acknowledgment," 109.

51. Ben Ratliff, "The Spiritual Serenity of Coltrane and the Scream," *New York Times,* Feb. 19, 2002.

52. Madhubuti, "Don't Cry, Scream," 338.

53. Troupe, "Ode to John Coltrane," 230, 237 (subsequently cited in the text).

54. Troupe does not specify exactly what he means by phrases such as "america's illusions." However, I would argue that Troupe's seemingly vague and subtle critique offers more room for readers to interpret how America has failed to live up to its purported principles from their own perspectives. Troupe, "Ode to John Coltrane," 234.

55. Shirley Anne Williams, "Blues Roots of Contemporary Afro-American Poetry," 187.

Chapter 5

1. Gates, *Figures in Black,* 32, 32–33.

2. Gates notes at one point, for instance, that Baker's appear to be "rather oversimplified, basically political criteria, which are difficult to verify." Gates observes that Gayle's criticism displays "an alarming disrespect for the diversity of the black experience itself and for the subtleties of close textual criticism." Gates, *Figures in Black,* 35–39.

3. Rowell, "Interview with Henry Louis Gates, Jr.," 445.

4. See Gates, *Figures in Black,* 31–41; Baker, *Blues, Ideology,* 64–112.

5. Benston, "Introduction," 5 (subsequently cited in the text).

6. Larry Neal, "Cultural Front," 26–27 (subsequently cited in the text).

7. Larry Neal, "Black Arts Movement," 29 (subsequently cited in the text).

8. Larry Neal, "Any Day Now," 57 (subsequently cited in the text).

9. Larry Neal, "And Shine Swam On," 653.

10. Larry Neal, "Ellison's Zoot Suit," 49.

11. See Thompson, "Literary and Critical Analysis," 248.

12. Semmes, *Roots of Afrocentric Thought.*

13. Rodgers, "Black Poetry—Where It's At," 7–16 (subsequently cited in the text); Rodgers, "Literature of Black," 5–11; Rodgers, "Breakforth, In Deed," 13–22; Rodgers, "Un Nat'chal Thang," 4–14.

14. The favorable comment on Rodgers's essay that Darwin Turner made was initially published in *Black World* magazine in July 1970. I cite from the version of the article published in Addison Gayle's *The Black Aesthetic*. See p. 72.

15. Ameer Baraka, "We Are Our Feeling," 5–6.

16. Usually, *Negro Digest/Black World* printed bylines for authors at the end of their essays. For some reason, no information is provided on Rodgers at the end. The statement appeared as the opening byline and offered no information about what books she had published or her affiliations. See Rodgers, "Black Poetry—Where It's At," 7.

17. See Ward, "N. J. Loftis' *Black Anima;* D. Smith, "Black Arts Movement and Its Critics"; Bolden, *Afro-Blue,* 18–36.

18. "Writers' Questionnaire," 48.

19. Larry Neal, "Social Background of the Black Arts Movement," 20.

20. Fabio, Untitled, 39.

21. Knight, Untitled, 38.

22. Larry Neal, untitled response, 35.

23. Fuller, "Black Writers' Views on Literary Lions and Values," 22–23, 24.

24. Fuller, "Black Writers' Views on Literary Lions and Values," 17.

25. LeRoi Jones, "Myth of a 'Negro Literature,'" 194, 195, 196, 197.

26. LeRoi Jones, "Revolutionary Theatre," 4–6.

27. LeRoi Jones, "In Search of the Revolutionary Theatre," 20.

28. Ameer Baraka, "Black Aesthetic," 5–6.

29. Stanley Crouch to Hoyt Fuller, Oct. 15, 1968, box 16, folder 12, Fuller Collection.

30. Stewart, "Development of the Revolutionary Artist," 8, 10.

31. D. Smith, "Black Arts Movement and Its Critics," 95.

Chapter 6

1. Gates and McKay, *Norton Anthology of African American Literature.*

2. Baker, "Black Arts Era, 1960–1975," 1848–49.

3. Gates and McKay, *Norton Anthology of African American Literature,* xxx.

4. Salaam, "Black Arts Movement," 74.

5. Some of those "events" include the extension of the Voting Rights Act of 1965 by the U.S. Senate in 1975, the election of political figures such as Maynard Jackson in Atlanta, and the selection of Muhammad Ali in 1974. Baker, "Black Arts Era, 1960–1975," 1848.

6. Also see Baker, *Journey Back,* 129–30.

7. Boyd, *Wrestling with the Muse,* 259.

8. Henderson, "Question of Form and Judgment," 19 (subsequently cited in the text).

9. Christian, "Literature since 1970," 2016.

10. Salaam, "Black Arts Movement," 74.

11. Gladwell, *Tipping Point,* 38.

Bibliography

"About the Cover." *Negro Digest* (February 1970): 92.

Alhamisi, Ahmed. "News." *Journal of Black Poetry* 1, no. 9 (1968): 87.

Alhamisi, Ahmed, and Harum Kofi Wangara, eds. *Black Arts: An Anthology of Black Creations.* Detroit: Black Arts Publications, 1969.

Amini, Johari. "Saint Malcolm." In Randall, *The Black Poets,* 230.

Bailey, Peter. "Nikki Giovanni: 'I Am Black, Female. Polite.'" *Ebony,* February 1972, 48–50, 52, 54, 56.

Baker, Houston. "The Black Arts Era, 1960–1975." In Gates and McKay, *Norton Anthology of African American Literature,* 1831–50.

Baker, Houston. "The Black Arts Movement 1960–1970." In Gates and McKay, *Norton Anthology of African American Literature,* 1791–1806.

Baker, Houston. *Blues, Ideology, and Afro-American Literature: A Vernacular Theory.* Chicago: University of Chicago Press, 1984.

Baker, Houston. "Critical Memory and the Black Public Sphere." In *The Black Public Sphere,* ed. The Black Public Sphere Collective. Chicago: University of Chicago Press, 1995. 5–37.

Baker, Houston. *The Journey Back: Issues in Black Literature and Criticism.* Chicago: University of Chicago Press, 1980.

Baker, Houston. "Our Lady: Sonia Sanchez and the Writing of the Black Renaissance." In *Black Feminist Criticism and Critical Theory,* ed. Joe Weixlmann and Houston Baker Jr. Greenwood, Fla.: Penkevill Publishing Co., 1988. 169–202.

Baraka, Ameer. "We Are Our Feeling: The Black Aesthetic." *Negro Digest* (September 1969): 5–6.

Baraka, Amiri [LeRoi Jones]. *The Autobiography of LeRoi Jones.* Chicago: Lawrence Hill Books, 1997.

Baraka, Amiri. "Black Art." In *Sonny's Time Now.* Newark: Jihad, 1965.

Baraka, Amiri. *Black Music.* 1968. Rpt. New York: Akashic Books, 2010.

Baraka, Amiri. "How Black Is *Black World?*" *Yardbird Reader* 5 (1976): 13–17.

Baraka, Amiri. *It's Nationtime.* Detroit: Black Forum, 1973.

Baraka, Amiri. *The LeRoi Jones/Amiri Baraka Reader.* Ed. William Harris. Berkeley: Thunder's Mouth Press, 1999.

Baraka, Amiri. "A Poem for Black Hearts." In Henderson, *Understanding the New Black Poetry*, 211–12.

Baraka, Amiri. "Toward the Creation of Political Institutions for All African Peoples." *Black World* (October 1972): 54–78.

Baraka, Amiri, and Fundi. *In Our Terribleness: Some Elements and Meaning in Black Style*. New York: Bobbs-Merrill Company, 1970.

Barbour, Floyd B., ed. *The Black Seventies*. Boston: Porter Sargent Publishers, 1970.

Barksdale, Richard, and Keneth Kinnamon. *Black Writers of America: A Comprehensive Anthology*. New York: Macmillan, 1972.

Baskerville, John D. "Free Jazz: A Reflection of Black Power Ideology." *Journal of Black Studies* (June 1994): 484–97.

Bell, Bernard W. *The Folk Roots of Contemporary Afro-American Poetry*. Detroit: Broadside Press, 1974.

Bell, Bernard W., ed. *Modern and Contemporary Afro-American Poetry*. Boston: Allyn and Bacon, 1972.

Benston, Kimberely. "Introduction." *Callalo: Larry Neal: A Special Issue* 23 (Winter 1985): 5.

Benston, Kimberely. *Performing Blackness: Enactments of African-American Modernism*. New York: Routledge, 2000.

Bolden, Tony. *Afro-Blue: Improvisations in African American Poetry and Culture*. Urbana: University of Illinois Press, 2004.

Bornstein, George. *Material Modernism: The Politics of the Page*. New York: Cambridge University Press, 2001.

Boyd, Melba Joyce. *Wrestling with the Muse: Dudley Randall and Broadside Press*. New York: Columbia University Press, 2003.

Branch, Taylor. *Parting the Waters: America in the King Years, 1954–1963*. New York: Simon and Schuster, 1988.

Breitman, George, ed. *Malcolm X Speaks: Selected Speeches and Statements*. New York: Grove Weidenfeld, 1990.

Brooks, Gwendolyn, ed. *A Broadside Treasury*. Detroit: Broadside Press, 1971.

Brooks, Gwendolyn. "For Dudley Randall (on the Tenth Anniversary of Broadside Press)." *Black World* (January 1976): 91.

Brooks, Gwendolyn. "A Further Pioneer." Introduction to *Don't Cry, Scream,* by Don Lee. Detroit: Broadside Press, 1969. 9.

Brooks, Gwendolyn. Preface. In *Poems from Prison,* by Etheridge Knight. Detroit: Broadside Press, 1968. 9–13.

Brown, H. Rap. *Die Nigger Die!* Chicago: Lawrence Hill Books, 1969.

Bullins, Ed, ed. *Drama Review* 12 (Summer 1968).

Bullins, Ed. *The Theme Is Blackness: "The Corner" and Other Plays*. New York: William Morrow and Company, 1973.

Bush, Joseph Bevans. "Trane's Tracks." *Negro Digest* (July 1968): 18.

Chapman, Abraham, ed. *Black Voices: An Anthology of Afro-American Literature*. New York: Mentor, 1968.

Chapman, Abraham, ed. *New Black Voices: An Anthology of Contemporary Afro-American Literature*. New York: Mentor, 1972.

"Chicago's OBAC: Portrait of Young Writers in a Workshop." *Negro Digest* (August 1968): 44–48, 79.

Christian, Barbara. "But What Do We Think We're Doing Anyway: The State of Black Feminist Criticism(s) or My Version of a Little Bit of History." In *Within the Circle: Anthology of African American Literary Criticism from the Harlem Renaissance to the Present,* ed. Angelyn Mitchell. Durham: Duke University Press, 1994. 499–514.

Christian, Barbara. "Literature since 1970." In Gates and McKay, *Norton Anthology of African American Literature,* 2011–20.

Clarke, John Henrik, ed. *Malcolm X: The Man and His Times.* Trenton: African World Press, 1990.

Collins, Patricia Hill. *Fighting Words: Black Women and the Search for Justice.* Minneapolis: University of Minnesota Press, 1998.

Coltrane, John. "Chasin' the Trane." *Live at the Village Vanguard/The Master Takes.* New York: Impulse!, 1998.

Cortez, Jayne. *Festivals and Funerals.* New York: Phrase Text, 1971.

Cortez, Jayne. "How Long Has Trane Been Gone." In *We Speak as Liberators,* ed. Orde Coombs. New York: Dodd, Mead, and Co., 1970. 13–16.

Crouch, Stanley. "Howling Wolf: A Blues Lesson Book." *Black World* (December 1970): 60–64.

Crouch, Stanley. Review of *Black Fire: An Anthology of Afro-American Writing,* ed. LeRoi Jones and Larry Neal. *Journal of Black Poetry* (Spring 1969): 65–69.

Crouch, Stanley. "Toward a Purer Black Poetry Esthetic." *Journal of Black Poetry* (Fall 1968): 28–29.

Davis, Arthur P. "The Poetry of Black Hate." *CLA Journal* (June 1970): 382–91.

Davis, Ossie. "Our Shining Black Prince." In Clarke, *Malcolm X: The Man and His Times,* xi–xii.

Dent, Tom. "Umbra Days." *Black American Literature Forum* (Autumn 1980): 105–8.

Dorsey, David. "Formal Elements of the Black Aesthetic in Poetry." CAAS Occasional Paper No. 9, Atlanta University, 1972. 1–22.

"Down deep, we should know." *Black World* (April 1976): back cover.

Emanuel, James A. "For Malcolm, U.S.A." In Henderson, *Understanding the New Black Poetry,* 235.

Evans, Mari. "The Black Woman." *Negro Digest* (September 1969): cover.

Evans, Mari. "A good assassination should be quiet." *Negro Digest* (May 1968): 24.

Evans, Mari. *I Am a Black Woman.* New York: Morrow and Company, 1970.

Ellison, Ralph. *Invisible Man.* 1952. Rpt., New York: Vintage Books, 1995.

Ellison, Ralph. "Remarks at the American Academy of Arts and Sciences Conference on the Negro American, 1965." In Chapman, *New Black Voices,* 402–8.

Fabio, Sarah Webster. "Tribute to Duke." *Black World* (January 1971): 42–45. Reprinted in Henderson, *Understanding the New Black Poetry,* 243–46.

Fabio, Sarah Webster. "Tripping with Black Writing." In Gayle, *Black Aesthetic,* 173–81.

Fabio, Sarah Webster. Untitled. *Negro Digest* (January 1968): 39.

Fabre, Genevieve, and Robert O'Meally, eds. *History and Memory in African-American Culture.* New York: Oxford University Press, 1994.

Fanon, Frantz. *The Wretched of the Earth.* New York: Grove Weidenfeld, 1961.

Feinstein, Sascha. *Jazz Poetry: From the 1920s to the Present.* Westport, Conn.: Greenwood Press, 1997.

Feinstein, Sascha, and Yusef Komunyakaa, eds. *The Jazz Poetry Anthology*. Blooming-ton: Indiana University Press, 1991.

Feinstein, Sascha, and Yusef Komunyakaa, eds. *The Second Set: The Jazz Poetry Anthology, Vol. 2*. Bloomington: Indiana University Press, 1996.

Ford, Karen Jackson. *Gender and the Poetics of Excess: Moments of Brocade*. Jackson: University Press of Mississippi, 1997.

Fowler, Carolyn. *Black Arts and Black Aesthetics: A Preliminary Bibliography of Articles and Essays*. Atlanta: Self-published, 1976.

Fowler, Virginia C. "Chronology." In *The Collected Poetry of Nikki Giovanni 1968–1998*. New York: William Morrow, 2003. xxxi–xliii.

Fowler, Virginia C. *Nikki Giovanni*. New York: Twanye Publishers, 1992.

Franklin, John Hope, and Alfred Moss Jr. *From Slavery to Freedom: A History of Negro Americans*. 6th ed. New York: McGraw-Hill, 1988.

Fulani, Richard. Review of *The Folk Roots of Contemporary Afro-American Poetry*, by Bernard Bell. *Black World* (September 1974): 51–52.

Fuller, Hoyt. "Black Writers' Views on Literary Lions and Values." *Negro Digest* (January 1968): 10–27, 81–89.

Fuller, Hoyt. "Editor's Notes." *Black World* (May 1970): 4.

Fuller, Hoyt. "An Important Beginning." *Black World* (September 1971): 82–83.

Fuller, Hoyt. *Journey to Africa*. Chicago: Third World Press, 1971.

Fuller, Hoyt. "The Negro Writer in the U.S.: Assembly at Asilmoar." *Negro Digest* (September 1964): 42–48.

Fuller, Hoyt. "Perspectives." *Black World* (December 1970): 65–66.

Fuller, Hoyt. "A Warning to Black Poets." *Black World* (September 1970): 50.

Garland, Phyl. *The Sound of Soul*. Chicago: H. Regnery Co., 1969.

Gates, Henry Louis, Jr. "Black Creativity: On the Cutting Edge." *Time*, October 10, 1994, 74–75.

Gates, Henry Louis, Jr. *Figures in Black: Words, Signs, and the "Racial" Self*. New York: Oxford University Press, 1989.

Gates, Henry Louis, Jr. *The Trials of Phillis Wheatley: America's First Black Poet and Her Encounters with the Founding Fathers*. New York: Basic Civitas Books, 2003.

Gates, Henry Louis, Jr., and Nellie Y. McKay, eds. *The Norton Anthology of African American Literature*. New York: W. W. Norton and Company, 1997.

Gates, Henry Louis, Jr., and Nellie Y. McKay, eds. *The Norton Anthology of African American Literature*. Second edition. New York: W. W. Norton and Company, 2004.

Gayle, Addison, ed. *The Black Aesthetic*. Garden City, N.Y.: Doubleday and Co., 1971.

Genette, Gerard. *Paratexts: Thresholds of Interpretation*. Trans. Jane E. Lewin. Cambridge: Cambridge University Press, 1987.

Gerald, Carolyn. "The Black Writer and His Role." In Gayle, *Black Aesthetic*, 349–56.

Gerald, Carolyn. Untitled. *Negro Digest* (November 1969): 24–29.

Gilbert, Zack. "Mirrors: For Martin Luther King Jr. (1929–1968)." *Negro Digest* (May 1968): 37.

Gilroy, Paul. *The Black Atlantic: Modernity and Double Consciousness*. Cambridge: Harvard University Press, 1993.

Gilyard, Keith. *Liberation Memories: The Rhetoric and Poetics of John Oliver Killens*. Detroit: Wayne State University Press, 2003.

Giovanni, Nikki. "Black Poets, Poseurs and Power." *Negro Digest* (June 1969): 30–34.

Giovanni, Nikki. *ego-tripping and Other Poems for Young People.* New York: Lawrence Hill, 1973.

Giovanni, Nikki. "For Saundra." In Randall, *Black Poets,* 321–22.

Giovanni, Nikki. "Nikki-Rosa." In *The Black Woman: An Anthology,* ed. Toni Cade. New York: Mentor, 1970. 15–16.

Giovanni, Nikki. "The True Import of Present Dialogue: Black vs. Negro." In Randall, *Black Poets,* 318–19.

Gladwell, Malcolm. *The Tipping Point: How Little Things Can Make a Big Difference.* New York: Back Bay Books, 2000.

Hall, James. *Mercy, Mercy Me: African-American Culture and the American Sixties.* New York: Oxford University Press, 2001.

Hall, James. "On Sale at Your Favorite Newsstand: Negro Digest/Black World and the 1960s." In *The Black Press: New Literary and Historical Essays,* ed. Todd Vogel. New Brunswick, N.J.: Rutgers University Press, 2001. 188–206.

Hampton, William E. "Fred Hampton: Martyr." *Black World* (May 1970): 46–48.

Harper, Michael. "Dear John, Dear Coltrane." In Henderson, *Understanding the New Black Poetry,* 238–39.

Harper, Phillip Brian. *Are We Not Men? Masculine Anxiety and the Problem of African-American Identity.* New York: Oxford University Press, 1996.

Harris, Middleton. *The Black Book.* New York: Random House, 1974.

Harris, William J. *The Poetry and Poetics of Amiri Baraka: The Jazz Aesthetic.* Columbia: University of Missouri Press, 1985.

Hayden, Robert. "1949 Runagate Runagate." *Negro Digest* (June 1966): 44–45.

Hayden, Robert. "1964 Runagate Runagate." *Negro Digest* (June 1966): 46–47.

Hayden, Robert. "El-Hajj Malik El-Shabazz." In Randall and Burrougs, *For Malcolm,* 14–16.

Henderson, Stephen. "The Question of Form and Judgment in Contemporary Black American Poetry: 1962–1977." In *A Dark and Sudden Beauty: Two Essays in Black American Poetry by George Kent and Stephen Henderson,* ed. Houston A. Baker Jr. Philadelphia: Afro-American Studies Program at the University of Pennsylvania, 1977. 19–36.

Henderson, Stephen, ed. *Understanding the New Black Poetry: Black Speech and Black Music as Poetic References.* New York: Morrow Quill Paperbacks, 1973.

Hernton, Calvin. "Jitterbugging in the Streets." In LeRoi Jones and Neal, *Black Fire,* 205–9.

Hill-Collins, Patricia. *Fighting Words: Black Women and the Search for Justice.* Minneapolis: University of Minnesota Press, 1998.

Hogue, W. Lawrence. *Discourse and the Other: The Production of the Afro-American Text.* Durham: Duke University Press, 1986.

Hurston, Zora Neale. *Their Eyes Were Watching God.* New York: Perennial Classics, 1998.

"In Memoriam: Martin Luther King, Jr., 1929–1968." *Negro Digest* (August 1968): 25.

Jackson, Blyden, and Louis D. Rubin Jr. *Black Poetry in America: Two Essays in Historical Interpretation.* Baton Rouge: Louisiana State University Press, 1974.

Jameson, Fredric. "Periodizing the 60's." In *The Sixties without Apology,* ed. Sohnya Sayyres et al. Minneapolis: University of Minnesota Press, 1984. 178–209.

Joans, Ted. "Jazz Is My Religion." In *The Jazz Poetry Anthology,* ed. Sascha Feinstein and Yusef Komunyakaa. Bloomington: Indiana University Press, 1991. 104.

Joans, Ted. "Let's Get Violent!" *Negro Digest* (September 1969): 23.

Johnson, Abby Arthur, and Ronald Maberry Johnson. "Charting A New Course: African American Literary Politics since 1976." In *The Black Columbiad: Defining Moments in African American Literature and Culture,* ed. Werner Sollors and Maria Diedrich. Cambridge: Harvard University Press, 1994. 369–81.

Johnson, Abby Arthur, and Ronald Maberry Johnson. *Propaganda and Aesthetics: The Literary Politics of Afro-American Magazines.* Amherst: University of Massachusetts Press, 1979.

Johnson, Alicia L. "To (2) Poets." *Negro Digest* (September 1969): 59.

Johnson, Charles. *Being and Race: Black Writing since 1970.* Bloomington: Indiana University Press, 1988.

Jones, Hettie. *How I Became Hettie Jones.* New York: Grove Press, 1990.

Jones, LeRoi [Amiri Baraka]. *Black Magic Poetry, 1961–1967: Sabotage, Target Study, Black Art.* Indianapolis: Bobbs-Merrill Company, 1969.

Jones, LeRoi. "The Evolver." *Negro Digest* (September–October 1968): 58–59.

Jones, LeRoi. "Foreword." In LeRoi Jones and Neal, *Black Fire,* xvii–xviii.

Jones, LeRoi. *Four Black Revolutionary Plays.* New York: Bobbs-Merrill Company, 1969.

Jones, LeRoi. *Home: Social Essays.* New York: William Morrow and Co, 1966.

Jones, LeRoi. "In Search of the Revolutionary Theatre." *Negro Digest* (April 1966): 20–24.

Jones, LeRoi. "The Myth of a 'Negro Literature.'" In *Black Expression: Essays by and About Black Americans in the Creative Arts.* New York: Weybright and Talley, 1969. 190–97.

Jones, LeRoi. "A Poem for Black Hearts." *Negro Digest* (September 1965): 58.

Jones, LeRoi. "The Revolutionary Theatre." *Liberator* (July 1965): 4–6.

Jones, LeRoi. "Sound for Sounding: A Preface." In *Black Boogaloo: Notes on Black Liberation,* by Larry Neal. San Francisco: Journal of Black Poetry Press, 1969. i–ii.

Jones, LeRoi. "Who Will Survive America? Few Americans Very Few Negroes No Crackers at All." *Negro Digest* (July 1968): 20–21.

Jones, LeRoi, and Larry Neal, eds. *Black Fire: An Anthology of Afro-American Writing.* New York: William Morrow and Company, 1968.

Jordan, June. "Poem." *Black World* (March 1973): 63–65.

Jordan, June. *Technical Difficulties: African-American Notes on the State of the Union.* New York: Pantheon Books, 1992.

Jordan, June, ed. *soulscript: Afro-American Poetry.* New York: Zenith Books/Doubleday and Company, 1970.

Karenga, Ron. "Black Cultural Nationalism." *Negro Digest* (January 1968): 5–9.

Kent, George. *Blackness and the Adventure of Western Culture.* Chicago: Third World Press, 1972.

Kent, George. "Notes on the 1974 Black Literary Scene." *Phylon* (2nd quarter, 1975): 182–203.

Kent, George. "Reflections on Stephen Henderson's *Understanding the New Black Poetry,* A Review-Essay." *Black World* (February 1974): 51–52, 73–77.

Kent, George. "Struggle for the Image: Selected Books by or about Blacks during 1971." *Phylon* (4th quarter, 1972): 304–23.

Kgositsile, Keorapetse William. "Acknowledgment." In *The Second Set: The Jazz Poetry Anthology, Vol. 2,* ed. Sascha Feinstein and Yusef Komunyakaa. Bloomington: Indiana University Press, 1996. 109.

Kgositsile, Keorapetse William. "Brother Malcolm and the Black Revolution." *Negro Digest* (November 1968): 4–10.

Kgositsile, Keorapetse William. "Lumumba Section." *Negro Digest* (July 1968): 46.

Killens, John Oliver. *The Cotillion; or, One Good Bull Is Half the Herd.* New York: Trident Press, 1971.

King, Woodie, ed. *Black Spirits: A Festival of New Black Poets in America.* New York: Random House, 1972.

Kinnamon, Keneth. "Anthologies of African-American Literature from 1845 to 1994." *Callaloo* 20, no. 2 (1997): 461.

Knight, Etheridge. "Elvin Jones: Jazz Drummer." *Negro Digest* (September–October 1968): 93.

Knight, Etheridge. "It Was a Funky Deal." In Randall and Burroughs, *For Malcolm,* 21.

Knight, Etheridge. Untitled. *Negro Digest* (January 1968): 38.

Kofsky, Frank. *Black Nationalism and the Revolution in Music.* New York: Pathfinder Press, 1970.

Lee, Don [Haki Madhubuti]. "Blackman/an unfinished history." *Black World* (May 1970): 22–23.

Lee, Don. *Dynamite Voices I: Black Poets of the 1960's.* Detroit: Broadside Press, 1971.

Leitch, Vincent. *American Literary Criticism from the Thirties to the Eighties.* New York: Columbia University Press, 1988.

Llorens, David. "Ameer (LeRoi Jones) Baraka." *Ebony,* August 1969, 75–78, 80–83.

Llorens, David. "One Year Ago." *Negro Digest* (February 1966): 67.

Llorens, David. "Poet Is Acclaimed Creator of Black Art, Is Writer-in-Residence at Cornell University." *Ebony,* March 1969, 72–78, 80.

Llorens, David. "Seeking a New Image: Writers Converge at Fisk University." *Negro Digest* (June 1966): 54–68.

Madhubuti, Haki [Don Lee]. "Don't Cry, Scream." In Henderson, *Understanding the New Black Poetry,* 336–43.

Madhubuti, Haki. *Groundwork: New And Selected Poems of Don L. Lee/Haki Madhubuti 1966–1996.* Chicago: Third World Press, 1996.

Madhubuti, Haki. "One-Sided Shoot-Out." *Negro Digest* (January 1970): 90–91.

Major, Clarence, ed. *The New Black Poetry.* New York: International Publishers, 1970.

Malcolm X. "Statement of Basic Aims and Objectives of the Organization of Afro-American Unity." In Chapman, *New Black Voices,* 557–63.

Marvin X. "Don L. Lee Is a Poem." *Negro Digest* (September 1969): 59.

Masiki, Trent. "Aesthetically Speaking: The Emergence and Survival of *Callaloo* (an interview with Charles Rowell)." *Poets and Writers* (January–February 2003): 25–29.

Mason, Ernest D. "Black Art and the Configurations of Experience: The Philosophy of the Black Aesthetic." *CLA Journal* (September 1983): 1–17.

McDowell, Margaret B. "Groundwork for a More Comprehensive Criticism of Nikki Giovanni." In Weixlmann and Fontenot, *Belief vs. Theory in Black American Literature,* 135–60.

McGann, Jerome J. *The Textual Condition.* Princeton: Princeton University Press, 1991.

Moreland, Charles. "a panther, named paul." *Black World* (September 1970): 72.

Morrison, Toni. "Behind the Making of the Black Book." *Black World* (February 1974): 86–90.

Morrison, Toni. "The Site of Memory." In *Out There,* ed. Russell Ferguson et al. Cambridge: The MIT Press, 1990. 299–305.

Moses, Wilson. *The Golden Age of Black Nationalism, 1850–1925.* Hamden, Conn.: Archon Books, 1978.

Mosher, Marlene. *New Directions from Don L. Lee.* Hicksville, N.Y.: Exposition Press, 1975.

Murray, Sunny. *Sonny's Time Now.* Newark: Jihad, 1965.

Neal, Larry [Lawrence P. Neal]. "And Shine Swam On." In LeRoi Jones and Neal, *Black Fire,* 638–56.

Neal, Larry. "Any Day Now: Black Art and Black Liberation." *Ebony,* August 1969, 54–58, 62.

Neal, Larry. "The Black Arts Movement." *Drama Review* (Summer 1968): 29–39.

Neal, Larry. *Black Boogaloo: Notes on Black Liberation.* San Francisco: Journal of Black Poetry Press, 1969.

Neal, Larry. "The Black Contribution to American Letters: Part II, The Writer as Activist—1960 and After." In *The Black American Reference Book,* ed. Mabel M. Symthe. Englewood, N.J.: Prentice-Hall, 1976. 767–90.

Neal, Larry. "The Cultural Front." *Liberator* (June 1965): 26–27.

Neal, Larry. "Don't Say Goodbye to the Pork-Pie Hat." In Henderson, *Understanding the New Black Poetry,* 290–93.

Neal, Larry. "Eatonville's Zora Neale Hurston: A Profile." In *Black Review,* no. 2, ed. Mel Watkins. New York: William Morrow, 1972. 11–24.

Neal, Larry. "Ellison's Zoot Suit: Politics as Ritual." *Black World* (December 1970): 31–52.

Neal, Larry. "Malcolm X—An Autobiography." In LeRoi Jones and Neal, *Black Fire,* 315–17.

Neal, Larry. "New Space/The Growth of Black Consciousness in the Sixties." In Barbour, *Black Seventies,* 9–32.

Neal, Larry. "The Social Background of the Black Arts Movement." *Black Scholar* (January 1987): 11–22.

Neal, Larry. Untitled response to questionnaire. *Negro Digest* (January 1968): 35, 81–84.

Neal, Lawrence P. "Development of LeRoi Jones." *Liberator* (January 1966): 4.

Neal, Lawrence P. [Larry Neal]. "Development of LeRoi Jones (part 2)." *Liberator* (February 1966): 18.

Neal, Lawrence P. "LeRoi Jones' *The Slave* and *The Toilet.*" *Liberator* (February 1965): 22, 23.

Nelson, Cary, ed. *Anthology of Modern American Poetry.* New York: Oxford University Press, 2000.

Nelson, Cary. "Murder in the Cathedral: Editing a Comprehensive Anthology of Modern American Poetry." *American Literary History* 14, no. 2 (2002): 311–27.

The New Wave in Jazz. 1965. Rpt., New York: Impulse, 1994.

Nielsen, Aldon. *Black Chant: Languages of African-American Postmodernism.* New York: Cambridge. 1997.

"OBAC—A Year Later." *Negro Digest* (July 1968): 92–94.

Okai, John. "The African." *Black World* (May 1970): 30–31.

Oren, Michel. "The Umbra Poets' Workshop, 1962–1965: Some Socio-Literary Puzzles." In Weixlmann and Fontenot, *Belief vs. Theory in Black American Literary Criticism,* 177–223.

Parks, Carole. "The Black Publishers." *Black World* (March 1975): 73–76.

Parks, Carole A., ed. *Nommo: A Literary Legacy of Black Chicago: 1967–1987.* Chicago: OBAC Writers' Workshop, 1987.

Parks, Carole A. "On Images and Control: The National Black Writers Convention." *Black World* (January 1975): 86–92.

Parks, Carole A. "Phillis Wheatley Comes Home: Report on a Poetry Festival." *Black World* (February 1974): 92–97.

Parks, Carole A. "Tenth Anniversary Celebration in Detroit: The Broadside Story." *Black World* (January 1976): 84–90.

Patterson, Lindsay, ed. *A Rock Against the Wind: Black Love Poems.* New York: Dodd, Mead, 1973.

"Perspectives." *Negro Digest* (July 1968): 49.

Plumpp, Sterling. "Decade (for Dudley Randall)." *Black World* (January 1976): 82–83.

Pool, Rosey E. "Robert Hayden: Poet Laureate." *Negro Digest* (June 1966): 39–43.

Porter, Lewis. *John Coltrane: His Life and Music.* Ann Arbor: University of Michigan Press, 1999.

Randall, Dudley, ed. *The Black Poets.* New York: Bantam Books, 1971.

Randall, Dudley, ed. *Black Poetry: A Supplement to Anthologies which Exclude Black Poets.* Detroit: Broadside Press, 1969.

Randall, Dudley. "Broadside Press: A Personal Chronicle." In Barbour, *Black Seventies,* 138–48.

Randall, Dudley. "A Different Image." In Randall, *Black Poets,* 142.

Randall, Dudley, and Margaret Burroughs, eds. *For Malcolm: Poems on the Life and Death of Malcolm X.* Detroit: Broadside Press, 1967.

Raphael, Lennox. "Roi." *Negro Digest* (August 1968): 84.

Redmond, Eugene. *Drumvoices: The Mission of Afro-American Poetry: A Critical History.* New York: Doubleday, 1976.

Redmond, Eugene. "A Planter of Trees." Introduction to *When I Know the Power of My Black Hand,* by Lance Jeffers. Detroit: Broadside Press, 1974. 9–11.

Redmond, Eugene. "Stridency and the Sword: Literary and Cultural Emphasis in Afro-American Magazines." In *The Little Magazine in America: A Modern Documentary History,* ed. Elliott Anderson and Mark Kinzie. Yonkers, N.Y.: Pushcart, 1978. 538–73.

Reed, Ishmael. *Mumbo Jumbo.* New York: Simon and Schuster, 1972.

Reed, Ishmael. "You Can't Be A Literary Magazine and Hate Writers." *Yardbird Reader* 5 (1976): 18–20.

Reid, Margaret Ann. *Black Protest Poetry: Polemics from the Harlem Renaissance and the Sixties.* New York: Peter Lang, 2001.

Riley, Clayton. "The Black Arts." *Liberator* (April 1965): 21.

Rivers, Conrad Kent. "Malcolm, A Thousandth Poem." *Black World* (September 1975): 47.

Robinson, William, ed. *Early Black American Poets.* Dubuque, Iowa: W. C. Brown Co., 1969.

Rodgers, Carolyn. "Black Poetry—Where It's At." *Negro Digest* (September 1969): 7–16.

Rodgers, Carolyn. "Breakforth. In Deed." *Black World* (September 1970): 13–22.

Rodgers, Carolyn. "The Literature of Black: Feelings Are Sense." *Black World* (June 1970): 5–11.

Rodgers, Carolyn. "Poems for Malcolm." In Henderson, *Understanding the New Black Poetry,* 347–48.

Rodgers, Carolyn. *Songs of Black Bird.* Chicago: Third World Press, 1969.

Rodgers, Carolyn. "Un Nat'chal Thang—The Whole Truth—US." *Black World* (September 1971): 4–14.

Rowell, Charles H. "An Interview with Henry Louis Gates, Jr." *Callaloo* 14, no. 2 (1991): 444–63.

Rowell, Charles H. "An Interview: With Larry Neal." *Callaloo: Larry Neal: A Special Issue* (Winter 1985): 11–35.

Rowell, Charles H., and Jerry W. Ward Jr. "Ancestral Memories: The Phillis Wheatley Poetry Festival." *Freedomways* (2nd quarter, 1974): 127–45.

Salaam, Kalamu ya. "The Black Arts Movement." In *The Oxford Companion to African American Literature,* ed. Trudier Harris, William Andrews, and Frances Smith Foster. New York: Oxford University Press, 1997. 70–74.

Sanchez, Sonia. "a ballad for stirling street." *Black Dialogue* (Summer 1970): 16.

Sanchez, Sonia. "a/coltrane/poem." In Henderson, *Understanding the New Black Poetry,* 274–78.

Sanchez, Sonia. *Homecoming.* Detroit: Broadside Press, 1969.

Sanchez, Sonia. "Liberation Poem." Broadside no. 34. Detroit: Broadside Press, 1970.

Sanchez, Sonia. "Liberation / poem." In Chapman, *New Black Voices,* 337.

Sanchez, Sonia. "Malcolm." In Randall and Burroughs, *For Malcolm,* 38–39.

Sanchez, Sonia. *Selected Poems, 1974.* Washington, D.C.: Watershed Tapes, 1974.

Sanchez, Sonia. Untitled. *Black World* (September 1972): 76–77.

Schulze, Robin, ed. *Becoming Marianne Moore: The Early Poems, 1907–1924.* Berkeley: University of California Press, 2002.

Scott, James C. *Weapons of the Weak: Everyday Forms of Peasant Resistance.* New Haven: Yale University Press, 1985.

Sell, Mike. "The Black Arts Movement: Performance, Neo-Orality, and the Destruction of the 'White Thing.'" In *African American Performance and Theatre History,* ed. Harry J. Elam Jr. and David Krasner. New York: Oxford University Press, 2001. 56–80.

Semmes, Clovis E., ed. *The Roots of Afrocentric Thought: A Reference Guide to Negro Digest/Black World, 1961–1976.* Westport, Conn.: Greenwood Press, 1998.

Shillingsburg, Peter. *Resisting Texts: Authority and Submission in Constructions of Meaning.* Ann Arbor: University of Michigan Press, 1997.

Smethurst, James Edward. *The Black Arts Movement.* Chapel Hill: University of North Carolina Press, 2005.

Smethurst, James. "'Pat Your Foot and Turn the Corner': Amiri Baraka, the Black

Arts Movement, and the Poetics of a Popular Avant-Garde." *African American Review* 37, nos. 2–3 (2003): 261–70.

Smith, David Lionel. "The Black Arts Movement and Its Critics." *American Literary History* (Spring 1991): 93–110.

Smith, Welton. "malcolm." In Jones and Neal, *Black Fire,* 283–91.

Smitherman, Geneva. "Black Power Is Black Language." In *Black Culture: Reading and Writing Black,* ed. Gloria M. Simmons and Helene D. Hutchinson. New York: Holt, Rinehart, and Winston, 1972. 85–91.

Smitherman, Geneva. "The Power of the Rap: The Black Idiom and the New Black Poetry." *Twentieth Century Literature* (October 1973): 259–74.

Spellman, A. B. "Did John's Music Kill Him?" In Henderson, *Understanding the New Black Poetry,* 261–62.

Stewart, James T. "The Development of the Revolutionary Artist." In LeRoi Jones and Neal, *Black Fire,* 3–10.

Sullivan, James D. "Killing John Cabot and Publishing Black: Gwendolyn Brooks's *Riot.*" *African American Review* 36 (2002): 557–69.

Sullivan, James D. *On the Walls and in the Streets: American Poetry Broadsides from the 1960s.* Urbana: University of Illinois Press, 1997.

Sutton, Charyn. "Poem for a Panther (For Johnny Huggins, killed in L.A.)." *Black World* (September 1970): 73.

Szwed, John F. *Jazz 101: A Complete Guide to Learning and Loving Jazz.* New York: Hyperion, 2000.

Thomas, Lorenzo. *Extraordinary Measures: Afrocentric Modernism and Twentieth-Century American Poetry.* Tuscaloosa: University of Alabama Press, 2000.

Thompson, Julius E. *Dudley Randall, Broadside Press, and the Black Arts Movement in Detroit, 1960–1995.* Jefferson, N.C.: McFarland and Company, 1999.

Thompson, Julius. "A Literary and Critical Analysis of the Role of Hoyt W. Fuller (1927–1981), *Negro Digest* and *Black World Magazine,* during the Black Arts Movement, 1960–1976." In *African American Sociology: A Social Study of the Pan-African Diaspora,* ed. James L. Conyers Jr. and Alva P. Barnett. Chicago: Nelson-Hall Publishers, 1999. 240–61.

Toure, Askia Muhammad. *Juju: Magic Songs for the Black Nation.* Chicago: Third World Press, 1970.

Toure, Askia Muhammad. "Notes from a Guerilla Diary." In King, *Black Spirits,* 220–22.

Trouillot, Michel-Rolph. *Silencing the Past: Power and the Production of History.* Boston: Beacon, 1995.

Troupe, Quincy. "Ode to John Coltrane." In King, *Black Spirits,* 230–37.

Turner, Darwin. "Afro-American Literary Critics: An Introduction." Originally published in *Black World* (July 1970): 54–67. Reprinted in Gayle, *Black Aesthetic,* 57–74.

Turner, Darwin, ed. *Black American Literature: Poetry.* Columbus, Ohio: Charles E. Merrill Publishing Company, 1969.

Van DeBurg, William L. *Black Camelot: African-American Culture Heroes in Their Times, 1960–1980.* Chicago: University of Chicago Press, 1997.

Van DeBurg, William L. *New Day In Babylon: The Black Power Movement and American Culture, 1965–1975.* Chicago: University of Chicago Press, 1992.

Walker, Margaret. *For My People.* New Haven: Yale University Press, 1942.

Ward, Jerry W., Jr. "A Black and Crucial Enterprise: An Interview with Houston A. Baker, Jr." *Black American Literature Forum* (Summer 1982): 51–58.

Ward, Jerry W., Jr. "Literacy and Criticism: The Example of Carolyn Rodgers." *Drumvoices Revue* 4, nos. 1–2 (1994–95): 62–65.

Ward, Jerry W., Jr. "N. J. Loftis' *Black Anima: A Problem in Aesthetics.*" *Journal of Black Studies* (December 1976): 195–210.

Ward, Jerry W., Jr., ed. *Trouble the Water: 250 Years of African-American Poetry.* New York: Mentor, 1997.

Weixlmann, Joe, and Chester J. Fontenot, eds. *Belief vs. Theory in Black American Literature.* Studies in Black American Literature, vol. 2. Greenwood, Fla.: Penkevill Publishing Co., 1986.

Wilentz, Ted, and Tom Weatherly, eds. *Natural Process: An Anthology of New Black Poetry.* New York: Hill and Wang, 1970.

Williams, John A. *The Man Who Cried I Am.* New York: Signet. 1967.

Williams, Shirley Anne. "The Blues Roots of Contemporary Afro-American Poetry." In *African American Literary Criticism, 1773 to 2000,* ed. Hazel Arnett Ervin. New York: Twayne Publishers, 1999. 179–91.

Williams, Shirley Anne. *Give Birth to Brightness: A Thematic Study in Neo-Black Literature.* New York: Dial Press, 1972.

Wilmer, Valerie. *As Serious as Your Life: The Story of The New Jazz.* Westport, Conn.: Lawrence Hill and Company, 1981.

Woodard, Komozi. *A Nation within a Nation: Amiri Baraka (LeRoi Jones) and Black Power Politics.* Chapel Hill: University of North Carolina Press, 1999.

Wright, Richard. "Blueprint for Negro Writing." In Gates and McKay, *Norton Anthology of African American Literature,* 1380–88.

"Writers' Questionnaire." *Negro Digest* (January 1968): 45–48.

Index